RUST

ONE WOMAN'S STORY OF FINDING
HOPE ACROSS THE DIVIDE

ELIESE COLETTE GOLDBACH

Quercus

First published in the USA in 2020 by Flatiron Books, New York

First published in Great Britain in 2020 by

Quercus Editions Ltd
Carmelite House
50 Victoria Embankment
London EC4Y 0DZ

An Hachette UK company

A CIP catalogue record for this book is available
from the British Library

HB ISBN 978 1 52940 279 7
TPB ISBN 978 1 5294 0280 3
Ebook ISBN 978 1 5294 0278 0

This is a true story, but some names and details have been changed and, to a limited extent,
certain incidental characters or events have been compressed or reordered.

10 9 8 7 6 5 4 3 2 1

Designed by Steven Seighman

Printed and bound in Great Britain by Clays Ltd, Elcograf S.p.A.

Papers used by Quercus are from well-managed forests and other responsible sources.

For my parents

1

Steel is the only thing that shines in the belly of the mill. The walk-ways, which were once the color of jade, have dulled to a sickly, ashen green. The cranes, once yellow, have browned with grime. Dust settles on everything—on walls and fingers, on forklifts and lunches, on train cars and coat jackets. Even the workers, who lumber through their long shifts, seem to be collecting dust.

I am one such worker. To the company, I'm known as *#6691: Utility Worker.* 6691 is a number given to new hires. Greenies. Fresh meat. When I first landed a job in the mill, one of the older employees congratulated me.

"You won the lottery," he said. "You're gonna make a lot of money." The man paused. He thought for a moment. He let out a long tapered breath.

"Just be careful," he said. "These machines will eat you up."

On most days, the mill looks like a nightmare. A tall chimney shoots an orange flame into the early-morning air. Smokestacks let out clouds of white steam. Train tracks divide the drained and dreary earth, and the brown water of the Cuyahoga River slogs toward the mouth of Lake Erie. Many of the buildings, which are covered in rust and soot, have taken on the blackish-red color of congealed blood. Inside those buildings, furnaces blaze and machinery churns and cranes screech under the weight of their loads. Inside those buildings, iron turns to steel. Billows of bright gas leap atop molten metal as it's poured into ladles standing upward of thirty feet tall. This leaping gas, which looks orange in the metal's glow, licks and whips in a devil's dance. Every inch of the mill is a screaming reminder: *This is the kind of place that will kill you. This is the kind of place where people have died.*

On one of my first afternoons in the mill, an old-timer told me a story about a woman he'd known. Like me, the woman was a Utility Worker. Like me, she probably felt grateful for her job in the mill.

One day, the woman set her gloves on a steel table near a conveyor belt. It wasn't anything out of the ordinary. Everyone set their gloves on that same table. The conveyor belt chugged along, loaded with steel cylinders that weighed twenty or thirty tons. On that particular day, the cylinders on the conveyor belt had been heavily coated in oil. The steel was particularly slick, and the conveyor belt tended to shudder when it moved. Just as the woman reached for her gloves, one of the cylinders slipped from the conveyor belt and pinned her body against the steel table.

"Imagine it," the old-timer said to me. "The weight of that steel. It just split her in half."

I didn't know what to say. I imagined my own body being crushed.

"She was still alive after it happened," the old-timer said. "That was the worst part. She was still alive. 'Get it off me,' she kept saying. 'Get it off me. Get it off me.'"

I looked down at my dirty hands. The grit of the mill seemed to bore its way into the creases on your palms. It got right down into your skin.

"When they finally got that steel off her," the old-timer said, "she died instantly."

The man paused and stared into empty air. He seemed to be looking at something very far away.

"Her body," he said, "her body just fell apart."

I wasn't supposed to be a steelworker. I wasn't supposed to spend my nights looking up at the bright lights on the blast furnace, which glimmered in the starless sky. I wasn't supposed to learn the language of the mill, telling men twice my age to *swing the rolls* or *jog the mill* or *clear the line*.

I attended an all-girls Catholic high school. I ran track. I played Beth in a school rendition of *Little Women*, and I was valedictorian of my graduating class.

The possibilities are endless, adults said to me when I was young. *You can do whatever you want in this world!*

Like a lot of kids who grow up in Cleveland, Ohio, I mostly wanted to leave.

In high school I often talked with my friends about our plans of future escape. We would travel far and wide to give ourselves culture. We would attend colleges in legitimate cities like San Francisco or Boston. The real world happened in other cities and other towns, and we wanted to build our lives somewhere—*anywhere*—but here.

As a native-born Clevelander, I had always viewed the mill as part of my landscape. It was a fixture, a backdrop, a given, much like the mountains of the Rockies or the cornfields of Iowa, and I can still remember driving past the rusty buildings on summer afternoons as a child. My father often took me on errands to pay bills or send packages or pick up groceries at the West Side Market, and we sometimes found ourselves near the orange flame that shot up from the mill's furnace.

I loved every minute of these afternoons with my father. The most mundane task felt like a mission when I sat in the passenger seat of his station wagon, which was the color of flushed skin. Together, we were Timmy and Lassie, Sandy and Flipper, Batman and Robin. We were sidekicks, comrades, kindred souls cut from the same mold.

One afternoon, as the station wagon crept toward the mill in heavy traffic, my father raised his middle finger at all of the idiot drivers who didn't deserve to be on the road.

"Learn how to merge, asshole," he said with a long honk of his horn.

I tried not to listen. The man who yelled at passing cars wasn't the father I usually knew. For the most part, he was a quiet, gentle man who indulged my every whim, but there was something about traffic jams that unhinged him. In those moments, it felt as if he were harboring another person inside. There was a contemptuous spirit lurking below his skin, and the slightest injustice had the power to release it into the world.

I cringed at every middle finger my father flicked into the air, but I fought the urge to sink into my seat and disappear. If I disappeared, then I wouldn't be his sidekick, so I did the only thing that made me feel more comfortable. Copying my father, I scowled at the other drivers on the road, but the traffic didn't ease despite our frustrations. With a sigh, he turned up the car radio, which was tuned to a fuzzy AM station. Rush Limbaugh was talking about all of the bad things Democrats were doing in America. I was too young to know much about the world, but I was drawn to Limbaugh's energy. He had conviction and charisma, like a preacher struck by the spirit, and I wanted to believe the things he said, even if I didn't understand them.

At the very least, I grasped the crux of Limbaugh's message: Being a Republican was good, and being a Democrat was not. My family believed some version of the same, except we added a heavy dose of religion into the mix. We were Republicans because God *wanted* us to be Republicans. Satan had corrupted the Democrats by tricking them into the sins of abortion, homosexuality, and, worst of all, feminism. Now the Democrats were trying to destroy everything that was good and moral in American society, and it was our job as Republicans to oppose them.

As the traffic inched forward, the station wagon drew closer to Cleveland's industrial valley, which was located just outside the center of the city. My father and I had driven this same stretch of highway many times before. It was one of the main arteries that wrapped around downtown Cleveland, and you could see the Terminal Tower and the Key Building looming to the north. If you looked south, however, you had a bird's-eye view of the industrial valley, which was often plagued by acrid smells. On some days, you might detect a vague odor reminiscent of decomposing fish. On other days, the scent of burnt rubber might linger in the air. On that particular afternoon, everything smelled like rotten eggs.

"Why does it always smell so bad around here?" I asked over the sound of Rush Limbaugh's tirade.

"It's sulfur from the steel mill," my father told me.

"Which one is the steel mill?"

My father smoothed his mustache with fingers that had grown plump with age. As a child, I often marveled at his ring finger, which was so fat that his wedding band wouldn't budge. His flesh had grown around the gold, forming a smooth indentation in otherwise calloused skin, and he used to joke that it was a good thing Catholics didn't believe in divorce.

"See all of those buildings in the valley?" he said.

I stared down at the old rusted buildings, some of which looked close to collapse. They stretched far off into the distance, like the remnants of a forgotten city. If there hadn't been smoke swelling from the smokestacks, I would have assumed they were abandoned.

"Yeah," I said, "I see the buildings."

"Well," my father said, "most of them belong to the steel mill."

"Really?"

"I think so. I know it's a huge place."

From my view on the highway, the mill looked like a cloaked villain, both sinister and mysterious. Nothing good could possibly come from buildings so decrepit, and the smokestacks made me nervous. My grandmother smoked two packs of cigarettes a day, and everyone told her that she was going to get cancer. If something as tiny as a cigarette could make you sick, then the rotten-egg chemicals the mill shot into the air would surely send you to an early grave.

I took a shallow breath and plugged my nose as the station wagon crawled forward. Rush Limbaugh boomed on the radio, railing against the Clintons, and I held my breath until my chest burned. I clenched my fists and wiggled in my seat, taking tiny gulps of air that were just big enough to keep me from passing out.

Like my grandmother's cigarettes, the mill belonged to a past I couldn't quite fathom at the time. It was the dividing line between the generations who had built America and the ones who were supposed to inherit it next. The word *Millennial* hadn't yet entered my vocabulary as I held my breath past the mill, but I already understood that my generation had been promised a better future than the one contained inside the sulfurous buildings of Cleveland's industrial valley. We weren't supposed to settle for trivial jobs that would provide us with nothing more than a paycheck, and adults encouraged us to pursue something more than the drudgery of blue-collar work.

If you can dream it, you can do it! they said. *The world is your oyster!*

As a child, I took the catchphrases and clichés to heart. The rust-covered buildings smelled of rot, not opportunity, so I stubbornly held my breath as my father honked his horn. I didn't care how long it took us to move through traffic, and I didn't care how badly my body wanted air. I was going to hold my breath as long as I could, because I didn't want the ugliness of the mill inside me.

When I was twenty-eight years old and months away from starting at the mill, I was still living on the outskirts of Cleveland. I had rented the only one-bedroom I could afford, an apartment that smelled like dead animals. It came with ugly burgundy carpeting and a mouse problem, which my landlord had remedied with poison. Now there were dead mice festering in my walls, so I had decided to pack a bag and visit my best friend in Washington, D.C. Unlike me, my friend had remained true to her adolescent wanderlust. She had escaped.

As I threw a fistful of underwear into a suitcase, I wondered what I'd done wrong. My friend and I had both gone to college. We had graduated with bachelor's degrees and turned a blind eye to our rising debts. Of course, we were both struggling in our own ways, even if my friend had managed to get out of Cleveland. She was barely making ends meet in an entry-level position in D.C., and I was painting houses for a living. Neither of us could afford to make payments on our student loans, and we wondered if we would ever be able to build meaningful lives for ourselves.

As teenagers, we had been told to follow our hearts and pursue our passions. She had chosen Chinese, and I had chosen English. Admittedly, English was an odd passion for me to pick, mostly because I didn't particularly like the subject in high school. I'd thought Shakespeare was dumb. Symbolism was a waste of time. Ten-page papers were invented by the Devil, and *The Great Gatsby* wasn't everything it was cracked up to be. Truth be told, I probably would have made a decent engineer. The STEM subjects came easily to me, but that was precisely the problem. Calculus didn't provide a challenge, which didn't jibe with the American ethos. We were a people who put our faith in hard work. *Earn what you have. Struggle to the top. Pull up your bootstraps and build yourself from nothing.* A true American passion needed to be conquered, like the ascent up a mountain, so I forsook engineering for English. I wanted to master the thing that I found most difficult.

Back then, my future job prospects didn't seem like cause for concern. For years, adults had assured me that people with college degrees could *always* find full-time work. It didn't matter what you studied; the degree itself was a golden ticket to a career, so I figured that a liberal arts diploma would do just fine. Then the Great Recession hit right after I got my bachelor's. I hadn't yet secured a job, and my prospects dwindled to nothing inside a Rust Belt that was hurting for available work. Even so, I wasn't worried. I still trusted the promises I'd been given in youth, so I enrolled in graduate school in the hopes of becoming a professor.

For three years I studied and went to classes. I deferred my student loans, which continued to accrue interest, and I earned a living by painting houses on the side. When the time came for me to get the degree, the college notified me that I had filled out one of the graduation forms incorrectly. Even though I had completed the coursework and finished the thesis, I needed to amend the form if I wanted my diploma. The problem seemed like a monumental hurdle as I was struggling with an unshakable bout of depression at the time. My life had followed a cascade of unpredictable events, and somewhere along the line I'd lost control. My low, often suicidal mood was only exacerbated by my anxieties about my future, so I ignored the graduation form for months. Inertia took hold, and the months turned to years. I continued to paint houses—I was unable to find work elsewhere—and now I was living inside an apartment filled with rot.

My couch had been someone else's trash. My kitchenware had been someone else's leftovers. My mattress, which I had salvaged from a friend's attic, was stained with someone else's menstrual blood. I was glad for a chance to escape the apartment, even if only to spend a few days with my friend in D.C., so I eagerly threw my suitcase into my tiny black hatchback and sped out of Cleveland.

When I arrived at my friend's place for the weekend, we went out and drank whiskey with two men she'd met in the city. The men were both lawyers on the fast track, and they seemed curious about my Cleveland heritage.

"So," one of the lawyers said. His thick brown hair was slicked back with just the right amount of gel. "What does Cleveland produce?"

"What do you mean?" I said.

"You know, Maine's got lobsters. Hawaii's got coffee. Virginia's got peanuts. What about Cleveland? What comes out of Cleveland?"

The man's question reeked of sarcasm. It was less of a question and more of a challenge. *I dare you to find something important that comes out of Cleveland, Ohio.* I sipped my whiskey and thought for a moment. I didn't know what to say. What *did* Cleveland produce? What made us important? What separated us from the rest? I couldn't think of anything, so I did what Clevelanders do best. I made a joke.

"What comes out of Cleveland?" I said. "Failure."

The joke got a good laugh. I laughed too.

"It's too bad that you got stuck in such a dead-end city," the lawyer said.

My fist tightened around my glass of whiskey. There's an unspoken rule among Clevelanders: Those who've been born and bred in the city can joke about its blunders, but outsiders had better keep their mouths shut.

"Listen," I said, "you don't know shit about Cleveland."

The man looked surprised, almost amused.

"We have all kinds of shit that you don't even know about," I told him, desperate for the right words. "We have the orchestra and the art museum and the lake. We have the fucking Cleveland Clinic."

The man took a long sip of whiskey. No doubt he was trying to discern whether or not I was joking. Truth is, he had struck a nerve. I felt torn about my city, my home, my heritage. I *did* feel stuck in Cleveland, but I also recognized the beauty of my hometown. It's a city nicknamed "the Mistake on the Lake." It's an underdog town marked by a spirit of dogged perseverance. Its people have a unique breed of gritty optimism in the face of dire odds.

I grew up in the nineties, when every Cleveland sports team carried with it an unbreakable curse. The Indians lost the World Series. The Browns packed their bags and headed to Baltimore. The Cavs weren't even on the map. Every year people always said the same thing: *This year's the year!* It didn't matter that they'd been saying the same thing for decades. Every year, they had a desperate hope. It might not seem like much—after all, it's just sports—except it's not just sports in Cleveland. It's a way of looking at the world.

Of course, the underdog mentality had its disadvantages. It could get so ingrained in your identity that you couldn't move forward. For years, people had crooned about my potential, but I was a product of my hometown. Every year, I told myself, *This year's the year I get my diploma!* Three years had already elapsed, and, like clockwork, I had fallen short of getting it done. Earning my graduate degree felt too much like a moment of truth. I had spent years trying to become proficient at the one thing I found most difficult. If I got the degree and failed to secure a job in academia—just as I had failed to secure positions in other fields—it would have meant that my years of study had been a wasted effort. It was better to fail on my own terms. It was safer to paint houses.

Before I went to work at the mill, it had never occurred to me that I didn't know shit about Cleveland, either. My hometown was more than just a city of blunders, but I didn't realize it as I talked to those lawyers from D.C. My half-baked defense had failed to persuade anyone, because I was only seeing half of the picture. I couldn't possibly defend Cleveland's spirit until I learned to appreciate its orange flame.

In a Rust Belt town, that flame isn't just a harbinger of weird smells and pollution. It isn't an anachronism, and it doesn't prove a lack of innovation. While people in cities like San Francisco or Boston might think of the flame as an embarrassment, it's something more than that to us. It's jobs and tax dollars. It indicates a thriving economy. *If that flame is burning*, steelworkers say, *then it means that Cleveland is doing all right.* The flame is very much a part of our history and our identity. It's a steady reminder that some things can stand the test of time, even in a world where nothing is built to last.

The mill itself has stood on the banks of the Cuyahoga River for more than a century. Back in the early 1900s, the river provided access to a wider world. Barges traveled the Great Lakes before shimmying up the river, delivering raw materials to the mill and transporting finished steel to anyone who would buy it. From the turn of the twentieth century until now, the mill has gone through booms and bankruptcies and name changes. It's been the colossally successful Republic Steel. It's been the ill-fated LTV. It's weathered depressions and recessions. It's survived fluctuating prices and foreign imports. It's adapted to new technologies and new markets and new demands. Even now, the mill keeps chugging along.

Inside its borders, men and women work long hours to make a living. It's a good living. Good benefits, good pay. One person's salary can feed a family, so the men and women chug along at the mill's rapid pace. They have bags under their eyes and dirt under their fingernails and fully loaded Mustangs beneath the rooftops of their garages. They work through the night. They work through the holidays. They work through marriages and divorces, birthdays and graduations, sicknesses, deaths. They keep the steel moving. They keep the production high. They work for ten hours, twelve hours, sixteen hours straight. If they don't do it, someone else will. A job in the mill is a coveted position. Hundreds, sometimes thousands, of people vie for a few open spots. They want what the mill offers. The livable wage, the good benefits, the union protection. They want to feed their families. They want the American dream, or what's left of it.

In the winter of 2015, as the holidays were swiftly approaching, my future didn't look very bright. The house-painting business always slowed from Thanksgiving until Valentine's Day, and I was strapped for cash. When an old friend asked me to paint a few rooms in the house he'd just bought, I jumped at the opportunity to make some quick money.

I lugged my drop cloths up his driveway on a cold gray morning, edging my way past a brand-new pickup truck. It was the tricked-out kind that costs money, which seemed odd to me. The last time I'd seen my friend, he had been working overtime just to pay off the loan on a shitty old Pontiac.

When I got to his door, he greeted me with a quick hug and a cup of coffee. He had the rich, buttery accent of someone who'd spent his childhood in Puerto Rico, and the two of us got to talking while I worked. We asked about each other's families and relationships, and we caught up on gossip about mutual friends. Eventually the conversation turned to our jobs.

"I started working at the steel mill a while back," he said, smiling proudly. A maze of freckles patterned his round cheeks, making him look younger than his thirty odd years. "I never would have been able to afford a house otherwise."

"The steel mill?" I asked with a pan of drywall mud in my hand. "No way. Do you work with the molten metal and stuff?"

"Kind of. I'm in steel producing, but I mostly just clean the tundishes."

I continued to patch cracks and holes as I talked, my drywall knife scraping against the walls like nails on a chalkboard.

"The what-dishes?" I said.

"The tundishes."

He went into a lengthy explanation about equipment I couldn't even imagine at the time. He talked about the *caster* and the *BOF* and these things called *tundishes* that apparently needed to be cleaned quite often.

"That's crazy," I said when he finished.

"Yeah, I know. I really don't mind it, though. It's a union job, so it's got great benefits and everything. I don't know how much you make as a house painter, but you should really think about applying."

I thought back to those ugly buildings that I had once driven past with my father.

I still didn't really know what a *tundish* was, but I was pretty sure that I didn't want to clean one.

"I don't think I'm cut out to be a steelworker," I said.

My friend turned and riffled through some papers on his dining room table while I finished fixing a crack in the ceiling.

"Here," he told me. "Let me show you something."

I set my drywall knife aside, and he handed me a crisp blue pay stub. I honed in on the section labeled *Gross Income.*

"Shut up," I said. "You make that much money?"

"Yep," he said with a smile.

Seeing my friend's paycheck was enough to make me forget about my childhood fear of the mill. When I finished painting his house, I doctored up my résumé and embarked upon a four-month-long application process that involved so many tests and background checks that I wondered if I had been recruited into the FBI. When the mill finally called me with a job offer, I accepted without hesitation. It was the first full-time offer I'd ever had, but it didn't damage my underdog persona. I was still an underemployed English major who had hopes of becoming a professor. I was still striving toward a goal that I was too afraid to attain.

When I accepted the offer, I called my friend to tell him the good news.

"Just be careful," he said after congratulating me. "Don't get caught up in all the money. I've seen it a hundred times. Someone smart comes to work in the mill. Maybe they could've been somebody someday, but they get used to all that money. They buy new cars and new houses. Before you know it, they're trapped."

I assured him that I wouldn't suffer the same fate. I was striving for financial stability and nothing more. Many months later, however, I sat behind the steering wheel of the brand-new car that I'd bought with my newly found income. I rode along the same stretch of highway that I had once driven down with my father.

The orange flame shot into the sky, and liberal pundits on the radio talked about all of the industrial workers in the Rust Belt who elected Donald Trump to the presidency. I hadn't been one of them, but I also fell into a slew of other demographics. I was college educated, a Millennial, a woman. But I was also now a steelworker. These people had become my people. Our country felt severed, as if crushed by a great weight, and I was straddling some invisible divide.

As I drove past the orange flame, I did the only thing that would befit a steelworker in my situation. I breathed deeply and raised my hand. Then, with great love and affection, I flicked that damned flame off.

2

The alarm on my phone rang at four in the morning, but the buzzer barely seeped into my dreams.

"Wake up," my boyfriend groaned from beside me. The words stuck in his throat, as if they were made of dried leaves, but I buried my head in my pillow. My mind hadn't yet made the full leap into consciousness, and it felt like the rooster crowing on my phone had pecked its way into my skull.

Tony shifted in the bed and gave me a quick jab on the shoulder, which roused me for a moment.

"Turn it off," he said. "Please, turn it off."

I opened my eyes long enough to hit the snooze button. My head felt dull and heavy, as it did on most mornings, so I rolled over beneath the warm sheets and pressed myself against Tony's back. His whole body emanated heat like a furnace, which felt heavenly on a cold, dark morning in early spring. It was a rare treat to wake up next to him. We had been dating for nearly a year, but we weren't living together. He was recovering from a failed marriage, and I was recovering from a difficult relationship with an ex-boyfriend. Combining households seemed like a monstrous step for two people who had each been hurt in their own ways, and neither of us was gunning to jump into something we might regret. While we usually only slept in the same bed on weekends, Tony had agreed to let me stay with him during my first few weeks at the mill. I had a tendency to sleep through my alarm, but he would wake up at the drop of a pin.

When the rooster crowed on the nightstand for a second time, Tony nudged me in the shoulder, nearly pushing me out of bed. As much as I wanted to ignore the alarm, I knew that my new job at the mill could undo years of financial hardship. It was a once-in-a-lifetime shot at stability, so I tore myself away from Tony's warmth and sank my feet into the plush carpeting that lay beneath the vaulted ceiling in his bedroom. I paused for a moment, pushing the carpeting between my toes. It felt downright luxurious, mostly because I knew there weren't any mouse droppings in it.

I had never been the type of person who envied material things, but I often found myself resenting Tony's place in the world. He was ten years older than me, and while he wasn't rich, he was worlds away from used mattresses and secondhand couches. He owned a modest house, a beat-up convertible, and a brand-new car, which he had purchased with cash, and his parents had paid for his undergraduate degree out of pocket.

When his mother first met me, she gestured toward his house and said, *You must be digging for gold*. It was meant to be a joke. Tony was a middle-school teacher, and his house wasn't particularly big or expensive. Even so, I cowered in my seat while his mother chuckled to herself. Any house that didn't smell like dead animals seemed like a mansion to me, and I didn't want to be seen as the type of person who expected something for nothing.

Now, after nearly a year of trying to fit into a family that was more well-to-do than my own, I was finally going to be making some serious money. I pulled my toes away from Tony's carpeting and headed for the cold tile of his kitchen to choke down a quick breakfast. My stomach churned with excitement as I kissed him goodbye and headed for the orange flame in my tiny hatchback. The air still stank of rotten eggs, but I didn't mind. Sulfur was the smell of shifting fortune.

My father had told me that the mill was a huge place, but I didn't understand its scope until I drove the winding road into the valley. The buildings stretched out as far as I could see. Warehouses rose out of the ground as if they'd been planted by the god of rust, and a pair of blue flames burned from a furnace with curved smokestacks. Steam billowed overhead, and a string of dump trucks rolled down the worn, pitted roadways.

The trucks were like nothing I'd ever seen before. Their tires were as tall as men, and their army-green bodies had been covered in a thick layer of dust. The squat rectangular windows on their cabs looked like squinted eyes, and their engines growled when given a little gas. At full speed, those trucks could've ridden to the other side of an apocalypse, but that wasn't where they were heading on my first day inside the mill. They were carrying slag to the pits on the far side of the property. The slag, I would learn, was a waste product of the steelmaking process, and it was so hot that it sizzled inside the truck beds, leaving a trail of steam in the air.

After parking in a gravel lot on the northern edge of the mill, I stood outside my car, mesmerized by the landscape. I couldn't help but feel that I had been sucked into a grisly version of the future where everything was gray. The asphalt was gray, and the pigeons that picked at the ground were gray, and the white security trucks that occasionally drove past were covered in a thick gray mud. The sky, which was still pink from the sunrise, provided the only color in the place, but even its blush felt like an intrusion.

The mill inspired the same fear and awe that one might feel when encountering an untouched wilderness, but I had to pull myself away from the sight. Orientation was about to start, and most of the other new hires had already filed into a tiny building that resembled an elementary school. There were four or five classrooms inside, each of which had a whiteboard, a projector screen, and several rows of desks. Thankfully, there were also two giant pots of complimentary coffee.

Once inside, I poured myself a cup and sat down in the designated classroom, where twenty-three other people were already waiting. We were a diverse group: young, old, black, white, Latino. The overall mix of people appeared to be a representative cross-section of Cleveland's demographics with one notable exception. There were only two other women in the room with me.

One of these women had already earned a reputation for herself. I had met her the day before, when I joined the other new hires at the union hall to sign tax forms and insurance papers. She had greeted the group with a confidence and an assertiveness that I envied in other women, but the rest of the new hires didn't share my admiration.

"How are you doing on this fantabulous morning?" she now said to a middle-aged man who had tattoos on his forearm.

"I'm fine, Amelia," the man said in monotone.

"Oh, you remembered my name!" Amelia squealed, tossing her long blond hair behind her shoulder. Everyone in the room had already pegged her as a valley girl, but I knew better. Deep down, Amelia was the type of woman who should have lived on a farm somewhere. She belonged to the smell of blackberry pies and early-morning dew. Her wide eyes were the color of freshly tilled dirt, and the extra weight she carried in her midsection suited her perfectly. She should have been digging her toes into the earth, not making friends inside a steel mill.

Amelia slowly scanned the room until her eyes fell on another man, who was trying to hide beneath the rim of his baseball cap.

"I don't know your name," she said, extending her hand. "I'm Amelia."

"Uh-huh," the man grunted without looking up.

Amelia withdrew her hand and put it on her hip, cocking her leg forward.

"Don't you have a name?" she asked.

The man pulled the baseball cap lower on his brow.

"Yeah," he said.

"And?"

"And what?"

Amelia appeared unfazed by the man's response. She ignored him and looked around the room for another target, eventually landing on me.

"What's your name?" she said as I took a sip of coffee.

Amelia walked closer to me, and I could feel everyone in the classroom looking at us. Most of the men seemed to view Amelia as a wild animal at a tea party—they thought she was totally out of her element—and they were probably wondering what she would say next.

"I'm Eliese," I told her with a smile.

"And what did you used to do before this, Eliese?"

"I used to be a house painter," I answered.

"Oh, wow, that's interesting," Amelia said, the pitch of her voice rising a few notes. "I used to work the night shift at a warehouse, but the pay was awful. I have a little boy, you know. I'm a single mom, and it was hard to make ends meet. I'm going to make twice as much money here, though. Aren't you just so excited about getting a job?"

"Yeah," I said. "I am."

An awkward silence settled between us. Amelia might have been gregarious and outgoing, but she was no match for an unabashed introvert.

"Well," she said after a long pause, "I'm going to get a bottle of water. You want one?"

"No, thanks," I told her, holding up my coffee.

Amelia smiled and turned to the rest of the classroom.

"Anyone want water?" she asked loudly.

No one answered.

"Come on," she said. "Cold, fresh bottled water. Anyone?"

Still no answer. Amelia shrugged and stepped out of the room. A few men craned their necks to make sure that she was gone.

"Oh jeez," one of the men said, not speaking to anyone in particular. "That girl is not gonna do well in the mill."

"Nope," another man responded. "I don't think she knows that the guys down here aren't gonna put up with all that bubbly shit."

It was true that Amelia's personality was a lot to handle, but I didn't think that she would be a bad employee. If anything, she was probably a hard worker. She was just going to be very effusive and excited about all of her hard work.

When Amelia finally returned with her water, the man who was moderating the orientation stood at the front of the room to get everyone's attention. He was a young union worker with baggy jeans and closely cropped hair. His white T-shirt was drawn tightly over his biceps, and his eyes were liquid blue. Compared to most of the men in the room, he was also relatively short. There were other seasoned union workers floating around the building that morning, and a few of them had already given the moderator grief about his height. They called him *shrimp*, and they asked if he needed a step stool to get into his pickup truck.

"We're watching safety videos today," the moderator said to the class. "We'll actually be watching safety videos for most of orientation. After these next two weeks, you'll never want to watch another safety video in your life."

"Hey, Gage," an older union worker called from the doorway, addressing the moderator. "You want a booster seat for the movie?"

Gage rolled his eyes and shook his head. I was surprised by the amount of calm he showed in the face of such a brutal insult.

"Don't pay any attention to him," he said to everyone in the class-room. "That's Jack."

"Maybe you want a sippy cup to go with your booster seat?" Jack said. He had the rough, hardened nature of someone who had been in the mill for decades. I would see a lot of him over the coming days, even though he didn't seem to have an official role in the orientation.

"Hey, old man," Gage said, turning toward Jack, "why don't you go tell the AARP about your Alzheimer's?"

Some of the new hires snickered at Gage's comeback, but it made me cringe in my seat. I glanced over at poor Jack, but the slur hadn't offended him. He laughed in a way that seemed almost self-congratulatory before walking away.

From the front of the room, Gage shook his head and pressed play on an old desktop computer. He hadn't been exaggerating about the safety videos. For the next two weeks, I would gather with the other new hires in this same classroom to watch more videos. Each one explained the many ways we could be injured inside the mill. We watched videos about arc flashes, which were random bolts of electricity that made you burst into flames. We watched videos about noxious gases, which could kill us without warning. We watched videos about confined spaces, which harbored the noxious gases, and we were told not to help a worker who had lost consciousness within a confined space. *That's how you get multiple deaths,* Gage said. *You go in to help a friend who's been gassed, and you end up getting gassed yourself.*

Gage offered us these nuggets of wisdom every so often, but mostly he just exchanged one video for the next. A middle-aged union official checked on us every now and then, but Jack provided the most consistent entertainment. Between videos, he sat in the back of the classroom and told us stories.

"I've seen a lot of shit down here in this mill," Jack said while we all took a coffee break. He didn't seem to be talking to anyone in particular, but I was sitting nearby and he happened to lock eyes with me. "I've been workin' down here longer than some of you've been alive. I've seen people get hurt. Hell, I've seen people get killed. You gotta watch your back, especially when you're an Orange Hat."

The seasoned steelworkers had a variety of names for new hires. They called us greenies, newbies, and fresh meat. Mostly, however, they called us Orange Hats. Every new employee at the mill wore an orange hard hat for approximately six months to distinguish them from the veteran workers, who wore yellow hard hats. The orange hard hats served two purposes. First, the bright color stuck out inside the mill. Veteran workers could easily identify inexperienced employees and offer them guidance, which provided added protection against accidents. Second, the orange hard hats let the bosses know that you weren't quite in the union yet.

In order to weed out any bad eggs that had slipped through the interview process, the union and company agreed to a probationary period for all new hires. As far as the company was concerned, we were at-will employees for our first 1,040 hours on the job. After completing those hours, however, we would be gifted with new, yellow hard hats to replace the orange ones. A yellow hard hat meant that you were officially in the union. While the bosses could fire an Orange Hat for the tiniest infraction, they would have to jump through bureaucratic hoops to fire a union-protected Yellow Hat.

"I've seen it time and again," Jack said, running a hand over his smooth chin. "An Orange Hat comes into the mill, and he thinks that he owns the place. Then he ends up getting hurt. Or, even worse, a Yellow Hat starts getting lazy about safety protocols. Then, one day, it bites him in the ass. Just remember, the mill can kill anyone at any time. I've seen it happen."

I smiled politely at Jack, whose small eyes were bordered by wrinkles. He had a square jaw and a furrowed brow, and he wasn't the type of man who worried about his receding hairline. At some point, he had simply shaved his entire head down to the skin. No sense in crying about what you couldn't change.

"One time, me and my buddy was out fixin' a crane," Jack said, inhaling deeply. He was still staring at me as if we were the only people in the room. "It was just routine stuff, but some idiot turned on the power before we got outta there. My buddy was bending over next to one of the wheels—you know, he had his head right there by the wheel of that crane—and the crane started moving. I tried to get to him, but I wasn't quick enough. That crane ran right over his head. Squashed the damn thing like a melon."

Jack blinked away a bit of moisture that was threatening to become a tear. He was a big, burly man with broad shoulders, and I wasn't sure how to comfort him. The violent death he had witnessed defied easy consolation, and the thought of it frightened me. When I first told my friends and family that I'd gotten a job at the steel mill, everyone looked at me with skepticism. *You might get cancer or lose a limb*, they warned. *It's a dangerous job. People die down there.* While I knew that the mill had its risks, I dismissed everyone's comments as hyperbole. After all, I already understood the hazards of physical labor. Painting houses wasn't a cakewalk either, and I had once broken a few bones when a sixteen-foot ladder kicked out from under me. I figured that the mill couldn't be any worse than that. I was simply exchanging one hazardous job for another, but Jack's story was making me reconsider.

"You don't forget something like that," he said. "I remember that whole day like it just happened, you know? Later that night, after my friend got crushed, I went home and went to bed, and something woke me up around two or three in the morning. My dog was barking like crazy, but I figured she was just yapping at one of the neighbors, so I rolled over and went back to sleep."

Some of the other new hires had started listening to the story, but Jack kept his eyes on me. He had begun stirring his coffee in an effort to keep his emotions at bay, and the tiny Styrofoam cup looked like a thimble in his big calloused hands.

"Well," he continued, barely taking a breath, "I woke up the next morning and I couldn't find my dog. She had one of those doggie doors, so I went outside to look for her, and I found her by the porch steps. She was as dead as dead could be. I always felt bad about it. I heard her barking, and I didn't go check. Maybe she was just barking at the neighbor, but I think maybe she was barking because she knew she was gonna die. I don't know why I didn't get up and check on her. Maybe I was just too messed up after my friend died. She was my favorite dog too. I've had a few of 'em over the years, and she was my favorite. She would always sit with me in my chair while I watched the sports station."

Everyone who had been listening to the story waited in silence while Jack stirred his coffee. I think all of us were expecting a happy ending. We wanted Jack to tell us that everything had gotten better after his dog died. We wanted closure. We wanted a moral at the end of all that misery, but Jack just sat back in his seat and crossed his arms. He was obviously done talking, and the rest of us looked around in confusion. Some people rolled their eyes, including Gage, who was sitting at the front of the room, but I just stared down at my hands.

"All right," Gage said with a sigh, "if story time is officially over, I'll play the next video. Luckily, it's the last one for today."

A brief introduction flashed across the screen, and the voice on the safety video began explaining the hazards of forklifts. *Forklifts can tip over and crush you. Forklifts can impale you. Forklifts can get stuck on railroad tracks, and then you might get hit by a train.*

I tried to pay attention to the video, but I couldn't stop thinking about Jack. A story as sad as his needed to *mean* something, but Jack's silence hadn't given any hints as to what that meaning might be. His dog had died, and his friend's head had been crushed by a crane. That was the moral and the story all rolled into one, and I really didn't know what to make of it at the time.

Later that night, long after I had pushed Jack's story to the far corners of my mind, Tony and I walked through a little park on the edge of Lake Erie to enjoy the sunset. The sky had turned the same shade of pink it had been when I watched the dump trucks roll past me in the mill, but the scene was far more idyllic now. A few wooden swings swayed on a grassy hilltop that looked down at the lake, and the leaves on the pear trees were just beginning to bud. Crocuses poked through the soft dirt, and a retriever jumped between its owner's legs, making a knot of its purple leash.

"How much do you love me?" I asked Tony as we navigated the crest of the hill.

He turned to me with a deadpan look in his eyes, as if I had posed the most serious question in the world.

"On a scale of one to ten," he said, "I maybe love you a two."

"No," I said. "You never love me."

"You're right," he told me. The look on his face hadn't changed, but his voice was light and playful. "I never love you. I was just trying to be nice."

I smiled at him. He was tall, dark-haired, and slender, and I was secretly afraid that he would realize how handsome he was. If he did, he certainly wouldn't want to be seen with a pale, plump Polish girl on his arm.

We had met each other on the Internet, which was the last place I ever thought I'd find someone. For years I had struggled to meet people in the world of house painters, which was often inhabited by potheads and alcoholics, so a friend had insisted that I try a dating website. I reluctantly agreed, and I hated every minute of it. The first man who had caught my eye tried to woo me with graphic images of tentacle porn, which seemed to confirm what I already believed to be true: I had wasted forty bucks on a dead end. I tried my best to laugh it off. My friends and I joked about Tentacle Porn Guy, and I figured the online dating experiment would go down as one more epic failure. Then I saw Tony's picture in the slush pile. He had thick-rimmed glasses and an infectious smile, which caught my eye immediately.

That's the one, I said to myself, even though the website's algorithms didn't agree. Tony and I were *almost* compatible, but I didn't care. I couldn't pass on that smile.

As we walked beside the lake, Tony stopped and pointed to a flock of birds that was floating on the water.

"Look," he said, "there are a few red-breasted mergansers."

The birds bobbed and paddled on the waves. The females were relatively unadorned, but the males looked striking. They had red eyes and white necks. Each tiny head was a cascade of black feathers, and their red breasts looked like flames in the water. Every once in a while, one of the birds dipped down below the surface in search of fish.

Tony stopped to watch for a moment, but I walked ahead of him in frustration. I've never been the type of person who smells the roses. I would much rather be pushing forward and moving ahead, but Tony preferred to pause. It was the least of our differences. He was a Virgo who valued restraint; I was a Scorpio who valued raw emotion. He was a morning person, and I was a night owl. Everything in his house had a place, and everything in my apartment was in a state of controlled chaos. We didn't even relate to our city in the same way. He had spent his life on the east side of Cleveland, and I had always lived on the west. Everyone in the city knew that the west side was the best side, but Tony had every intention of staying in his east-side corner of the world. We might as well have been named Capulet and Montague, except Clevelanders would have never presumed to give themselves such timeless titles.

I stopped a few feet ahead of Tony and waited. The sun had already disappeared beneath the horizon, and the clouds were turning salmon and orange. Tony looked over at me.

"Just one more minute," he said.

"Okay," I answered, trying to contain my restlessness.

I stared out over the lake, which rippled slightly beneath the clouds.

The red-breasted mergansers had turned into tiny silhouettes in the fading sunlight. They rode gently on the water until the whole flock suddenly took flight. Together they skimmed the surface of the water, and even I had to admit that there was something beautiful about the way they floated across the auburn sky. Tony walked over to me and took my hand. Sometimes it seemed like our relationship wouldn't survive our differences, but there were just enough moments like this one, when our differences made us recognize the things we would have missed on our own.

It was the kind of relationship I never would have envisioned for myself growing up. I wasn't supposed to join dating websites or take long walks on Lake Erie with a man I imagined myself marrying, much like I wasn't supposed to work at the mill. Such trivialities were meant for boring girls, but I was destined for something greater. When I was young, I believed that God had called me to become a Catholic nun, like Mother Teresa, and I fully intended on healing the sick and feeding the poor. I was willing to go wherever the Spirit sent me, so long as he didn't send me to Cleveland, and I was willing to do Christ's bidding, so long as he gave me something in return. Mother Teresa had won the Nobel Peace Prize. Ronald Reagan had given her the Presidential Medal of Freedom. I, too, craved national recognition and international accolades. I wanted shrines built in my honor. I wanted my face on the cover of *Time* magazine.

These visions of grandeur seemed entirely feasible to my childhood self. Growing up Catholic had given me a sense of wonder, and I believed in the magic of it all: the miracles, the visions, the unlikely tales embellished over generations.

In fourth grade I received a chain letter that promised exactly this kind of magic.

If you send this letter to nine people within nine days, it said, *you'll get a special miracle from St. Therese of Lisieux.*

Most people would have seen the message as a scam, but I was a sucker for miracles. I typed the letter up on the family computer, and I addressed all of the envelopes. Then I forgot about it. The letters sat on a desk until the ninth day, when I suddenly remembered the deadline. I found my father, who had just gotten home from work. He barely had time to take off his shoes before I accosted him at the door.

"We have to go to the post office," I pleaded, the stack of letters in my hand. The white envelopes felt crisp and perfect between my fingers, and my mind raced at the thought of letting a miracle go to waste.

"The post office is almost closed, but we can go tomorrow," my father said in the same chipper tone he always used with me. He had a way of treating me gently, even when he was breaking my heart.

I tried to explain just how dire the situation was. If we didn't go to the post office *right now*, then I wouldn't get the miracle and God would be mad at me. My father probably had a million other things to do, but we hopped into his station wagon and arrived at the post office just before they locked their doors.

A few days later I sat in the basement reading about whales when I was overcome by the smell of roses. The scent was potent and fresh. I looked everywhere to see if I could find its source, but there wasn't anything in the musty basement that would have produced such a strong aroma. I breathed deeply. The letter had promised a miracle from St. Therese of Lisieux, who was often called the Little Flower. In statues, St. Therese was always depicted with a bouquet of roses. I went upstairs to find my dad, who was drinking his morning coffee in the living room. I plopped down beside him on our blue gingham couch and smiled.

"I got the miracle," I told him excitedly.

"Well," he said with a glint in his eyes, "what was it?"

I stared up at him for a moment. There was something about his smile that made me think he already knew the answer, but I didn't give it much thought. He was my father, which meant he was all-knowing, so it stood to reason that he already knew what the miracle would be.

"It smelled like roses," I answered, and he smiled even wider.

"It's pretty cool that you got a miracle from your favorite saint," he said with a wink, but I didn't put two and two together. I just rushed back down to the basement to see if there were any more miracles to be found.

I barely noticed the smell of sulfur when I arrived at the mill for another day of orientation. The sun was just beginning to rise, and most of the other Orange Hats were already sitting in the classroom, waiting for the safety videos to start. It was just shy of six in the morning, and everyone except Amelia looked sleepy despite the complimentary coffee. Many of us had worked normal jobs before coming to the mill. We'd gotten used to standard forty-hour workweeks, and we weren't yet accustomed to the mill's wild schedule. In the life of a steelworker, the daily nine-to-five doesn't exist. Nearly everyone works twelve-hour shifts and mandatory overtime, and nearly everyone swings between nights and days. Some people get to work at three in the morning and leave work at three in the afternoon. Others become so exhausted from the swing shifts that they find it difficult to decipher dawn from dusk. Many Americans might say that six in the morning is early, but a steelworker knows that *six in the morning* is a relative term.

As I sipped my first cup of coffee, I listened to a conversation Amelia was trying to strike up across the room.

"Who are you?" she said to a man who looked to be in his early thirties. He had a kind smile and caramel skin, and Amelia hovered over him as he sat quietly in his chair.

"I'm Sam," the man replied. He was one of the first people who didn't roll his eyes when Amelia asked him a question, which made me take note.

"Hi, Sam," Amelia said, flipping her hair like always. The words came out effortlessly, as if there weren't a self-conscious bone in her body. "What did you used to do before this?"

"Oh, I worked for FedEx," Sam told her, and the two launched into a conversation that I would have struggled to keep afloat. In a matter of seconds, Amelia learned that Sam had twin toddlers, one boy and one girl, who were the result of a long struggle with infertility. The twins had been an accident—Sam and his wife had given up hope when they conceived out of the blue—and now Sam hoped to buy a new house with his job at the mill.

I watched Amelia from the far side of the room, admiring the poise with which she extracted this information. For most of my life, I had marveled at extroverts, although I never wanted to be one. I preferred to sit quietly in the background, watching and listening, which was odd for someone who craved recognition as a child.

When Amelia had learned all about Sam's home life, she turned to a man who was sitting nearby. The man had these large brown eyes that should have belonged to a philosopher, and while he was more withdrawn than Sam, he still seemed willing to indulge Amelia's extroverted whims.

"How about you?" she said, smiling. "What's your name?"

"I'm Charlie," the man told her. His voice was low and smooth, like smoke from a pipe.

"You got kids?" Amelia asked. It was one of the main get-to-know-you questions that surfaced during orientation. *What did you do before all of this? Do you have kids?* I didn't mind the first question, but I hated the second. I always detected a hint of disappointment when I answered no.

"Nope," Charlie answered, "I don't have any kids. At least not yet."

"Oh, that's too bad," Amelia said with a sigh. It was the same sigh I'd heard countless times before, and it always issued from the mouths of people who believed that everyone was cut out to have children.

Ever since I hit my mid-twenties, I had started to sense that people pitied me for being childless and unmarried. When I was twenty-four, people said, *Oh, you've still got time to have some babies.* Now that I was twenty-nine, people had started to say, *Oh, you better hurry. You're running out of time.* It didn't matter that I had made a very conscious decision not to have children, at least for the time being. I had been diagnosed with bipolar disorder at the age of eighteen, and I wasn't sure I wanted to pass those genes on to the next generation. I also wondered what kind of mother I'd be.

Since my diagnosis, my life had felt like a tireless string of down-falls and disasters. I went through depressive periods, which made me sluggish and suicidal. I went through manic periods, which made me impulsive and irrational. Worst of all, many of my episodes had characteristics of both mania and depression. Rather paradoxically, the two extremes could exist together in what was called a mixed state.

I wished that the highs of mania and the lows of depression would cancel each other out, but this kind of logic doesn't exist inside the mind. The extremes only amplify one another. The mania fills you with an overwhelming need to get up and move, but the depression makes it impossible to climb off the couch. You're completely immobilized by sadness, and the inertia makes your skin crawl. You grow more and more irritable with every passing moment, and eventually the irritability tips the scales. The mania takes over and your impulses reign. Maybe you yell at a loved one or a friend, or maybe the mania drives you off the couch and into an electronics store where you spend all of your rent money on a professional-grade DSLR camera with all the trimmings. You certainly can't afford it—and you've never had any inclination of becoming a photographer before—but none of that matters. You are destined to become the next Robert Mapplethorpe, because Robert Mapplethorpe's birthday is two days before your birthday, which means that his soul has been reborn into your body. When you come back home with your new camera, you sit on the couch and realize that you are too depressed to take any pictures. You're completely immobilized by sadness, but your skin is still crawling, and the cycle begins again.

Doctors would tell me that mixed-state bipolar disorder is one of the most dangerous forms of the disease. Depression brings suicidal thoughts, and mania adds impulsivity. When people with mixed-state bipolar disorder have the will for death, they are more likely to have the energy to follow through. In the midst of such an episode, it often feels like you're at the mercy of a fickle mind. You are a helpless observer strapped to a missile that's hurtling toward a sleepy city. You are a cricket chirping into a void. You are a puppet on a string, and you are the drunken ventriloquist who makes the puppet talk, and you are also—strangely—the voyeur who's watching the show from the window. It was the kind of disease that made you question your ability to raise children.

My mind wandered as Amelia continued to talk with Sam and Charlie. Gage fumbled around with the desktop computer at the front of the room. He was apparently having trouble finding the first safety video of the day, and the complimentary coffee was beginning to take effect on all of the sleepy Orange Hats. Everyone was growing livelier, and a few conversations had sprung up in various pockets around the room. I wasn't quite awake enough to participate, so I listened absently to a nearby exchange between a young man and his neighbor, whose brown hair was speckled with gray.

"Man, I wonder what we're gonna be doing down here," the older man said. He was tall and lanky, and he had the air of someone who thinks he knows more than everyone else. "I hope they don't send me to Iron Producing. My friend told me it's the worst."

The younger man appeared more timid than the first. He ran his palm over his black hair in a gesture that seemed to me like a self-conscious tic.

"Actually, I already know what I'll be doing," the younger man said. "They told me that I'm going to the Railroad."

"Oh, wow." The older man sighed. I could tell by his tone that the younger man's placement in the Railroad had instantly earned his respect. "So, you're one of the Railroad guys? I heard that a few people were going there."

The majority of new hires, myself included, didn't yet know what kinds of jobs we'd be doing inside the mill. The entire steelmaking operation was massive—it spanned nearly 950 acres—and the twenty-four new employees in the room would be divided up and sent to various departments scattered throughout that huge space. Each department was responsible for a different aspect of the steelmaking process, and all of us were eager to find out where we were going. Only a handful of new employees already knew their fates, and they were all destined for the Cleveland Works Railroad, which was also known as the CROW. These employees had undergone a more extensive physical examination than the rest of us, and they would soon be taken away for a separate orientation just for Railroad workers.

The CROW was owned by the same company that owned the steel mill, and it was primarily responsible for transporting steel and materials between the various departments within the mill. While employees of the CROW were still considered steelworkers, they were also part of the nationwide brotherhood of railway workers. They were entitled to a better pension than the rest of us, and they went through a much more intensive training program. Not only did they have to memorize the intricate network of tracks within the mill, they also had to learn how to jump on and off moving trains without getting killed. These Railroad employees might have enjoyed some extra retirement benefits, but they had one of the most dangerous and physically demanding jobs inside the mill.

"I heard that the Railroad is no joke," the older man said. "I think that the last person who died down here was working on the Railroad."

A concerned look spread across the younger man's face.

"Really?" he said. "Are you sure?"

"Yeah, I'm pretty sure it was a Railroad guy who died," the older man said. He seemed completely oblivious to the younger man's growing trepidation. "My friend told me about it a little while back. I guess there was a big snowstorm or something, and this guy was riding on the front of a train. He was just out there in the open, which wasn't weird or anything. That's just what those Railroad guys have to do sometimes. They hop up onto this little platform and cling to the front of the train while it's still moving. That's just part of the job or something. You'll have to do it too, I guess."

The older man's voice was growing more animated with every word, and the other people in the room were beginning to turn their attention to the conversation. Meanwhile, the younger man was trying to mask his unease.

"Well, anyways," the older man said, "this guy was riding on the front of the train, and there was this big snowstorm. I don't have to tell you how bad the weather gets around here."

The older man paused and glanced around at his growing audience. He took a deep breath and leaned forward, as if to build tension.

"So the snow was really coming down," he said. "It was one of those storms where you can barely see your hand in front of your face, and all of those trains are just big hunks of metal, and all of that metal gets icy real quick. Well, the guy slipped on all of that ice. He fell right on the tracks, and the train just kept on going. I heard it split the guy right down the middle."

The older man leaned back in his seat, and the room settled into a brief silence.

"I remember when that happened," Gage said from the front of the room.

He had finally found the first video, which was cued up and ready to go, but he'd gotten caught up in the conversation just like everyone else.

"I was down at the mill when it happened," Gage continued. "Everyone was really upset, because the company just left the body on the tracks for hours. Apparently, they were waiting for people to come out and investigate what happened. I think that there always has to be an investigation after a death, but it took them forever to get it done. The body was just sitting there in the snow."

I thought back to the story that Jack had told us about his friend. The incident with the crane had been just as horrific and frightening as the train accident, but it happened back when Jack was a much younger man. I was probably just a child at the time, if I had been born at all, and so much had changed over the years. Things were supposedly safer now. We had OSHA. We had mandatory safety videos. I figured that workplace fatalities happened to Jack's generation, not mine, but the story about the Railroad accident seemed to prove me wrong. Gage had been working in the mill when the accident had occurred, and he wasn't a grizzled old man. He was barely in his thirties.

"How long ago did this happen?" I asked.

"I'm pretty sure it was back in 2013," Gage said.

"You mean that it happened three years ago?" I blurted out, barely masking my surprise.

"Yeah, I guess it's been about three years," he told me. "I remember feeling really sorry for that guy. I think he was still pretty young. He'd only been working down here for a little while. He probably had a family and a wife and everything."

All of the Orange Hats in the room had grown quiet. Even Amelia was speechless. The talk of death had piqued our interest, but we weren't motivated by morbid curiosity. All of us had been ecstatic about landing a job in the mill. We had hit the jackpot. We had scored a union job, and we were going to make loads of money. Then we started watching a barrage of safety videos that outlined the many ways we could be hurt in the mill, and the people narrating those videos didn't just mention injury. They talked about death. They told stories about people getting electrocuted to death, people getting crushed to death, and people falling to their deaths. Those videos started to scare us, so we tried to hold them at arm's length. We told ourselves that they were just videos. They were *supposed* to scare us so that we would develop a healthy respect for the machinery.

Still, we were worried. We wanted to know just how likely we were to die inside the mill, and the story about the Railroad gave us a grim answer. The man's death wasn't separated by time or distance, and it wasn't told to us by a faceless narrator in a movie. The death had occurred in our city and in our mill, and it had happened only three years prior. Suddenly all of the fears we'd been keeping at bay came rushing into view, and we hung on every ugly detail. It wasn't curiosity or irreverence, and it wasn't an odd form of masochism. We were all trying to divine what had sealed this particular man's fate. If we could just understand *why* he died, then we might be able to predict whether our own futures would come to the same end.

On the other side of the room, the young man who was destined for the Railroad had grown quiet and nervous. He stared down at his hands with wide eyes, and the older man finally seemed to realize that a story about a train-related death wasn't quite the pep talk that a future Railroad employee wanted to hear.

"Hey," the older man said. "Don't even worry about what happened to that guy. Don't let it scare you or nothing. You look young and fit.

You can handle it. I mean, you can't be older than twenty-five. Am I right?"

"I'm twenty-one," the younger man said.

"Shit. You're twenty-one, and you've already got a job at the mill? You've got it made. You'll be buying a house before you turn twenty-three. Don't even think about what happened to that guy. It was just a fluke thing, you know?"

I didn't realize it at the time, but the older man was right. In the mill, you couldn't think too long about what had happened to the man who died on the Railroad. If you did, you'd be paralyzed. You just had to keep pushing forward. You had to keep striving for a good living. You had to keep saving for that house. You had to keep your wits about you if you wanted to avoid doing something stupid. You had to keep calm if you wanted to avoid a tragic misstep, and you had to keep looking at your surroundings if you wanted to avoid the fluke that might kill you. True, the fluke might come for you anyway. There are some accidents that can't be divined. There are some fates that can't be understood. The future is a very uncertain thing, and you can't always predict the end you'll meet.

When I was growing up, money was often tight, but my mother knew how to stretch a dollar. She worked her own bit of magic within the family, although I didn't always appreciate it as a child. Every year, she budgeted the family's expenses to a T, making sure that there was enough to pay for piano lessons and Catholic schooling for my sister and me. This was no small feat considering that my mother worked part-time as a dental hygienist and my father worked as a retail manager at a pawnshop. She could pinch pennies and conjure dimes, but her role in the family went far beyond the monthly balance sheet. She was also the disciplinarian, the secretary, and the cook. She was the overseer who made sure my sister and I did our chores. She gave the epileptic dog its daily dose of phenobarbital. She rolled everyone out of bed in the morning, and she made sure our lunches were packed. In our family, my mother was the gear that made everything run, but she wasn't too rigid to bend.

Once, when I was quite young, she missed Sunday Mass for the sake of a ratty yellow blanket that I used to carry everywhere. The tattered piece of fabric was practically part of my body, and I wouldn't even stand for it to be washed. As we walked out of the house that morning, the blanket caught on the door handle. The yellow fabric ripped down the middle, and the bottom fell out of my stomach. I cried so loudly that neighbors probably thought that I had broken a leg, so my mother kneeled down in front of me and wiped away my tears.

"It can be fixed," she told me. "It can be sewn."

We both stayed home from church that morning, which was practically unheard of in our family, and I waited as my mother sewed the blanket in the basement. She reinforced the hole with several layers of thread, making sure there weren't any gaps that could unravel, and she let me watch cartoons on the couch when she was finished. While the fabric would always retain a scar, my mother's stitching was good. With my father, she had created a world where the most devastating hole could be mended with a mother's needle. It was a place where miracles could happen if you just made it to the post office on time, and it made me believe that even the improbable could be possible.

Years after the torn blanket, when I was about nine years old, I sat next to my mother at Sunday Mass. My father and sister were there too, and everyone was listening to the priest, who lectured from the pulpit. As usual, my attention had been drawn elsewhere. I focused on a statue of the Virgin Mary, which stood above the tabernacle on the right side of the church. The Virgin had flawless skin and open palms. Her tiny feet balanced atop a miniature Earth.

"Mary," I prayed silently, "if I'm supposed to become a nun, give me a sign before Mass is over."

Even at the age of nine, I needed to be assured of my destiny. I wanted proof. While my desire to become a nun might have been rooted in childhood visions of fame, it was also deeply spiritual. I felt something unspeakable welling up inside me. This *something* felt like a rush of beads pinging on a glass tabletop, or a wildfire torching old trees to allow for new growth. It was quiet and urgent, whisper-like and fierce. I didn't know its name, but the religious life seemed to be the only vocation worthy of its power. Looking back, I'd call it hunger.

The service ambled along, and I stared at the statue of the Virgin. I wanted the clay to come alive and tell me that I was destined for greatness, but no matter how hard I stared, the Virgin wouldn't move.

"Please, please, please," I prayed, "give me a sign."

I dreaded the Virgin's silence. If she didn't give me a sign, then it meant that I wasn't chosen. I would end up just like everybody else. I had watched the ways in which adults seemed to move through the world. They went about their days with downtrodden resignation, as if life had beaten something out of them. They weren't just cogs in the wheel; they'd fallen off the wheel completely. It seemed as if they no longer believed that they were an integral part of anything, and I didn't want to suffer the same fate.

The priest stood in front of the congregation and spread his arms. My stomach tightened.

"The Mass is ended," he said. "Go now in peace to love and serve the Lord."

The organist began playing the final hymn.

"Please, Mary, please."

Some of the congregants gathered their belongings and snuck out the back door.

"Please."

When the organ fell silent, my mother and father turned to leave. Tears itched at the corners of my eyes, but I fought them back. The Virgin had communicated through her silence: *You are not as important as you think.* My parents headed toward the church exit, and I followed. As I resigned myself to my own mediocrity, I heard a woman's voice behind me.

"Okay, goodbye," the voice said.

I looked around. The surrounding pews were empty. The aisle was clear except for my mother, my father, and my sister. There were no other women within earshot. I pulled at my mother's arm.

"Did you hear that?" I said.

"Hear what?"

"That woman."

"What woman?"

"Never mind."

I looked back at the statue. It must have been the Virgin who spoke. *Okay, goodbye*, she'd said. That must have been my sign. I smiled. Maybe I had been right all along. I had been chosen for a great and impossible thing, and the beauty welling inside me was real.

My excitement didn't last long, however. I was skeptical, even as a nine-year-old. Right after I heard that voice, I began questioning. Perhaps I'd heard an echo. Perhaps I'd heard a passing conversation. What kind of message was *Okay, goodbye*, anyway? Couldn't the Mother of God think of something better to say? I craved a second sign that would confirm the first. Better to be safe.

"Mary," I prayed as I walked out of the church that morning, "if that was you who spoke, let me see doves today."

Doves seemed like an optimal solution. It was something specific. It was something I could expect. Asking for two signs in one day felt excessive, so I didn't want to ask for something completely world-altering. Doves were improbable but not impossible.

On that particular Sunday, my family was heading out on our yearly vacation. As my father drove to a local state park, I thought of nothing but doves. I watched the sky and scanned the power lines. My stomach tightened at every flutter of wings, but only robins and pigeons appeared. When we finally reached our hotel, I grabbed my backpack and jumped out of the car. I searched the bushes for doves.

"What are you looking for?" my mother asked.

"Nothing," I said.

"Well, come on, we don't have all day."

I followed her reluctantly into our hotel, but I stopped in the doorway. In the middle of the lobby stood an enormous birdcage. The burnished brass bars curved toward the ceiling. Inside the cage crooned a handful of off-white birds.

I ran over to my mother, who was already checking in.

"Mom," I said. "Mommmm."

"Hold on, Eliese."

"No, Mom, I just have to ask you something. Please."

"What is it?"

"What kind of birds are those?"

She turned around.

"I don't know," she said. "They look like mourning doves."

I walked back to the cage and watched the birds. They skittered between thin branches and flapped their clipped wings. Some searched for seeds at the bottom of the cage. I smiled, and my heart raced. I gripped my backpack with furious excitement.

Morning doves, I thought to myself.

It would take years for me to realize that the doves were *mourning*, not *morning*. On that perfect summer afternoon, I still believed in my own quiet magnitude.

3

Catholicism wasn't just a source of miracles and mysteries for me as a child. There was always another side of the equation. Good existed alongside evil, and the Devil was constantly thirsting for our souls. He wanted to bring us down to hell by any means possible. He could trick us and deceive us. He could torment us, afflict us, and possess us. My desire to become a nun was a matter of salvation, for myself and others. It was a battle cry in the epic struggle of *good* and *evil*, which was especially important in modern times. More than anything, however, I had this nagging premonition that my future would be fraught with hardships that others wouldn't have to endure. I sensed that the demons would always be at my heels, and I would become the frayed rope in a heavenly tug-of-war between God and the Devil.

One night, when I was eleven, I tossed and turned in bed while the rest of my family slept. My older sister was tucked away in the bedroom next to mine, and our parents had retired to their room across the hall. The winter wind beat against the side of the house, and the furnace rumbled in the basement. Everything else was eerily quiet, and I couldn't stop my mind from racing. I turned on the little lamp next to my bed and riffled through a stack of books that had accumulated on my dresser. There were Agatha Christie novels from the library, which I liked but didn't always understand, and nonfiction books about horses and dolphins. It took a while, but I eventually found my Bible. As I crawled beneath the covers, I opened to the book of Revelation and started reading.

I had been curious about Revelation ever since I learned that it foretold the coming apocalypse, but I had been scared of what I might find. I was afraid that the book would confirm what I already believed to be true: The apocalypse would happen in my lifetime, and abortion was to blame.

Throughout my childhood, my parents never failed to remind me that God swiftly destroys every civilization that sanctions the killing of children. The Mayans sacrificed babies to pagan gods, so our God wiped the Mayans off the face of the Earth. The cities of Sodom and Gomorrah turned a blind eye to infanticide, so God punished them with fire. The Third Reich killed children in concentration camps, so God made them lose the war.

Seventy years, my parents used to say. That was the maximum amount of time it took for God to exact his vengeance. Sometimes he performed the dirty work more quickly, as he had done with the Nazis, but one thing never changed: The offending civilization was always wiped out within a span of seventy years.

According to my parents, America's clock was already ticking. The countdown started when *Roe v. Wade* was decided in 1973. I added up the numbers and found that America would be destroyed sometime on—or before—my fifty-seventh birthday.

Growing up, I had been taught that America was the best country on Earth. The United States was the pinnacle of mankind and the champion of freedom, and its demise would be the end of everything. Goodness, civility, and democracy would go out the window. If America crumbled, there would be nothing left to fill the void. In my kid brain, America was all that mattered. Its destruction *was* the apocalypse.

My stomach turned as I read Revelation. There was a pale horse who brought death wherever he walked. A dragon hissed into the world and wiped away the stars with his tail. Battles raged in Heaven and on Earth, and people died in all sorts of horrific ways. At some point in the book, a beast emerged from the sea.

"It had ten horns and seven heads, with ten crowns on its horns," the Bible said.

I didn't yet understand symbolism, and I was terrified. I imagined the beast in gruesome detail. He would look like a serpent, but he would be as swift and fierce as a lion. His eyes would be green, and his seven necks would twist into knots.

"One of its heads had been mortally wounded," the scripture said about the awful creature, "but this mortal wound was healed. Fascinated, the whole world followed after the beast."

The miraculously healed wound scared me most. Miracles were supposed to be God's domain, but the beast belonged to the Devil. His miracle was just a bit of trickery, and it frightened me to think that people could be duped by an evil thing that posed as something good. I was afraid that I might unwittingly fall for the Devil's wiles. After all, evil was already in my midst. Millions of Americans were under Satan's spell. My parents called them *Democrats*, and they were traipsing blindly toward the "end of days."

I had tried my best to understand these Democrats by parsing together bits of wisdom I'd heard from my parents and talk radio. Apparently, Democrats thought that *good* and *evil* were relative terms. They practiced New Age philosophies that condoned all sorts of immoral behavior. They believed that every person was on par with God himself, just as Lucifer had done before the Fall. Democrats wanted to destroy American democracy by instituting global socialism, whatever *that* meant. They wanted to ruin our economy with NAFTA, whatever *that* was. They did drugs. They did yoga. They believed in gay rights, which I was taught was an abomination. They believed in feminism, which undermined the God-given sanctity of women. Worst of all, Democrats defended abortion. In doing so, they were invoking an apocalyptic wrath on the rest of us.

I read the book of Revelation straight through to the end, and I was too afraid to sleep when I finished. I couldn't stop worrying about the beast. The following afternoon, I logged on to the Internet and researched Revelation on the family computer. Even in the mid-nineties, the Internet already held a wealth of apocalyptic literature that was certain to terrify a little Catholic girl who wanted to become a nun. I visited website after website, trying to ensure that I wouldn't be crushed when the rest of America met her fate. The sound of her fall would be deafening, and the cries of the Democrats would echo that much louder.

I spent hours of my childhood worrying about hellfire, but my wildest imaginings did nothing to prepare me for the mill's molten metal and the suffocating heat of the furnace. The amount of power it took to make steel was mind-bending. Safety videos about heavy machinery didn't do justice to the ominous growl of the Hot Mill, which had more horsepower than 100 supercharged Corvettes. Hulking cranes were always rumbling overhead. Forklifts whizzed around every corner, and trains crept silently along the tracks with crushing intensity.

I finally began to understand the force of the mill at the end of orientation, when a few union officials came to give the Oranges Hats a tour. We all piled into vans that drove along the dusty streets, weaving between warehouses and furnaces I couldn't yet name. Amelia sat in the passenger seat of my van, while Sam and Charlie were in the back. I had plopped down next to a window in the middle seat, which gave me an unobstructed view of the landscape.

To the north, I could see the crumbling remains of a bridge that had been demolished years ago. The concrete pillars that once supported the bridge had been left intact, as if the demolition men had taken mercy on a line of old wounded knights. The warriors that now remained loomed like sentries on the edge of the mill. Graffiti marred their cracked bellies, and chunks of concrete had gone missing from their pockmarked sides. Their hulking forms looked slumped and dejected, and their heads were tangled messes of rebar forever pointing at the orange flame.

As the van drove into the heart of the mill, Amelia turned around in the passenger seat to address the other Orange Hats. Like everyone else in the van, she was dressed in what steelworkers called *greens*.

The uniforms were composed of a pale green pair of pants and a pale green jacket, both of which were heat resistant and fire retardant. The greens were also immensely thick and scratchy, and Amelia picked at the cuffs of her jacket as she prepared to speak.

"I heard that most of us are going to be working in the Hot Mill," she said, hinting at the mystery that was still weighing on everyone's minds. Orientation was nearing a close, and we still didn't know where we would be working inside the mill.

"That's not what I heard!" another newbie shouted from the back seat. He seemed intent on proving Amelia wrong. "I heard that a lot of people are going to Steel Producing."

Amelia shook her head and shuddered.

"I definitely don't want to go to Steel Producing," she said.

"It's better than Iron Producing," the newbie told her.

As I had come to learn, there was an unofficial hierarchy of departments inside the mill. Iron Producing was the worst place to work, followed closely by Steel Producing and the Hot Mill. The Quality Control Department and the Grounds Maintenance Department weren't too shabby, and the Transportation Department wasn't bad either. Working in the Water Treatment Plant was heavenly. Working in the Powerhouse was not. There were also a few departments dedicated solely to electrical and mechanical maintenance, but you had to be a mechanic or an electrician to work there.

"Steel Producing might be better than Iron Producing," Amelia agreed, "but nothing's as nice as Finishing."

A hush fell over the van at the mention of the word *Finishing*. It was the Shangri-La of the steel mill. It was where everyone wanted to go. There wasn't any molten iron in Finishing. There weren't any noxious gases. The department was clean and relatively safe, and the old-timers often called it the Country Club.

Amelia turned to the union official who was navigating our van through a maze of semitrucks.

"Is Finishing really as nice as they say it is?" she asked him.

The driver was in his early thirties, and when he wasn't carting new hires around he worked as the Safety Advocate in the Finishing

Department. Each department had one of these union-elected Safety Advocates. They protected workers from the company men, who sometimes asked us to perform dangerous tasks in questionable conditions. The Safety Advocates made sure we had water in the summer and heaters in the winter. They provided us with personal protective equipment, and they suggested new safety protocols when the old ones went out of date.

The Safety Advocate thought about Amelia's question for a moment, while everyone else in the van fiddled with their orange hard hats and safety glasses. We had to wear both when entering any building inside the mill, and none of us were used to carrying them yet. Some people balanced their hard hats awkwardly in their laps, while others tried to stow them under the seats. A few people had already donned their safety glasses. Some had put the glasses in their pockets or perched them on the crowns of their heads. Over the course of several weeks, those hard hats and safety glasses would become extensions of our bodies. We would learn to tuck the hard hats effortlessly beneath our arms, and we would become experts at flipping the safety glasses on and off without a second thought. In the van, however, we all looked painfully inexperienced.

"You'll find that every department has its pros and cons," the Safety Advocate said after a long pause. The answer seemed to me like a copout. Throughout our orientation, Jack had told us about Finishing. *Iron Producing is as close to hell as you'll ever get*, he had said, *but Finishing is practically paradise. That's where you want to go. There's nothing better in the mill.*

I let my gaze wander out the window and spotted a building that looked like a grisly amusement park, with two parallel cylinders that rose up from the roof. Each cylinder climbed steeply into the air, bent abruptly, and headed back to the ground—much like the first hill of a roller coaster—and a pair of blue flames danced like pyrotechnics nearby. The flames came from the tops of two chimneys, and they were nothing like the orange flame I remembered from my childhood. While the orange flame had shot angrily into the sky, these blue flames lapped gently in the breeze.

"We're not going to Iron Producing today," the Safety Advocate said, gesturing to the foreboding building as he rounded a corner, "but you can see it in the distance."

As we looked on from the relative comfort of the van, the Safety Advocate tried to explain the department's role in the steelmaking process. "In Iron Producing, they make iron from iron ore," he said, turning his head slightly so that everyone could hear.

All throughout orientation, I had been excited to learn more about the steelmaking process. I wanted to know the chemistry of it. I wanted to understand the physics. My curiosity was so strong that it even outweighed my fear of being the center of attention.

"How exactly is the iron made?" I asked.

The Safety Advocate stopped at a set of railroad tracks and glanced at me for a moment. He had a quizzical look on his face, and I started to wonder if I'd asked a stupid question.

"They put a bunch of ingredients into a blast furnace," he said, "and iron comes out."

I wanted more detail, so I blurted out another question. "What kinds of ingredients do they use?"

The Safety Advocate shrugged and continued driving down the road. "They put pellets into it, I think. And they add coke, of course."

"But how does that produce iron?"

"The blast furnace heats it up into iron, I guess."

It wasn't the answer I was looking for, but I stopped asking questions. I had inadvertently stumbled upon an important truth inside the mill. Most steelworkers didn't know how steel was made. Not really, anyway. Everyone knew the few steps they were personally responsible for, but most couldn't explain the finer details.

In general, however, the Safety Advocate had gotten it right. To make iron, pellets of iron ore and limestone are melted together with coke inside a blast furnace. The coke produces extreme heat and reacts with carbon dioxide to produce carbon monoxide. The carbon monoxide then combines with iron oxide to produce iron. This molten iron, which smolders hot and orange, isn't quite steel yet. It's rife with impurities, and its carbon content is still far too high. To become steel, the molten iron travels inside train cars that vaguely resemble horizontal pop bottles on wheels. These train cars carry the iron to one of several Basic Oxygen Furnaces, or BOFs, inside the Cleveland mill, which are collectively known by workers as Steel Producing.

Our tour officially began in Steel Producing. The van slowed to a stop next to a huge rust-colored building, and we all stepped out into a parking lot that was covered in tiny flecks of graphite. Graphite was everywhere in Steel Producing. It accumulated on handrails and window ledges, shimmering in the sun at certain angles. As we walked across the parking lot, I noticed that pieces of graphite were even floating through the air. The little specks had escaped from the building, and now they glittered to the ground like black snow.

There were two Steel Producing Departments inside the mill—#1 Steel Producing and #2 Steel Producing—but they essentially did the same thing. They both turned iron into steel, and they each sat on opposite banks of the Cuyahoga River. The Safety Advocate had brought us to #1 Steel Producing, which was located on the river's east side. It was also home to the mill's signature orange flame, which was called a flare stack in the world of steelmaking. The fire burned away the highly toxic gases that came from the furnaces, turning them into carbon dioxide and water vapor before releasing them into the atmosphere.

The Safety Advocate pointed to a tall chimney. "That's where the flame comes from."

The fire wasn't burning that day, but I imagined that the view from the ground would have been particularly impressive. The chimney towered several stories high. I had to strain my neck just to get a glimpse of the top.

After pausing to admire the source of the flame, the Safety Advocate led us into the building that housed a large section of #1 Steel Producing. We walked single file through a maze of staircases and catwalks that defied logic. There were multiple levels and dead ends. There were stairways that led nowhere and doorways that opened into thin air. Seasoned employees used the catwalks to navigate the space without walking beneath the cranes that carried vats of molten iron, but the labyrinth was treacherous to anyone who wasn't familiar with its quirks.

Eventually one of the catwalks opened onto an observation deck that overlooked the two Basic Oxygen Furnaces in #1 Steel Producing. The furnaces looked like a pair of giant carafes standing side by side, except steelworkers didn't call them *carafes*. They referred to the furnaces as *vessels*.

"Oh, good, we're just in time," the Safety Advocate said, ushering us into the observation deck. The space was barely bigger than a walk-in closet, and it took a good deal of jostling before everyone got settled.

The taller Orange Hats stood in the back to allow the shorter ones among us a good view of the furnace, and most people apologized self-consciously whenever they bumped into someone else. By the time we were all inside, the tension in the observation deck buzzed like a current. We were standing shoulder to shoulder with people we barely knew, a recipe for unease, and I was squashed beside the wall on the far end of the room.

"They're about to charge a heat," the Safety Advocate said, pointing to direct our attention to one of the vessels. It was tilted forward, revealing an interior that was glowing hot, and a crane was heading toward it with a big boxlike contraption on its hooks.

The crane itself was nothing like I'd expected. When I imagined the cranes during orientation, I thought that they would be similar to the ones I'd seen beside construction projects in downtown Cleveland. I imagined an impossibly tall boom attached to a pendulous cable, but when I looked over at this looming monster, I quickly noticed that these cranes—called gantry or bridge cranes—were different.

To understand the workings of a gantry crane, you need only think of a claw-machine game in an arcade. Children maneuver a little claw over a pile of tightly nestled stuffed animals. The claw moves in two directions. It can go left and right, or it can go forward and backward. When a child has the claw just where she wants it, she presses a button. The claw descends and hopefully grabs a prize. The gantry cranes moved in a similar fashion, except the prizes were massive and the person behind the controls wasn't standing safely on the ground. The crane operators always rode in a tiny cab that was attached to the body of the crane, and I didn't envy the operator who was sitting in front of the red-hot furnace.

"That crane is going to pour scrap metal into the vessel," the Safety Advocate said in a booming voice that barely overpowered the clicks and groans that were coming from the crane's motor.

We watched in silence as the contents of the boxlike contraption slowly tilted into the furnace. The falling metal screeched and sizzled as it fell inside, and a waft of angry noxious steam swirled up into the air.

"Every heat of steel starts with a load of scrap," the Safety Advocate explained, but I knew better than to ask why. "It'll be a few minutes before anything else happens. You always have to let the scrap sit in the vessel for a while. You want to burn away any moisture. If you don't, then you're likely to have an explosion."

"An explosion?" Sam said from the far side of the room, a hint of concern in his voice.

"Yeah," the Safety Advocate told him. "If you pour molten iron onto water, it'll explode."

This was one of the ten commandments of the steel mill: You could put water on molten metal, but you couldn't put molten metal on water. The heat from the metal would quickly turn the water to steam, and the sudden pressure from the steam would cause the metal to explode.

If any of the other Orange Hats were worried about this possibility, they didn't show it. Everyone acted calm and aloof, and I tried my best to do the same. Even though I had only been a steelworker for a few days, I already sensed that the mill wasn't a place where you indulged in your fears. The jobs had to get done. The steel had to be made. If something scared you, then you just had to suck it up and move forward. You had to take that fear and twist it around in your mind until it resembled something like confidence.

Everyone on the observation deck waited in silence while the crane exchanged the boxlike contraption for a giant bucket—known as a ladle—full of molten iron from the Blast Furnace. The iron sloshed around in the ladle, and it was so bright that you could barely look at it without hurting your eyes.

The crane moved cautiously, centering the ladle in front of the furnace, and my breath caught in my throat when it slowly tipped the molten iron onto the scrap. Even from a distance, I could feel the dry heat that rose from the furnace when the iron was poured inside. For the longest time, I had assumed that I understood why the Devil was equated with fire. Fire burned. Fire turned flesh into ash. Fire licked around in the pit, resembling demons and pitchforks, but I had never really seen hell until I looked into that furnace. The bright orange gases whipping up from the vessel moved so quickly that they created a mirage of tortured bodies and twisted souls. Half-skinned faces rose to the surface only to disappear in a split second. The tails of demons thrashed about, and monsters came up for air.

I was so hypnotized by the sight that I completely forgot my fear of a potential explosion. The crane completed its task without incident, but I kept staring into the vessel until the Safety Advocate's voice roused me.

"That's about it," he said. "The rest of the process isn't very interesting."

For the next several minutes the mixture of iron and scrap would be inundated with oxygen to decrease its carbon content, and various chemical blends, called fluxes, would be thrown into the molten metal to reduce impurities like sulfur and phosphorus. This was where the magic happened, in the Basic Oxygen Furnace, after the crane had done its job, but the reactions occurred deep inside the vessel, completely out of view.

The Safety Advocate ushered us off the observation deck to continue our tour. I followed the other Orange Hats through a doorway that was coated in graphite, while the swirling hell within the furnace slowly turned iron to steel.

The noise overwhelmed everything. Gears rumbled. Machinery clunked and roared, and cranes screeched overhead. Thuds fizzled through the air whenever a red-hot slab of steel entered the mill, and a thundering growl echoed on after. Steam hissed from the heat, and something that sounded like a waterfall was rushing in the distance. It was the only noise I had ever heard that felt really, truly cacophonous.

We were standing face-to-face with the Hot Mill, which was the next step in the steel's journey and on our tour.

The steel came to the Hot Mill in thick slabs that were roughly thirty feet long, three feet wide and several inches thick. These huge hunks of metal were raw and unfinished and—to be salable—needed to be stretched into long pliable sheets.

Like a lot of the lingo in the mill, the word *sheet* didn't begin to describe the sheer size of this steel. Just like the word *ladle* actually described a towering vat of molten metal, and the word *spoon* described a long trident that would befit a demon, the sheets that the mill produced were absolutely massive. The largest ones literally stretched for miles. They weighed more than forty horses, more than three elephants, more than seven SUVs. Each sheet contained an incredible amount of metal, which could be turned into the doors of countless microwaves or the sides of numerous washing machines. The steel might one day become guardrails or brackets. It could be transformed into pipes, cars, or lawnmowers, but first the thick slabs had to be stretched into thin sheets by the Hot Mill.

The Orange Hats and I huddled in a semicircle near the entry end of the Hot Mill, an eerie, vacant aura filling the cavernous space. Overlooking this particular mill were a series of small boxes two stories up, which were known as pulpits. Every pulpit had a wall of windows that allowed the workers to keep an eye on the machinery, and most of the buttons that controlled the mill were located inside. While these pulpits allowed workers to do their jobs in relative safety, they also made it so there wasn't a soul in sight. Everyone was up in the pulpits, but the Orange Hats and I stared at the mill from the floor. The machinery was the only thing moving on the ground, like giant metal creatures with a life of their own.

From what I could tell, the Hot Mill didn't seem much better than Steel Producing. The ground was again covered in graphite, and the lights were incredibly dim. Small fires burned beside a raised conveyor belt, and everything smelled like grease.

The Safety Advocate, who was standing nearby, walked in front of us and began shouting something. I could see his mouth moving but couldn't hear a word over the noise. He kept talking, presumably to explain what the mill did, but I didn't catch any of it. If I had, I might have learned that there are many mills inside the larger Cleveland steel mill. In the most basic terms, a mill was a piece of equipment that compressed the steel in between two rotating cylinders. Each had a different objective—the Hot Mill elongated hot steel, the Tandem Mill elongated cold steel, and the Temper Mill rolled the steel to harden it—but every mill contained a pair of rotating cylinders that smashed the steel like huge metal-crushing rolling pins.

Workers in the Hot Mill unload the steel slabs from the train cars that have come from Steel Producing. They reheat these slabs in a furnace until the steel is approximately 2,300 degrees Fahrenheit. While this is an incredibly high temperature that turns the steel a smoldering shade of orange, it's not hot enough to melt it. The slabs retain their shape but become far more pliable. The glowing-hot slabs are then sent down the conveyor belt, where they are pressed between several sets of industrial-sized rollers, each of which is attached to a ten-thousand-horsepower motor. The pressure generated by the rollers in the Hot Mill stretches the slabs into long, thin sheets of steel, which is no small feat. A typical slab is usually about thirty feet long and nine inches thick. In a matter of minutes, thirty feet becomes *three thousand* feet, and nine inches turns to millimeters.

The Safety Advocate continued to lecture the other Orange Hats about the Hot Mill, but I watched as a red-hot slab of steel hurtled down the conveyor belt. It entered the rolling pins with a boom. I winced at the noise. There was something violent about the process, as if the steel were being tortured, but I was also fascinated by the way it stretched and thinned. It was like Play-Doh in a pasta machine, but all of that Play-Doh needed somewhere to go. You couldn't let it pile up at the end of the mill, and you couldn't transport thousands of feet of steel without condensing it first. So the mill turned the steel into coils.

By far, the word *coil* was the one I heard the most during orientation. Jack told us to watch out for the coils. He told us not to get crushed by the coils. Every time he used the word, it brought to mind something looped and frilly and beautiful. I thought of spirals, curlicues, or giant bows made of metal, but I couldn't have been more wrong.

At the end of the Hot Mill, each sheet of steel was curled around a horizontal spool that was approximately two feet in diameter. The spool rotated with great speed and great tension, winding the steel onto itself like a bobbin. Within seconds, thousands of feet of steel could be turned into a manageable cylinder that stood five or six feet tall. When this cylinder was released from the spool, there was a two-foot-wide hole in the center of its diameter. In the language of the steel mill, the cylinder was called a *coil* and the hole was called an *eye*. Cranes could slip their hooks into the eye of the coil and lift it from the floor, allowing tons and tons of steel to be handled and shipped with relative ease.

After watching a few more slabs turn to coils in the Hot Mill, the Safety Advocate led us out into the bright sun, which felt particularly garish after adjusting to the dimly lit mill. We took off our hard hats and stowed them awkwardly under our arms before hopping into the van.

While some of the coils from the Hot Mill would be sold immediately, many others would go to another department for more processing.

The Safety Advocate put the key in the ignition and turned around. "Next stop, Finishing."

The Finishing Department was everything the old-timers said it was. The Country Club. The Retirement Home. Goddamned Paradise. The lights were brighter. The air was cleaner. The yellow bodies of the cranes seemed *yellower.*

The Safety Advocate started explaining something to me and the other Orange Hats, but I wasn't really listening. I couldn't stop looking at the floors. They had been painted light gray, and they were accented by a series of jade-colored walkways indicating the safest path of travel. There wasn't any graphite or fire. Everything else seemed to glisten too. The yellow handrails weren't dusty, and the doorways weren't covered in grime. I couldn't find a drop of oil or a spot of rust, and even the dark blue machinery looked flawless.

"What did the Safety Advocate say?" I whispered to Charlie when I finished admiring the floors. Charlie was the only Orange Hat who looked at home in his new uniform. He wore his hard hat well.

"We're in the Hot Dip Galvanizing Line," Charlie told me.

I nodded in thanks before turning to the Safety Advocate, who was still talking.

"All of the steel that comes to the Hot Dip has been through the Pickle Line and Tandem Mill," he said, making a sweeping gesture with his hand. He seemed to be suggesting that the Pickle-thing and the Tandem-whatever were far away.

I looked around at the other Orange Hats, who nodded as if they understood what the Safety Advocate was talking about. I tried to do the same, but I was lost.

"Every coil that comes to Finishing starts out in the Pickle Line," the Safety Advocate said, and I perked up to listen to his explanation of the process.

He told us that workers in the Pickle Line unwound each coil and sent it through a stream of hydrochloric acid, which washed away any surface-level impurities that were left over from the Hot Mill. From there, the steel passed through the Tandem Mill, where several sets of rolling pins elongated it even further. After the Tandem Mill, the steel could go any number of places. Some of the tandem steel was sold directly to customers. Some of it passed through a Temper Mill, which provided strength and uniformity, and other steel was galvanized to prevent rust. No matter what path a sheet of steel took, it was eventually spooled back into a coil that gleamed under the fluorescent lights. These finished coils would then be loaded onto train cars and semitrucks that were destined for customers across the country.

"The Hot Dip is the newest part of the mill," the Safety Advocate told us, leading us down the jade-colored walkways. "It's the moneymaker."

Galvanized steel, it turned out, could command a higher price than other types of steel, and employees in the Finishing Department often received healthy bonuses as a result. It was the icing on the cake of a department that was already heaven, so I whispered a little prayer.

"Please, let me get into Finishing."

I repeated the mantra as the Safety Advocate shuffled us toward the exit. In the distance, a worker in a yellow hard hat fired up a detergent-filled Zamboni. The little machine drove silently over the pristine floors, moving in tight serpentines, mopping up any marks our footprints had made.

As orientation came to a close, Jack finally got his moment in the spotlight. The company wanted every newbie to receive some hands-on training to augment the safety videos, and Jack was their guy.

As the person in charge of everything related to boom lifts, Jack took me and a small group of Orange Hats to a massive warehouse on the south side of the mill. The building could have held several mansions inside, and a cool breeze was coming from an open truck dock. In the cavernous space, I felt like a ball of dust blowing slowly across the floor.

A thin tarp had been draped from the ceiling to divide one side of the building from the other, and I didn't envy the person who put it up there. The ceiling was at least four stories high, and the fabric was torn in places. The dim fluorescent lights cast haunting shadows over the whole scene. It looked like something out of a horror film, and I could almost imagine a serial killer slashing through the tarp with a big bloodied knife.

Jack led us through a big hole in the fabric and stopped in an area of the building that felt like a land of forgotten parts. Random tools sat on abandoned tables, as if the person wielding them had suddenly disappeared. Huge pieces of machinery had been scattered across the floor. There were shafts that no one wanted, and there were gears with nothing to grind. You could find kinked cables and rusty bolts, and every so often you stumbled upon an oily pair of gloves. I waited with the other Orange Hats while Jack riffled through a twisted pile of safety harnesses. When he had finally freed a harness from its knots, he turned to us with an air of authority.

"This is how you put the harness on," Jack said, buckling himself into a bright blue contraption that went around his legs and shoulders.

"Just make sure it's not too loose," he explained.

"How loose is too loose?" one of the Orange Hats said.

"If you fall out of it, it's too loose."

When Jack handed me a harness, I tightened it as much as I could.

For the rest of the morning, he took each of the Orange Hats up in the boom lift individually, and I watched as the first few people had their turns. The lift was a truck-like contraption attached to a long articulating arm. When operating the lift, you stood inside a basket that was fixed to the end of the arm. From there, you could drive the lift like a vehicle. You could turn in tight circles or go in reverse, or you could do what the boom lift was intended to do. With the right combination of levers, the articulating arm would extend upward and raise you into the air, allowing you to reach great heights without a ladder. With a boom lift, mechanics and electricians could reach precarious positions in relative safety, mostly for the purpose of fixing cranes. That's the reason Jack was running the class. He worked as a maintenance man in a department called Crane Repair.

When it was finally my turn, Jack showed me the power switch and explained how to check the boom lift for damage. Then we both climbed into the basket and clipped our harnesses to a rail.

"These are the controls that bring the boom up," he said. "Go on, give it a try."

I pressed the levers that Jack showed me, and the articulating arm started to move. Our little basket climbed in the air. It rose twenty feet, thirty feet, forty feet, and more.

"Take it as high as it'll go," Jack said.

The basket was starting to wobble, and the world below was looking smaller and smaller. I don't know exactly where we stopped, but we were high enough that a fall would've been fatal. While my harness was theoretically there to stop me from hitting the ground, I wasn't eager to try it out.

"See this lever?" Jack asked.

"Yeah." I was secretly hoping that the lever would bring us back to the ground.

"This lever tilts the basket forward," Jack told me. I wondered why anyone would want to tip the basket forward. "Give it a try. Tip it as far as you can handle."

The basket shuddered when I pressed the lever, and Jack must have seen a worried look flash across my face.

"Don't worry," he said, "that's normal."

I wasn't so sure, but I kept pressing the lever anyway. The basket began to pitch forward, and it wasn't long before I was struck with vertigo. It felt like I was going to tumble right off the side, so I looked over at Jack to see if I'd gone far enough.

"Keep going!" he said, laughing maniacally. His eyes had grown wide with excitement, and his mouth was twisted into the gaping smile of a madman.

"Keep going! Show me that you've got what it takes to be a steelworker!"

Jack chuckled to himself. It seemed that the pitch in the basket had made him completely deranged, but I was too afraid of falling to take much notice. I've always had an immense fear of heights, ever since I was a child. Back when I worked as a house painter, it took me years to tackle anything taller than a six-foot ladder. I refused to walk on roof lines, and my heart beat wildly whenever I climbed higher than a few feet.

As I tipped the basket of the boom lift forward, I looked up at the ceiling. I knew that the small group of Orange Hats was watching from the ground, but I would have lost my nerve if I looked down and tried to find them. Later that day I talked with those other Orange Hats and learned that Jack had done this same trick with all of us. He wanted everyone to tip the basket as far as it would go, as if this were a sacred right of initiation. He wanted to make sure that we had what it took to work inside the mill.

In truth, I wasn't quite sure that I *did* have what it would take to be a steelworker. I didn't bleed iron, as Jack surely did, and rust didn't cling to my bones. I had spent my whole life in Cleveland, but I'd learned about the mill from the sidelines. I read about the Rust Belt in books and magazines. I heard about it from pundits and economics professors, and I'd come to believe that the Rust Belt was the collection of tidy metaphors that everyone else wanted it to be.

"Come on!" Jack shouted. "Don't stop!"

I kept pressing on the controls, and the basket kept tilting forward. It was the spring of 2016, and Donald Trump was making his climb to the presidency. In a matter of months, reporters would be looking at the Rust Belt and scratching their heads. They would search through their best metaphors to explain what had happened, and I would think back to the story that Jack told me at the beginning of orientation. I was wrong to think that the story didn't impart a message. Jack hadn't been quick enough to save his friend from the wheel of the crane, and he hadn't walked outside to save his dog, and whatever guilt connected those two events didn't deserve to be dressed up or watered down. Sometimes you just had to let things be what they were.

The basket was pitched at a precipitous angle, and Jack just cackled.

"Keep going!" he howled.

I didn't want Jack to call me *soft* or *yellow*, which seemed like the kind of thing he was liable to say, so I tilted the basket even more. I would keep going, even if I wanted to puke. I would learn how to make steel, even if it wasn't the job I'd envisioned for myself, and I would finally learn how to answer those smug lawyers in Washington, D.C. If they came up to me today and asked what Cleveland produces, I would know what to say. *Steel.* Steel comes out of Cleveland. Tons and tons of steel. It's not sexy. It's not exotic. It's dirty and hot and loud, but somebody has to do it. We feed the appliance industry, and we supply the auto industry. We make the types of steel that will be transformed into frames and innards and underbellies. We make the strong stuff. The TRIP grades. The dual-phase steels. The HSLA steel. We make the types of steel that don't collapse under pressure. What we make isn't glamorous, but it keeps you safe. What we make isn't fancy, but it keeps you moving.

"I can't do any more," I called to Jack as I eased off the controls.

My heart was beating wildly, and my sweaty hands were clinging desperately to the side of the basket. Jack, on the other hand, was completely calm. He wasn't sweating or breathing heavily, and he didn't have a look of terror on his face. He might as well have been enjoying a picnic at the park.

"That was pretty damned good for a first-timer," he said with a smile. "Now bring us back down."

Later that afternoon, I sat in the classroom with the other Orange Hats while a middle-aged union official straightened a few sheets of paper. The room was completely quiet, and everyone looked nervous. We knew that this was the moment of truth. The union official was going to tell us our job assignments.

"Anderson," the union official said.

The man named Anderson raised his hand.

"Hot Mill," the union official said.

He continued on down the list of names.

"Clark, Steel Producing."

"Collins, Hot Mill."

"Evans, Steel Producing."

I glanced over at the people whose names had already been called. The ones who had been directed to the Hot Mill didn't betray any emotion, but the ones who were slated for Steel Producing looked gravely concerned.

Please, I thought, *not Steel Producing, not Steel Producing.*

The union official called Amelia's name, and her hand shot up with a flourish.

"Right here and ready to go," she told him.

"Hot Mill," the union official said without emotion, and a look of

disappointment spread across Amelia's face. Like me, she was probably hoping for the bright lights of the Country Club.

"Edwards," the union official continued. "Hot Mill."

"Finnegan, Hot Mill."

"Goldbach," the union official said at last.

"Here," I answered.

The man didn't look up from his paper. He just read the verdict.
"Finishing."

4

If there was one thing I believed as a child, it was this: My father didn't deserve to be cataloged as *ordinary*.

In his twenties, my father had attended Indiana University Bloomington to become a jazz drummer. He studied briefly at a conservatory in Switzerland, and he had even been credited on a few LPs. For a while, he lived as a struggling musician in a cockroach-infested apartment in New York City. He taught John Cougar before the star began performing under the name Mellencamp, and he taught Melissa Etheridge before she became a hit. My father had even done a brief stint with the Cleveland Jazz Orchestra, but his dreams of hitting it big had largely evaporated by the time I was born. Throughout my childhood, he worked as the manager of a pawnshop.

Back then, I didn't comprehend the disappointment that might attend this twist of fate. I didn't see the unachieved ambitions or the failed dreams. To me, the pawnshop was a fascinating place to find yourself. It was chock-full of curiosities.

Sometimes I went to work with him on summer afternoons, and I delighted in all there was to see and touch. There were buckets of coins on the floor and trays of jewelry on the chairs. Stacks of paper reached up to the ceiling, and rows of baseball cards littered the desks. Sports pennants were draped over seat backs, and loose jewels were scattered on tabletops. Everywhere you looked, there was some sort of priceless artifact that needed to be appraised. Even the bathroom was a marvel. The toilet seat was made of pennies.

While my father knew how to buy jewelry, gemstones, and Beanie Babies, he mostly specialized in old American coins. The coins were my favorite too. They smelled earthy and metallic, and many had been minted before I was born.

One morning, when I was still in grade school, my father took me to work with him for the day. I plopped down at a tiny desk that he had cleared, and he set a bucket of nickels in front of me. Without instruction, I went to work. I already knew what I had to do.

The nickels weren't just any nickels. They were Buffalo nickels, and I was looking for a 1937 D. Some coins in that mint had been printed with a defect. The buffalo, which usually had four legs, had only three legs on some 1937 Ds, and my father told me they were quite expensive. I scoured through the coins, not realizing that three-legged Buffalo nickels were so rare that I was basically on a snipe hunt. To me, it didn't matter that I always left the pawnshop without striking it rich. A treasure only had value because it was difficult to find.

"Is this one?" I asked, walking up to my father, who was grading Morgan dollars at his desk.

The nickel was particularly worn, so my father held it up to a microscope and inspected it closely. He removed his glasses to get a better view of the coin, revealing a pair of eyes that were small and squat, much like my own.

"Nope," he said, and my heart sank. "Not the right mint."

I went back to my desk with a sigh. There were still hundreds of coins to sort through, so I picked out another handful and went to work. An AM radio played in the background, and the man's voice was giving me a headache.

"The Indians have a good shot," the man said. "This might be their year, but their bull pen needs work."

I hated sports radio—the men were always too animated and aggressive—but I didn't want to ask for a different station. I admired my father, and I wanted to be like him. If that meant I had to listen to men jabber about the Indians, then so be it.

At lunchtime, my father and I both took a break from our work. I wandered back to his desk, which was covered in Morgan dollars.

"Can I pick one up?" I asked with my hand already poised over a coin.

"Sure," my father said. He was sitting back in his chair, enjoying a sandwich. "Go ahead."

The coin felt cold between my fingers, and I swooned when I read the date: 1881. The coin was more than a hundred years old, and I studied it with reverence. An eagle with outstretched wings graced the back of the dollar, but my attention was drawn to the strange portrait that had been depicted on the front. The person on the coin had a long straight nose and curly hair. It didn't look like any president I'd ever seen.

"Who's this supposed to be?" I asked my father.

"It's Lady Liberty," he told me with a bit of mustard on his cheek.

I wrinkled my nose. "Really? It doesn't look like a lady."

"Yeah." My father laughed, glancing at the coin. "I guess you're right."

"Why does she have leaves in her hair?" I said, noticing a crown of foliage that had been woven into Liberty's curls.

"I think they're supposed to be laurel leaves," my father said. "They're a symbol of peace."

I let out a long sigh. Of course they were *laurel* leaves. My older sister's name was Laurel, and she always seemed to outdo me in everything. Even her name was better than mine. We had been born five years apart, and it often felt like I was living in her shadow. I developed a fiercely competitive spirit as a result. If Laurel got all As, then I had to get all A+s. If she could play an instrument, I had to do it better. If she could sing, I had to hit a higher note. Even when I managed to surpass everything Laurel had already done, my teachers and relatives usually undermined my hard work.

Oh, they'd say, *you can tell she's Laurel's sister!*

While I did my best to keep up with my sister, I sometimes found it difficult to stifle my sharp tongue or curb my stubbornness. Laurel, on the other hand, seemed to achieve perfection without effort. I was glad that she was off playing basketball with her friends. It gave me a chance to be alone with my father, where the two of us could search for treasure all afternoon.

I looked down at the Morgan dollar, trying to ignore the laurel leaves. Lady Liberty's silver cheek had been worn smooth, and there were a few dings on her skin. Above her head were three words in a language I didn't understand. *E pluribus unum.* It only added to the coin's mystery.

In the mind of an imaginative child, the Morgan dollar possessed a strange bit of magic. It connected me to everyone who had ever touched it. Hundreds—perhaps thousands—of people I had never met were all tied together across time and distance through this tiny bit of metal. As I turned the coin over in my hands, I tried to imagine all of the old-fashioned people who had once carried it in their pockets. They had probably gone about their lives without ever wondering where the coin would be in a hundred years. Maybe they had purchased sugar or horses with that very same coin. Maybe they had bought flour or music boxes.

In that tiny pawnshop on the outskirts of Cleveland, the piece of silver in my hands was more than a collectible. It was a living piece of history. One day, far in the future, the coin might pass through other fingers that hadn't even been born yet. It would see many more generations of Americans, all of whom would stare down at the strange woman with curly hair, wondering who she was. I turned the Morgan dollar over in my hands one last time. To me, the coin felt like a great and important intersection. It was a crossroads between what we were and who we might become.

On my first day in the Finishing Department, I felt lost. I had never been on my own inside the mill before. No one stopped me at the guard station. No one questioned me when I parked my car. Jack wasn't there to tell me stories, and I had already forgotten where I was supposed to report for work.

I lingered in the parking lot for a while, paralyzed by the huge expanse of the mill. Semitrucks crept down the roadways, laden with steel coils, and the warehouses stretched on without end. A tall white tower loomed above the Hot Dip Galvanizing Line, and the blue flames of the Blast Furnace burned in the distance. I watched as a forklift barreled down the road, weaving around the trucks, and I recalled the safety videos I had watched during orientation. *Forklifts can impale you. Forklifts can crush you.* I wasn't ready for this place. I wasn't a steelworker, even though my orange hard hat indicated otherwise. I didn't know how to navigate the dangers. I wasn't sure I could keep myself safe.

I waited in the parking lot for a moment longer. Both Sam and Charlie had been placed in Finishing with me, and I was hoping they would show up and guide me through the mill. I wanted to follow, not lead, and both men appeared more self-assured than I was. Already, the mill had made me timid. I usually loved to put myself in physically demanding environments. I had hiked part of the Appalachian Trail. I had scrambled up cliffs without a rope. I had hopped on the backs of unruly horses without a second thought, but the bone-crushing equipment of the mill made me feel small and breakable.

After a while, I gave up hope of finding Sam and Charlie. There was no sign of them, so I started walking. A few golf carts zoomed past as I tried to remember where I was supposed to go. Every cart was loaded with Yellow Hats, most of whom were starting or ending their shifts, but I was too afraid to ask for directions. Some of the Yellow Hats stared at me with suspicious eyes, and others hummed along without a second thought. I tried to keep my head down. I didn't want anyone to know that I was lost.

"Hey!" a man yelled from behind me, but I kept staring at the pavement. I assumed he was talking to someone else. "Hey, you. Orange Hat."

I looked up to find that one of the golf carts was idling at my heels.

"Want a ride?" The man was sitting in the passenger seat, and he had a childish glint in his eyes despite his gray beard.

"Sure," I told him.

I hopped onto the back of the golf cart, clutching my lunch in my hand.

"Where are you going?" the driver said. He was a middle-aged man with wispy brown hair and slightly hunched shoulders.

"I'm supposed to find the shipping boss. I think his name is Jeremy."

"Oh," the man in the passenger seat said, glancing over at the driver. "*Jeremy*. She's in for a treat."

"Why?" I asked, suddenly concerned. "Is he mean or something?"

"No," the driver said, stepping on the gas. "He's just . . . *Jeremy*."

The golf cart zoomed down the road, bouncing on a few potholes as it went. I came to learn that the etiquette regarding golf carts in the mill operated on two key rules. First, you never called them *golf carts*. You called them *buggies*. Second, you didn't dare touch a buggy that "belonged" to someone else. For the most part, all of the buggies were affiliated with certain jobs inside the mill. So, the Wrappers in the A-Building had their own buggy, and there would be hell to pay if anyone other than a Wrapper in A-Building took that particular buggy. That buggy was *theirs*, more or less. While most steelworkers would offer you a ride if they saw you walking from the parking lot, they turned into bloodhounds whenever a buggy went missing. People padlocked their buggies when they left the mill. They hid the batteries and took off the tires.

"So, what's your name, anyway?" the man in the passenger seat said. The ends of his gray hair were sticking out from the bottom of his hard hat, and he was giving me a wide smile. "My name's Luke, but everyone calls me Gunner."

"Gunner?" I asked.

"Yep."

The driver of the buggy shook his head, which made Gunner roll his eyes.

"I see you shaking your head at me," Gunner told the driver before turning his attention back to me. "Don't mind him. He gets really uptight sometimes."

The buggy sped around a curve, narrowly dodging a forklift that was heading in the opposite direction. My fingers tightened around my lunch box, but Gunner seemed completely oblivious to the near miss.

"So, how long have you been working in the mill?" he asked.

"I just got done with orientation," I told him. "This is my first day in the actual mill."

"Oh boy," he said. "Well, just make sure you follow the rules while you've got that orange hat. If you do that, you'll be fine. Did they tell you where you're gonna be working?"

"Gunner," the driver said, obviously annoyed, "where do you think she'll be working? She's going to see Jeremy."

"I just wanted to make sure," Gunner huffed. The two men were acting like an old married couple. "You don't have to jump down my throat."

The bickering was beginning to make me uncomfortable, but I tried my best to ignore it.

"They said I'll be in the Shipping Department for now," I told the men. Just as there were different *mills* inside the *mill*, there were also different *departments* within the *departments* inside the mill. The Shipping Department was one such department that fell under the umbrella of the Finishing Department.

"See? I was right," Gunner told the driver. I almost thought he was going to stick out his tongue.

"Well, we're here," the driver said, stopping in front of a warehouse. "Just go through that door. You'll find some offices inside."

I thanked both of the men, waving self-consciously as they drove away, and then I stepped through a rusted door that squealed when I opened it. Jeremy's office was located in a tiny building that had been built inside the warehouse, as if someone had decided that the mill needed a Russian nesting doll. This building-inside-a-building housed a few other offices, all of which opened into a narrow hallway that smelled like freshly brewed coffee. I was met by Sam and Charlie when I went inside.

Jeremy hadn't arrived yet, so we all stood in the hallway, lusting after a box of doughnuts that was propped open in the break room. A map of the mill had been posted on the wall, and I studied it with exaggerated interest. I was glad to be in the mill with people as friendly as Sam and Charlie, but we still didn't know each other well. Two weeks of orientation was barely enough time to forge friendships, and I could tell that the men felt just as awkward as I did.

"Hey," Sam said, breaking the silence that had settled between us. "Did you guys see your first paycheck yet?"

"I don't know," I told him. "I haven't looked at my account."

"I got mine," Charlie said, giving Sam a knowing look. "They deposited it last night."

"Holy shit, right?" Sam laughed.

"Yeah. Holy shit."

As we talked about the salaries at our previous jobs, a tall man with thin hips and sleepy brown eyes walked down the hall. He approached us tentatively.

"You must be my new hires," he said. "I'm Jeremy, your boss."

I had expected a big, burly foreman, but Jeremy looked like the kind of man who should have been selling car insurance. His hand felt soft and limp when I shook it, and he had the self-conscious air of someone who doesn't like being the tallest person in the room.

After making our introductions, we followed Jeremy into his office, which was surprisingly large. A sizable desk sat at the back of the room, leaving a big empty space near the door that was begging to be filled. The desk was littered with papers, and a picture of Jeremy's wife and kids sat in one corner.

"Now that I have a few extra hands, I want to get some cleaning done around here," Jeremy said, getting straight down to business. "That's all I want you guys to do for a few weeks. Just stop in here every morning, and I'll give you a few tasks."

That particular morning, Jeremy told us that we would be sweeping. I breathed a sigh of relief. The task didn't sound too difficult, and it certainly seemed safe. We would be contending with dust bunnies, not booming mills that could swallow our limbs.

"I want to offer you guys a word of caution," Jeremy said, growing suddenly serious. "Don't let this place change you. I've seen it happen to a lot of people. They start out as great employees, but the culture gets to them. After a year or so, they start getting obstinate and lazy. They just become different people."

"Don't worry," Charlie said, cradling his orange hard hat like a baby. "That won't happen to us."

"No way," Sam added. "We're just thankful for the job."

We assured Jeremy that we understood the value of hard work. We were willing to toil for our paychecks, and we couldn't imagine how anyone would do otherwise. Jeremy nodded, but there was a weary look in his eyes. I sensed that he had heard the same thing before.

"Well," he said, pulling a yellow hard hat out from under his desk, "let's see if we can find you some brooms."

We exited the office, and then the warehouse, before crossing the same road I had driven down with Gunner. Jeremy led us across the street and into a long building that served as the main hub of the Shipping Department.

The Hot Dip Galvanizing Line, which had the glistening floors that we'd walked across during orientation, was located at the south side of this building, and the Shipping Department was located in the north. While the two operations were housed in the same building, they each constituted a separate department. They were managed by different bosses, and you could clearly see where the Hot Dip ended and the Shipping Department began. A line had been drawn with dirt. Whereas the Hot Dip was squeaky-clean, the Shipping Department looked faded and worn. Jeremy wanted to change all of that.

While sweeping had initially sounded like an easy task, I hadn't considered the sheer size of the building. It was at least a tenth of a mile long, and sweeping the floors would probably take a week or longer. Jeremy showed us where to find the brooms and quickly scuttled back to his office. I set to work with Sam and Charlie, all of us toiling like the model employees we had promised to be.

If getting into Finishing was like winning the lottery, then getting into Shipping was like winning the lottery and finding buried treasure on the same afternoon. Everyone wanted to work in Shipping. The jobs were relatively easy, and Jeremy rarely ever came around to give you grief. The thing that appealed to me most, however, was the relative safety of the place. From what I could tell, there were really only a few things that could kill you in Shipping: the cranes, the wrapping machines, and the boredom.

On that first day in the mill, the boredom hadn't yet hit me. Charlie, Sam, and I swept without stopping for the first few hours of our shift, and we quickly learned that it was a Sisyphean task. We would start clearing a section of the floor, and our brooms would kick dust into the air. By the time we moved on to the next section, all of the dust had settled on the section we'd just finished. The perfectionistic demon on my shoulder wouldn't stop badgering me. I kept going back and re-sweeping the settled dust.

"It's useless," Charlie said. "You're never going to get it all up."

"Yeah," Sam told me. "Let's just keep moving forward. It still looks better than when we started."

I resisted them at first, but I eventually had to agree. Even when I swept a second or third time, the dust always found its way back to the ground. I moved forward with the two other Orange Hats and tried to ignore the dust that fell to the floor behind me, but I had trouble shooing the demon from my shoulder. Part of me was still a little girl trying to outdo her sister. I wanted Jeremy to walk through the doors and tell me that I was the best steelworker he'd ever seen, but I knew the other Orange Hats were right. The mill would never be perfect, and we still had a lot of floor left to sweep. The building stretched on forever. Semitrucks were constantly flowing in and out of the doors, leaving fresh dirt on the ground, and no amount of sweeping could rid the air of their exhaust.

I bent diligently over my broom, working as fast as possible to keep up with the other Orange Hats. I wasn't really paying attention to the trucks—or anything, really—when I felt a hand on my shoulder. It was Sam. He pointed up at the ceiling. A crane rumbled past, carrying a steel coil in its jaws. I had gotten so involved in the task at hand that I had almost walked right underneath it. I nodded to Sam in thanks and cursed myself for not following one of the cardinal rules in the mill: *Don't ever walk under a crane that's carrying a load.*

For my first few weeks in the mill, navigating around the cranes felt a lot like learning how to cross the street all over again. You still had to look *left* and *right* when you walked, because semitrucks and forklifts were always passing nearby, but you also had to look *up* at the cranes. They were constantly moving steel, and they posed one of the most persistent threats in the Shipping Department.

While most operators did their best to stay safe, close calls certainly happened. Sometimes the cables snapped for no apparent reason, and a steel coil would come crashing down to the ground. Sometimes the cranes went rogue, moving of their own volition. Sometimes the power went out, which could be deadly. While logic might suggest that a loss of power would make the crane stop moving, the opposite would happen. The cranes didn't have a very effective braking system, and the huge machines were mostly stopped by *plugging*, a technique that halts the crane's current trajectory by forcing it to move in the opposite direction. Without power, the crane operator couldn't plug. If the crane was moving at the time, the momentum would carry it straight into a wall.

I watched as the crane loaded its coil onto a semitruck. In one fluid motion, the operator swooped forty thousand pounds of steel through the air without hesitation. The coil descended toward the truck, eventually settling onto its bed like a robin's egg in a nest of feathers. As dangerous as the cranes could be, there was also an understated grace about them. They swam through the sky with unspeakable force, moving great loads with little effort, and I often found myself mesmerized by their movements.

My thoughts were interrupted as Charlie approached Sam and me. "Do you guys want to go get some water?" We were all sweating, even though it wasn't particularly warm in the building, and our necks were coated in dirt. All three of us were so thankful for the mill's paycheck that we'd been working without rest, and the thought of water was heavenly. Without another word, we all dropped our brooms to the ground and started walking toward the break room.

I followed behind the two other Orange Hats and stared up at the ceiling in search of cranes.

"Hey, look," Sam said. "There's Jack."

I adjusted my gaze back toward the ground, expecting to see the old crazed steelworker who had almost tipped me out of the boom lift, but there wasn't anyone else nearby.

"Where's Jack?" I said.

"There," Sam said, pointing toward the wall of the building. "See?"

It took me a second, but I finally understood what he was talking about. Someone had drawn a caricature of Jack's head on the wall, and it was an uncanny likeness. With a few swipes of black marker, the artist had perfectly captured Jack's square jaw, his bald head, and his tiny eyes. The caricature's mouth was open, as if offering advice, and Jack's last name had been written beneath the portrait for clarity. Clarity seemed unnecessary, though. The face unmistakably belonged to Jack.

These little portraits of Jack were the last I'd ever see of him. He worked in a different department, which meant we didn't have much opportunity to cross paths. The mill was so huge that you rarely interacted with people who weren't in your department. You might see former coworkers at union events—or maybe you'd run into them at the dive bar around the corner—but that was about it. I would never talk with Amelia again, and I wouldn't see Gage until years later, when I happened to wander into #1 Steel Producing. Even the old friend who showed me his paycheck—the one who prompted me to apply at the mill in the first place—might as well have worked on the other side of the moon. He spent his days in #2 Steel Producing, and we only talked to each other through the occasional text message.

Jack was never far from my mind, though, because the caricatures were everywhere in Finishing. You could find them on doors and walls and girders. A few faces had been drawn right onto the machinery that we used to make steel. For the most part, Jack's face was the only piece of graffiti on a given surface. Other times, however, an impossibly large penis had been drawn next to Jack's open mouth.

In the corporate world, you might report the phallic doodles to the company's HR Department and seek mediation, but that kind of thing would never fly in a union shop. In the mill, *snitches got stitches* and *scabs were lower than dirt*. If you had a problem with the penises that a union brother or sister drew on the wall, you sure as hell didn't go to the company. You hashed it out between yourselves. You dealt with it mano a mano. You could get your committeeman involved if things got hairy, but you could never tattle to the boss.

Long after I'd learned the ropes of the mill, I had to navigate one of these situations myself. One of the old-timers had started calling me QuackQuack. He snickered whenever he said the name, and I tried to ignore it at first. The man was notoriously miserable and annoying, and most people didn't put much stock in the things he said.

"I figured out why he calls you QuackQuack," a female steelworker told me during one of our shifts. The woman had a nickname of her own, courtesy of the old-timer. He called her Tackle Box, which was supposedly a reference to the woman's facial piercings. She had gauged ears and a nose ring, so the reasoning behind the nickname ostensibly made sense, but she was also absolutely gorgeous. She was knockdown beautiful, even without makeup, and there was always part of me that wondered if the old-timer wasn't also referring to a different kind of box he'd like to tackle.

"Okay," I said. "Why does he call me QuackQuack?"

"Are you sure you want me to tell you?" she asked. There were a few other steelworkers within earshot, and she didn't want to embarrass me.

"Yeah," I said. "Tell me. How bad can it be?"

"He said that you waddle when you walk. Like a duck. Those were his words, not mine. I don't think you fucking waddle."

It wasn't something that any woman wanted to hear. I had struggled with body image and eating disorders for most of my life, so the comment hit particularly close to home. Still, I knew better than to show any emotion other than indifference. I shrugged.

"Dude," I said, "I should totally get a rubber duck and put it on his chair."

The woman and I both laughed, and the other steelworkers who were sitting nearby chimed in.

"Oh my gosh," one said, "you should get a bunch of ducks and line them up by his computer and stuff."

"That would be amazing," another steelworker said.

"Yeah." I laughed. "I'll put a note next to all the ducks that just says, 'Quack quack, motherfucker.'"

We all joked about the nickname for the rest of the afternoon. You couldn't let things get to you in the mill. If people said that you waddled, then you had to own it. If they drew penises next to your face, then you had to open your mouth and laugh.

A few days later the old-timer visited me at my workstation. His hair was beginning to thin, and he walked with a swagger that didn't befit a man in his sixties.

"Hey, QuackQuack," he said with a sly smile on his face.

"Hey," I mumbled in response. I wanted to show this old buzzard that I wasn't going to put up with his nonsense, but I couldn't do it right after he'd used the name QuackQuack. That would have been suicide. It would've proven that the nickname had gotten to me, so I let the old-timer talk while I bided my time. He started spouting some incoherent nonsense about how women are gold diggers.

"You women just want to be taken care of," he told me. "You women only have money in mind."

You women, you women. When he finally stopped to take a breath, I rolled my eyes and raised a middle finger.

"Whoa, whoa, whoa," he said, taking a few steps back in surprise. "You're flicking me off?"

"Yeah."

"Right to my face?"

"Yeah. What are you gonna do? Cry about it?"

Earning respect in the mill was a subtle art. You had to take your bruises without tears, but you couldn't be too passive. You had to prove that you were just as tough as the other guy. If you didn't, you would always be seen as easy fodder.

The old-timer walked away after I flicked him off, and he avoided me from that day forward. He no longer had the nerve to insult me to my face, but that didn't really solve anything. He continued to call me QuackQuack behind my back. At best, it seemed like a lateral move.

For as long as I could remember, my life felt like a struggle to figure out where I fit in relation to men. I wasn't sure how to get my way without being seen as demanding. I wasn't sure how to express myself without being seen as needy. I wasn't sure how to be assertive without being seen as a bitch. Even as a child, boys confused me. They had the best toys. They had the best games. They moved their bodies with easy confidence, and I wanted to be just like them. In first grade, the boys and I played Star Wars under the desks at school, chopping each other with fake lightsabers and falling to the ground when our bodies had been struck. By fourth grade, everything had changed. The world got divided up into *boys* and *girls*, and everyone was obsessed with the same stupid questions: Who liked you? Who kissed you? Who wrote you love letters at lunchtime?

Strange gossip traveled the halls. Kids tittered about sex. They joked about *doing it*. They were all privy to knowledge I didn't understand, so I tried to listen closely. My understanding of birth control came from the popular girls in my class, who used to pretend that SweeTarts were "pregnancy pills." My knowledge of anal sex came from incredulous tales told around the lunch table. I learned about masturbation from the *Catechism of the Catholic Church*. I learned about condoms from advertisements. An opinionated sixth grader explained missionary style to me, and my grandfather's *Playboy* taught me about breasts.

I knew better than to ask my parents about any of it. They had worked hard to keep me and my sister sheltered from media that might be construed as sinful. In our house, *sinful* also meant *sexual*. While we certainly didn't exist in a bubble, Laurel and I were encouraged to watch programs like *Antiques Roadshow* and *Dr. Quinn, Medicine Woman*. *The Simpsons* was off-limits, as was *The Golden Girls*. Both were considered too racy. *Seinfeld* was allowed, but only because my father liked to watch it. Nirvana was the Devil's music. MTV was the Devil's mouthpiece, and anyone who listened to Metallica was certainly under the Devil's spell.

Ultimately, though, it didn't matter how diligently my parents tried to shield me. By the age of ten, I was already guilty of one of the most grievous sins imaginable. I had committed a *sexual* sin while playing *Oregon Trail* with a boy in computer class.

The boy and I had been paired together by our teacher, who often partnered boys with girls to reduce the risk of misbehavior. We both sat quietly in front of an old Apple computer while our teacher handed out floppy disks. She warned us about the sacred hole in the disk's center.

"If you touch the hole," she said, "you'll ruin the disk. Anyone who touches the hole will go to the principal's office."

The boy slipped our disk into the computer, unworried. *Oregon Trail* popped up on the screen, and we opted to be the Banker from Boston. As our wagon crept slowly along the trail, the boy put his hand on my knee. His fingertips sent a delightful tingle up my spine. The teacher patrolled the opposite side of the room, and our wagon stopped beside a river.

"*Do you want to ford the river?*" the computer asked.

"*Yes.*"

The boy inched his hand up my thigh, and I froze. His fingers, which had felt so lovely on my knee, now grazed the elastic of my underwear. I didn't want him to go any farther, but I wasn't sure how to make him stop. No one had ever warned me about these kinds of situations, so I tried to remedy the problem in the only way I knew how right then. I chose to hunt along the Oregon Trail. Everyone knew that hunting was the best part, and I figured that it might turn the boy's attention away from my underwear. I aimed the gun at the white animals that darted across the screen. I shot a buffalo, which sank into a blob. I fired at a deer and missed.

"Do you want to try?" I said to the boy, pushing the keyboard in front of him.

"Not really," he told me.

He slipped his fingers beneath my underwear, moving clumsily.

A rabbit darted across the screen, but I was too distracted to hit it. I wanted the boy to stop, so I looked over at him and shook my head.

"No," I whispered.

He just smiled. I pulled the keyboard in front of me and stared blankly at a cluster of deer. If I couldn't make the boy stop, then I would brace myself like I did before a needle prick at the doctor's office. Eventually the discomfort would pass.

When a buffalo walked into view, I killed it on the first try. I looked back at the boy, hoping for his approval, but he wasn't watching the computer. His eyes were fixed on me. There was something in his stare that frightened me. He looked vacant and ravenous and wild. As a child, I didn't recognize that look, but I would come to know it as I aged. I would see that look in the eyes of other men. Men in bars. Men on street corners. Men in the workplace. They were the eyes of a man sizing you up as nothing more than a void to relieve his pressure.

The computer notified me that my hunting session had ended. As usual, I had killed more than I could carry. The little wagon continued its journey along the trail, and the teacher walked past our seats. With surprising speed, the boy withdrew his hand. He pulled the keyboard in front of him and stared at the screen with exaggerated intensity. Up until that point, I hadn't really comprehended the weight of the boy's hand beneath my underwear. It made me uncomfortable, but I didn't realize how wrong it had been. The boy's sudden change in demeanor made it clear that whatever we had been doing could get us into serious trouble. I didn't like getting into trouble. I prided myself on being an obedient student, and I felt guilty for breaking a rule I couldn't quite articulate.

"Don't tell anyone," the boy whispered after computer class.

His insistence further solidified my guilt. I knew about sins of omission. If you saw someone doing something wrong, you were supposed to stop them. If you didn't, it was just as bad as doing the wrong thing yourself.

A few weeks later I went with my family to receive the sacrament of reconciliation at our church. My parents waited in line behind me and Laurel. Eventually we would each take a turn inside a tiny wooden booth, where we would tell a priest all of our sins and shortcomings.

Going to confession was a normal occurrence in my family. We went every so often, which was the recommended practice for all Catholics. Everyone was encouraged to confess their sins as a way to grow closer to God, but there were some instances when confession was absolutely required. According to Catholic teaching, there were two types of sin: mortal and venial. The venial sins were tiny lapses and minor misdeeds, while mortal sins were serious transgressions that landed you in hellfire. God could forgive venial sins during Mass, but mortal sins were different. You absolutely had to confess those to a priest, or else they stained your soul. If you died with a mortal sin against your name, you would wind up spending the rest of eternity with the Devil.

As I waited for my turn in the confessional, I stared down at the yellow sheet of paper someone had given to me when I first entered the church. It was an Examination of Conscience, which listed the many ways a person could violate the Ten Commandments. The Examination was intended to help people recall their sins, but I stared solely at the Sixth Commandment: *Thou shalt not commit adultery.*

My Catholic grade school had taught me that you didn't have to actually commit adultery to break the Sixth Commandment. The rule covered all manner of sexual sins, including sex outside of marriage. You didn't even need to have sex in order to break the commandment. Anything more than an innocent kiss counted as a sin against God.

Have you been impure with someone else? the yellow paper taunted. *Have you engaged in inappropriate touching?*

Sins against the Sixth Commandment were considered mortal sins, which made my palms sweat. Even though I didn't have a word for what had happened with the boy in computer class, I knew that the area of my body beneath my underwear was the sexual part of my body. I knew in my gut that the boy and I had done something very wrong that involved sex outside of marriage, so I reasoned that we'd violated the Sixth Commandment.

My sister, who was waiting in line ahead of me, entered the confessional. I was up next, and I started to panic. I didn't want to tell the priest about what had happened with the boy, but I also knew that I didn't have much of a choice. If you consciously withheld a single sin from the priest, then your whole confession was considered null and void. God would refuse his forgiveness, and the mortal sin would still be a black mark against your soul. If I wanted to avoid the eternal punishment, then I would have to tell the priest about *Oregon Trail*.

By the time it was my turn in the confessional, I felt sick to my stomach. I sat down in front of a balding middle-aged priest. We both made the sign of the cross.

"Forgive me, Father," I said in the customary way, "for I have sinned."

The priest looked down at his lap while I told him my sins. I listed the normal misdeeds you would expect from a child. Fighting with my sister. Disobeying my parents. Not praying enough. When I uttered all the sins I could remember, I paused.

"And," I said, "I was impure with a boy in computer class."

I said it quickly, rushing through the words. The priest kept staring at his lap.

"For these and all my sins," I told him, "I am sorry."

The priest remained silent for a moment. He shifted in his seat, and the wooden chair creaked beneath him.

"That was a very honest confession," he said at last. "For your penance, pray one Our Father, one Hail Mary, and one Glory Be. You can say your Act of Contrition now."

I recited the prayer of contrition that I'd been taught in school, and the priest gave me his blessing. After he'd dismissed me from the confessional, I kneeled down and prayed my penance, feeling just as confused as ever.

I still felt like the meek girl who confessed her sins to a priest when I met Tackle Box for the first time. I was walking through the Shipping Department to get a bottle of water when I heard her cursing.

"I can't believe those assholes sent me to do this bullshit," she said to no one in particular as she walked around a coil that had been placed on a pair of elevated rollers. Half of her head was shaved, and the other half was a shock of blue that fell past her shoulders. She appeared to be a few years younger than me, but she carried herself with a level of confidence I'd never been able to muster.

"I fucking hate this shit," she said again, shaking her head.

While Tackle Box usually worked in the next building over, in a place called the Temper Mill, her boss had sent her to Shipping to do cutbacks. The job involved cutting off the damaged end of an otherwise perfect coil, which was accomplished by unwinding it on rollers and then hacking off the marred steel with a guillotine.

I watched her from the corner of my eye as I edged past, not wanting her wrath to fall on me. Her sharp tongue and furrowed brow intimidated me, but an old crane operator walked up to her with his arms crossed. He had a mop of gray hair and a lazy eye, and he watched her like a spectator at a zoo.

"Boy, you've got a tongue," the crane operator said, smiling.

"Fuck off," Tackle Box hissed as she slowly unrolled the coil.

The man threw his head back and laughed. "I'm gonna watch out for you," he said, wagging his finger.

Tackle Box just glared at him. "Bite me."

The man chuckled to himself and walked away, while I slipped past Tackle Box undetected, breathing a sigh of relief as I darted into the shanty where the water was kept.

In the mill there were three different types of small break rooms—known as shanties, booths, and pulpits—that had been built inside the main buildings that housed the steelmaking equipment. Since the main buildings were so incredibly large, it was impossible to heat them in the winter or cool them in the summer. The shanties, booths, and pulpits provided a tiny space where workers could sit down and escape from the elements.

Pulpits were the largest of the three, and I had seen a few during my tour of the Hot Mill. They were two-story structures that housed the knobs and buttons that controlled a certain section of machinery, and they usually had a bathroom, a microwave, and a refrigerator. Pulpits were mostly found in areas that contained an actual mill, so there weren't any in Shipping. There were, however, a few booths, which were similar to pulpits. The booths also had knobs and buttons that controlled machinery, but they were markedly smaller. They rarely contained a bathroom, and they were never two stories high. Shanties, on the other hand, didn't contain any important pieces of equipment whatsoever. They were simply a place for steelworkers to rest, confess their troubles, and gossip about the goings-on at the mill.

The shanty I walked into after my brief encounter with Tackle Box was one of the biggest in the Shipping Department, and it also served as a hub of social activity. This Social Shanty was big enough for two refrigerators and a conference table, which was made of fake mahogany. No matter how many times you wiped down the table and the surrounding chairs, your paper towel always came away black. The grime was so pervasive that you eventually gave up trying to eradicate it. The dark color of the fake mahogany hid the dirt well enough, and sometimes ignorance was bliss.

Sam and Charlie were already rummaging through the fridge when I stepped inside, and some of the workers who were gathered around the table had started to come alive.

"What do they have the Orange Hats doing today?" an old-timer asked. He was tall and broad-shouldered with a captivating smile, and everyone called him the Godfather.

"We've been sweeping," Sam said.

The Godfather raised an eyebrow. "Sweeping? They need to be training you as Banders. Then you can make more money."

"I don't know," Sam said, shrugging. "It sounds like we'll be cleaning for a while."

The Godfather leaned back, as if appraising me and the other Orange Hats. "Well, you guys must be doing a good job. You're all filthy."

"Yeah," Charlie said, "I just blew my nose and a bunch of black stuff came out."

"Hold on," a second old-timer interrupted, standing up from his chair. I had already seen this particular old-timer walking through the department, and I had assumed that he would be gruff and surly. He vaguely resembled the Crypt Keeper from *Tales of the Crypt*, but it turned out that few people in the mill were more helpful in providing guidance and advice.

"Nobody gave you dust masks before you started?" he asked.

"No," Sam said.

The old-timer grunted in disgust.

"Well, that's Jeremy for you," he said. "You can't always trust some of these brain-dead bosses. They're your best buddy when they want something done, but when push comes to shove, they don't really care about your safety."

The man rummaged through some filing cabinets and found a box of dust masks. While there was certainly a lot of pettiness that took place within the union, it wasn't all bad. Union workers looked out for each other. They warned one another of nearby dangers, even if they didn't like each other personally. If the bosses gave you trouble, your fellow union workers rallied behind you. There was a feeling of family about it. People threw holiday parties. They took up collections for sick or injured workers. They organized breakfasts on Saturday mornings and cookouts on the Fourth of July.

"Here," the old-timer said, handing us the dust masks. "If you need more, just ask some of the people around here. They're bound to have a few squirreled away."

We thanked him and grabbed a few bottles of water, but the Godfather stopped us when we started to head back to our brooms.

"Wait a second," he boomed. "Where are you all going?"

I glanced over at Sam and Charlie. They both had blank looks on their faces.

"We're getting back to work," I said.

The Godfather shook his head and laughed. "You guys barely took a break. Sit down. Enjoy your water. You don't want to get overheated."

For a moment no one moved. Sam and Charlie stared at each other, as if asking permission to follow the Godfather's direction. All three of us had come from jobs where breaks were strictly monitored, and we'd been taught not to dally in our work. It felt wrong to kick up our feet when we were making so much money, but the Godfather insisted.

"You guys should count your blessings," he said as we sat down around the mahogany table. "You started out in the Country Club. Back in my day, everyone had to hack it in the Coke Plant before they could even dream of Finishing."

I unscrewed the cap on a fresh bottle of water. "The Coke Plant?"

"Yeah." He sighed. "We used to make our own coke down here, and it was no picnic. The Coke Plant made the Blast Furnace look like a merry-go-round."

Many of the old-timers in the Shipping Department had been making steel for thirty or forty years, and they'd had to pay their dues in the now-defunct Coke Plant before qualifying for better positions. *"Hell" ain't even the word for it*, they'd say when reminiscing about the Coke Plant, and there was nothing exaggerated about the description. Treacherous ovens. Shoddy stairways. Rogue fires. Coke dust on your face and in your lungs. If you weren't shoveling load after load of coke, you were walking atop tall batteries that were hot enough to melt the soles of your shoes. In those days, most folks barely lasted a few hours on the job. People came to work sober and left work drunk. Prostitutes lingered around the mill and waited for the dirty desperate men to climb out of the coke pits and into their arms. Ex-convicts and displaced persons arrived by the busload to take the jobs that no one else wanted, and arguments were solved with fists and two-by-fours.

Of course, things were different now. You could get fired in a heartbeat for laying a hand on another worker, and there was a corporate-sponsored focus on safety. Safety training. Safety audits. Cabinets full of personal protective equipment. Companies had to pay heavy fines if they endangered the lives of their workers in the name of production, and no one had to slog through the coke pits in Cleveland anymore. The operation had been shuttered in 1992, shortly after the Clean Air Act was amended in 1990. It was too expensive to bring the equipment up to environmental standards, so the company decided to get its coke from other sources. Even with all of the changes, though, the mill had its risks. During my first few years at the mill, there were cuts, contusions, acid burns. One man barely survived a fall into the basement of the Tandem Mill. A few workers got stuck inside cranes after a fire started. They had to be rescued with boom lifts and taken to the hospital for smoke inhalation. There was the young mechanic who fell through a lance hole onto one of the vessels that was used to make steel. He broke his ankle, his knee, and his pelvis. Had he fallen a moment sooner, he would have landed in molten metal. Had he fallen a moment later, he would have bounced off the side of the vessel and fallen another sixty feet to his death. It's true that the old-timers started during slightly rougher days, but the present was plenty rough on all of us.

I drank my water quickly as the Godfather regaled us with stories about the Coke Plant. All of a sudden he stopped mid-sentence and looked at the corner of the room.

"Uh-oh," he said, "the boss is having a fit."

My stomach sank at the word *boss*. I didn't want Jeremy to see me and the other Orange Hats taking a break. It would confirm the warning he'd given us earlier: *Don't get lazy.* I turned around, expecting to be met with a disappointed gaze, but Jeremy was nowhere to be found.

"What boss?" I asked.

The Godfather chuckled. He walked over to the corner of the room, where a fax machine was in the process of printing out a few pages.

"Did you think that Jeremy was the boss?" he said. He grabbed the newly printed papers and slapped the fax machine a few times. "*This* is the boss."

Indeed, someone had written *THE BOSS* on the fax machine in permanent marker. It turned out that Jeremy seldom entered the buildings where his employees worked, and he usually gave directions via the fax machine. The Godfather didn't give Jeremy's fax so much as a glance. He just crumpled it up and threw it in the trash. Like many old-timers, he wasn't about to take directions from a mild-mannered pencil pusher who let a fax machine do his dirty work. Jeremy had to earn respect, just like the rest of us, and he was doing a poor job of it. Most of his employees had literally crawled through the coke pits. They spent their days walking beneath the cranes that could kill them.

They risked injury and accident, but their boss was too afraid—or too lofty—to come to the Country Club and give them directions. *Screw Jeremy*, they said. They saw a cowardly boss, and Jeremy saw obstinate employees. The fax machine sat somewhere in the middle, pumping out well-crafted memos that didn't mean shit to the people on the floor.

It took me and the other Orange Hats the better part of a week to sweep the floors, after which Jeremy gave us a new directive.

"I want you guys to clean the rail dock in 43-Building," he said while we gathered in his office one morning. We were still new employees, so Jeremy was offering us more guidance than he gave to the seasoned workers. We hadn't yet been subjected to the memos, but they wouldn't be far off.

"There's some wood and metal down in the rail dock that needs to be thrown away," Jeremy continued.

The rail dock in question was a long recessed pit inside one of the buildings that housed the Shipping Department. A set of train tracks ran down the length of this pit, which allowed train cars to come into the building. Once inside, a crane would load the cars full of steel coils that would then be sent to customers.

"Don't kill yourselves," Jeremy said. "Use a forklift to pick up one of those gray dumpsters. Then you can drive the dumpster along the rail dock and throw stuff inside."

It was a good piece of advice. The rail dock was several hundred feet long, and the forklift would certainly make things easier. The plan was simple enough. Two of us would go down into the rail dock and hurl debris up to the edge. The third person, who would drive the forklift along the edge of the rail dock, could then put the debris into the dumpster.

We told Jeremy that we could handle it and elected Charlie to drive the forklift. While he went to find a dumpster, Sam and I put a blue light on the entrance of the dock to let Railroad workers know that the tracks were closed. In the world of the mill, blue lights meant that

people were working in a precarious spot. Maybe workers were standing in a rail dock, or a crane was being repaired, or some other unusual
maintenance event was taking place. You didn't mess with a blue light.

When Charlie finally returned with a forklift and a dumpster, I
was surprised to see that he drove the vehicle directly into the rail
dock. I couldn't help thinking about what Jeremy had said to us earlier
that morning. He told us to drive the forklift *along* the rail dock, not
into it.

Maybe I should say something, I thought.

I quickly reconsidered. Charlie had worked at a hardware store, so
he already had a good deal of experience with forklifts. He certainly
knew more about them than I did, and Sam didn't seem concerned
about driving the vehicle down the dock. I was probably just being a
perfectionistic English major who thought too much about language.
Besides, the train tracks in the rail dock were flush with the ground.
Even though the wheels of the forklift straddled the tracks, there was
no way the vehicle could get stuck.

The three of us cleared a ten-foot section of the dock, and then
Charlie drove the forklift forward a few feet. We cleared the next
ten-foot section, and so on. We worked slowly down the length of
the dock, picking up pieces of wood and metal that had been carelessly flung into its depths. As we inched along, I noticed that the train
tracks were no longer level with the ground. They seemed to be getting higher and higher with every ten-foot section.

Maybe I should say something, I thought for a second time.

And once again I reconsidered. The two men were probably aware
of the rising tracks, and they didn't need some woman worrying about
a stupid, inconsequential detail.

Charlie kept driving the forklift forward, and we kept hoisting debris into the dumpster. After we'd cleared another ten-foot section,
Charlie gave the engine a little gas.

"Shit," he said through the open window.

The tires were spinning on the dirt, and the forklift wouldn't budge.
He tried again. Still nothing. Lo and behold, the tow motor had gotten stuck on the railroad tracks.

"Shit, shit, shit," Charlie said, exiting the cab.

"Don't worry," Sam told him, ever the optimist. "We'll get it out."

Together, we tried wedging the forklift free. We tried giving the wheels traction with plywood. We tried rocking it back and forth. We spent the better part of an hour trying to dislodge the forklift, but the damned thing wouldn't move. There was only one option left: We had to tell the old-timers what had happened. At first they seemed annoyed. We had pulled them away from their coveted downtime, and they rolled their eyes in annoyance. After a few minutes they started to laugh. They knew exactly what to do. They called a huge dump truck, which was able to pull the forklift free.

"I wonder whose bright idea it was to drive a forklift in the rail dock?" an old-timer said to me after the incident. He looked me up and down. By his tone, I could tell that he thought he knew exactly whose bright idea it had been.

Another man pulled me aside.

"Don't worry about this little blunder," he said. "You're not gonna get in trouble over this, but let it be a lesson to you. Think things through next time. Use your head."

More men told me the same thing: I needed to be a little smarter the next time around.

Sam and Charlie didn't receive these kinds of lectures. The other steelworkers simply joked with them.

"Welcome to the wonderful world of making steel!"

"That'll be the first of many!"

"Next week you'll be laughing about this!"

When I tried to join in on the jokes, all of the old-timers paused for a second. They looked at me with the same telling stares. I wasn't supposed to joke. I was the woman in the group, so it had certainly been my fault.

While there were other women who worked in the mill, we were definitely a minority. There were some men who still saw female workers as a quota that the company was trying to fill. They thought that women were token employees, at best, and they usually didn't trust our judgment. If we had an idea or an opinion, these same men always asked another man to confirm what we'd just said. There was a good deal of mansplaining, and there were offhanded comments that came straight out of the 1950s.

One man told me that I needed a manicure. Another told me that I would never find a husband until I learned how to cook, and still another was perplexed by the fact that I didn't have children. There were some men who ogled the young female employees. There were others who refused to train women, because they were afraid of being accused of sexual harassment or rape.

One afternoon, as I was walking to the Social Shanty for a bottle of water, the same crane operator who had heckled Tackle Box wrapped his arm tightly around my shoulders. His lazy eye looked a little too far to the left, and his touch made me uncomfortable.

"You're too pretty for this job," he said as my whole body tensed. "You should find a man to take care of you."

While not all of the men in the mill had these outmoded views, more than a few certainly did. I told myself that their attitudes weren't conscious or malicious—and I was probably right most of the time—but the underlying sexism was difficult to ignore. It seemed to have tangible effects too.

"Did you hear what happened with Amelia?" Sam asked me after we'd been working at the mill for a few months.

"No," I said. "What happened?"

Neither of us had seen the bubbly single mother since orientation, but rumors spread like wildfire in the valley, giving new meaning to the term *rumor mill*.

"I heard that she got fired," Sam told me.

I shook my head in disbelief. "Really? What happened?"

"I guess she was working as a Burner over in the Hot Mill," Sam explained. "She wasn't wearing a protective visor, and the bosses saw her."

"That's it?" I asked. "That seems like a stupid reason to fire somebody."

"Well, I think it happened a few times. She gave them some attitude about it, so they fired her."

"Wow, that sucks," I said, and Sam nodded in agreement.

Amelia's fate gave me pause. I had seen other Orange Hats—all of whom were men—break petty rules like this, and they were usually forgiven. I knew an Orange Hat who got caught leaving his shift a little early, but there were no repercussions. I heard of another Orange Hat who took a long nap on a picnic table. The main boss in the Finishing Department woke him up angrily, but the Orange Hat didn't lose his job.

When I heard about Amelia, I thought back to what some of the other new hires had said during orientation: *The guys down here aren't gonna put up with all that bubbly shit.*

I wondered whether Amelia had been singled out by the Hot Mill bosses, many of whom were men. I wondered if some of those bosses had hounded Amelia in a way that they wouldn't have hounded their male counterparts. If they *had* picked on Amelia unfairly, she was certainly the type to stick up for herself. In the Rumor Mill, people said that Amelia had *attitude*. Maybe she was just being assertive. Maybe she was just calling bullshit. Maybe she wasn't the *right* kind of woman for the mill.

If there was a difference between me and Amelia, it was this: I was, in fact, the right kind of woman. This wasn't exactly a compliment. When the men blamed me for the incident with the forklift, I wanted to tell all of them that it wasn't my idea. *I* was the one who'd noticed the rising tracks. *I* had been smart this time around, and they were simply making assumptions based on my gender. I didn't dare say anything, though. I sensed that many of the men in the mill wouldn't take kindly to a woman who accused them of being somewhat sexist. Even if I explained my position in a polite, rational way, I was pretty sure that it wouldn't go over well. At best, I might get an eye roll. At worst, I might be ostracized. If I wanted to save face with the old-timers, then I had to take the fall for the two other Orange Hats. Afterward, I decided to work even harder to prove that I was better than what the men assumed of me. As it turned out, the right kind of woman was the kind who didn't protest too much.

Thankfully, the mid-century expectations touted inside the mill ended with every shift. My relationship with Tony felt far more egalitarian than what many men in the mill seemed to prefer. Tony was a teacher, and I was a steelworker. He cooked, and I did the dishes. When we went shopping, he browsed while I crossed my arms impatiently. He preferred fluffy feel-good movies, and I liked to watch stuff blow up. Between the two of us, I was the decision maker and the risk taker. With my income from the mill, I would also become the breadwinner.

After my bad day with the forklift, I went over to Tony's house to spend the night. We played a few rounds of dominoes at the dining room table while his dog sniffed at our feet. I was losing at dominoes, as always.

"I want to play a different game," I said with a smile.

"Yeah," he said, rolling his eyes playfully, "you'll hate this game until you start winning. Then you'll think it's the best game in the world."

"But I never win, so we should just play a different game."

It was a running a joke between us. I was a sore loser and an ungracious winner, which was no doubt a residual symptom of my childhood competitiveness with my sister. Still, Tony and I had both found a way to laugh about it.

I put a domino down on the table and took a sip of beer.

"Did you hear that Trump won a few more primaries?" I asked.

Tony and I didn't talk politics very often, because it usually ended in a fight. It wasn't that we disagreed. Quite the contrary. We both considered ourselves liberal, and we had both come from Republican Catholic families. While we tended toward Democratic candidates in national elections, we sometimes found appealing Republican candidates on the local level. In many ways, we could be described by the dirtiest word in American politics: *moderates*. For some reason, however, talking about politics often led to fights in which we disagreed about the reasons we agreed.

"Yeah, I heard about the primaries," Tony said, taking his turn. "I'm telling you, he's going to get the nomination."

"I still can't believe that. I mean, it's Donald Trump. He can't be president."

"Yeah, but he keeps winning."

I thumbed through my dominoes, trying to figure out what to play next. In my mind, the Trump run was just a publicity stunt meant to solidify his brand. All of the outlandish things he said were just meant to get people talking, and all of that talking was just meant to sell more merchandise and more hotels. He couldn't possibly win the presidency. After all, he was doing little more than grandstanding.

"I don't know," I said. "Maybe you're right. Maybe he'll get the nomination, but there's no way he'll actually win in November."

"Well," Tony said, "he's already gotten way farther than anyone would have predicted. Maybe we'll all be surprised."

"No way," I told him, shaking my head.

I couldn't find a domino to play, so I picked one from the pile. Tony, on the other hand, had a high-scoring move ready to go.

"If Trump gets the nomination," I said, "he'll lose."

"We'll see. Personally, I think he'd be awful for our country. I'm seriously afraid of what he'll do to the environment."

If there was one issue that weighed most on Tony's mind, it was environmental policy. While he certainly wasn't a single-issue voter, he had a soft spot for trees and furry things. He recycled meticulously. He cringed at plastic bags. He donated to all kinds of animal rights groups, and he was always looking for new ways to reduce waste. I, too, was a nature lover, which made me rather conflicted about my new job at the mill. I wondered what kind of responsibility I bore by earning a living in an industry that was inherently hard on the environment.

In orientation, the company told us about their dedication to protecting and improving local ecosystems. They made us memorize fancy acronyms that summarized their environmental policies, and they told us about all the ways they complied with various EPA regulations.

There were posters in the Finishing Department that depicted idyllic scenes of happy sea turtles and towering windmills. According to one poster, the company's mining activities on the Brazilian coast hadn't impacted local sea turtle populations. According to another poster, steel was an integral component in the construction of new green energies. The posters pacified me. For my first few days on the job, I abandoned whatever guilt I had about working in the mill. Caring for the environment was the company's responsibility, and they had it under control.

After a few more games of dominoes, Tony and I watched our nightly episode of *Star Trek* and went to bed. The following morning, I walked into the Social Shanty and waited for my shift to start. Sam and Charlie were already there, planning our next cleaning task. A few other steelworkers were sitting around the table, drinking coffee and reading newspapers.

"How are you liking it so far?" a woman said to me. She sat at a desk near the door. Her blond hair had been cut into a messy bob, and she spoke with the raspy voice of a smoker.

"It's okay, I guess," I told her. "So far we've just been cleaning."

"Well, don't let them work you too hard. Feel free to have some coffee. I made a pot over there."

I went over to a ramshackle coffeepot that sat on a small table at the edge of the room. The pot looked crusty and burnt, but I had never been known to turn down coffee. After pouring myself a cup, I gathered a few empty water bottles that were scattered on the table. Water bottles like these were everywhere. You couldn't actually drink the tap water in the mill, presumably because the pipes were too old and corroded. Whatever chemicals were floating in the tap water weren't fit for human consumption, so the company provided us with an endless supply of bottled water.

I took the empty bottles to a blue garbage can just outside the Social Shanty. The can was always filled with plastic bottles, so I figured that it was the recycling bin.

"Why do you always walk all the way outside to throw away your trash?" the woman at the desk said to me when I returned.

"It was plastic. I was putting it in the recycling bin."

The woman laughed. A few of the other steelworkers joined her.

"There's not a recycling bin," someone said.

"Where do you guys put plastic, then?" I asked.

"It goes in the trash. Like everything else."

I sat down at the table and sipped my coffee, while the other steel-workers went back to their newspapers. For the next few weeks I tried to collect every bottle I could find. I put them in bags, which I hauled away from the mill and recycled at home. No matter how many bottles I collected, however, there were always hundreds more that seemed to pile up overnight. Eventually I gave up on my recycling crusade. It was too daunting and frustrating, and it felt pointless. I started throwing my bottles in the trash like everyone else, but I was careful not to let it slip to Tony. He would have been mortified.

As I sat with the other steelworkers in the Social Shanty, Sam and Charlie informed me of our plan for the day. We were supposed to do some painting in one of the other warehouses in the Shipping Department, but there was no sense in rushing through it. If we did, then Jeremy would just give us more work. Better to get our fill of caffeine and pace ourselves.

While the three of us nursed second cups of coffee, the woman who had been sitting at the desk got up and left the room. The other steelworkers who were sitting around the mahogany table suddenly looked up from their newspapers.

"Hey, Orange Hats," one of these steelworkers said. "Be careful with some of the people around here." The man nodded toward the woman's desk. "I don't want to name names, but be careful who you trust."

The other workers muttered in agreement.

Even though there was a general feeling of camaraderie among steelworkers, there were more than a few dysfunctions in this family of steel. That old-timer was right: Not everyone could be trusted, and some union workers wouldn't think twice about stabbing you in the back. Some people tattled to the bosses. Others sucked up and tried to get ahead. Others seemed intent on making the mill miserable. The woman at the desk was rumored to be a snitch.

"Yeah," another old-timer piped up, "Dog Face will sell you out in a second."

"Dog Face?" I said.

"Yeah. That's what we call her."

"Oh," I said, "that's an awful name. Don't call her that."

The words came out before I had time to think. The man who had used the nickname was old enough to be my father. He could've harped on me for coming to the woman's defense. After all, I was just a newbie who hadn't yet absorbed one of the unspoken rules of the mill. You weren't supposed to point a finger at a problem and identify it directly.

You couldn't say that you didn't like being called QuackQuack, and you couldn't say that people were misjudging you because you were female, and you certainly weren't supposed to reprimand old men for referring to a fellow woman by a derogatory name. In the mill, you were supposed to bottle up the problem and let it come out in an un-related way.

If someone calls you QuackQuack, you flick him off for some other reason. If someone misjudges you because you're a woman, you work harder to prove yourself. You believe, for a moment, that it solves something, but the guy still calls you QuackQuack behind your back and people still assume that you're a ditzy woman who doesn't think things through. The problems still exist; they just morph into some-thing else.

When I told the old steelworker not to call the woman Dog Face, I wasn't met with criticism or disapproval. The man shrugged, looking nearly contrite.

"Eh," he said, "I guess it's not the best name in the world. You still shouldn't trust her, though."

The man quickly changed the subject and started talking about union matters with the other Yellow Hats who were sitting around the table. My protests had stopped him from using the name, at least

for the moment, but whatever confidence had inspired me to reprimand the old steelworker didn't last long. I eventually found that Jeremy's warning had merit. The culture of the mill did change me, and
I wouldn't realize it until I got into a spat with the very woman I had
once defended as an Orange Hat.

For most of my time at the mill, I rarely interacted with the woman.
We were cordial whenever we crossed paths in the locker room, but
we certainly weren't friends; I didn't trust her for a second, but we
certainly weren't enemies. After I'd been in the union for more than
a year, a fellow employee told me a juicy bit of gossip. The woman
who people called Dog Face—the notorious snitch—had accused me
of snitching on her. Apparently, someone had told a boss that she'd
been smoking cigarettes in the bathroom. For whatever reason, she
assumed that I was the tattletale. I was dumbfounded. Why in the
world would she think me a snitch when I was the one person who'd
stood up for her?

The day after I heard the gossip, I discovered that someone had
cut the locks on my lockers and stolen everything inside. Inside the
mill, cutting a lock was the ultimate taboo. The union didn't cut a
lock without the approval of the company, and vice versa. For workers,
cutting a lock—*any* lock—could land you in the Human Resources
Department. It was a matter of safety. Whenever a machine was ser-
viced inside the mill, workers placed a personalized padlock on the
mechanisms that de-energized the equipment. Locks were placed on
off-switches and valves, which prevented the machines from being
turned on while someone was in harm's way. If you cut a personalized
lock and reenergized a machine, you could kill someone. As a result,
cutting locks—even in the locker room—was strictly forbidden unless the union and the company went through a lengthy procedure to
ensure that no one would be harmed in the process, but the woman
who people called Dog Face was known to wield a pair of renegade
bolt cutters from time to time. When I first started in the mill, she
cut someone's locks to free up a pair of lockers for me. Now that my
own locks were cut, I assumed she had done the same thing to me out
of spite.

Thankfully, there wasn't much to take from my locker. Some clothes, some boots, a few toiletries, a blow-dryer. The material losses didn't irk me much, but the violation of the theft did. Inside the mill, your locker was the only private space available. It was a tiny extension of yourself. To defile that space felt strangely aggressive.

When I found that the woman had broken into my lockers, I knew better than to say something to my boss. I told my committeeman that someone—*maybe one of the janitors*—had broken into my locker and taken my company-issued work boots. He agreed to get me a new pair of boots, and that was that. You didn't snitch, plain and simple. I did, however, consult a handful of other union workers, all of whom had grown into trusted friends.

"Maybe I should just go talk to her," I said. "You know, I can just explain that it was a big misunderstanding."

"No way," everyone warned. "Do not, under any circumstances, go and talk to her. At best, you'll just look guilty. At worst, you'll get into a fight that might end in HR."

I took their advice to heart. I bottled up my anger and let it fester. Every so often, I ranted about the incident to those same union workers.

"I can't believe she broke into your shit," they told me.

"Yeah," I said, wrinkling my nose. "Fucking Dog Face."

Sometimes the mill had that effect on me. If I wasn't careful, it could suck me down.

5

After sleeping at Tony's house for my first few weeks at the mill, I decided to go back to my tiny apartment and try my luck at getting out of bed on my own. The cool spring air wafted through an open window as I curled up beneath my warm comforter and fell into a heavy, dreamless sleep. When the alarm went off the following morning, I didn't notice it at all. By the time I finally rolled over and looked at the clock, it was already a quarter to six.

My stomach dropped. Even though my shift wasn't scheduled to start for another fifteen minutes, I was late by mill standards. The long trek from the parking lot to the Shipping Department always took at least ten minutes, and every morning I stopped at the locker room to get dressed in my uniform and hard hat. If I wanted to be at my post by six o'clock sharp, then I had to be at the mill by half past five at the latest. Time and again, Gage had told us the same thing during orientation: *Do. Not. Mess. Up.* In particular, he told us to be punctual. *The company hates when people are late*, he said. *They'll fire an Orange Hat in a heartbeat.*

I quickly pulled on some clothes and brushed my teeth before hopping into my tiny beat-up hatchback. The sun was just starting to rise, and there weren't many other cars on the road. As I sped down the city streets, I glanced over at the clock. It usually took only a few minutes to get to the mill from my apartment, and the company probably wouldn't fire me if I arrived on the premises by the start of my shift.

Jeremy might give me a slap on the wrist for not being dressed and ready to work, but I would likely be given a second chance. I gave the hatchback as much gas as it could handle and hoped for the best.

I can't lose this job, I thought to myself as I raced along the highway. I repeated the same words over and over again, as if trying to break a curse. *I can't lose this job.*

There was more at stake for me than just money. My job as a steelworker was the first full-time work I had ever secured, and the Great Recession wasn't the only reason it had taken me so long to find it. For years I had been worried that my bipolar disorder would inevitably get in the way of a career.

After receiving the diagnosis as a teenager, it felt like I was constantly cleaning up the pieces left in the wake of my disease. When my erratic moods wreaked havoc on my academic performance as an undergraduate, I found ways to work around my failures. I asked for extensions and took incompletes. My professors knew me as an otherwise responsible student, so they were willing to accommodate me when I got sick. They realized that my inability to perform wasn't born out of laziness or procrastination, and their flexibility allowed me to graduate with honors.

The same pattern continued in graduate school. My mixed episodes would come and go, but professors saw my potential. They made exceptions. They accepted late work and treated me kindly, but then a landslide hit. Just as I was entering my last year of graduate school, I began one of the worst bipolar episodes of my life. I was overcome by the familiar mix of mania and depression, and my delusions were off the charts. I couldn't shake the feeling that I had killed my parents, and I sometimes drove past their house at night to make sure they were still alive. I told a priest that I was possessed, begging him for holy water and an exorcism. I sent crazed emails to my thesis director, telling him that I wanted to drape the local Burger King in thousands of dollars of red fabric to help people "experience art."

It's like I'm watching myself disappear, I wrote in one of these emails.

Friends abandoned me. My parents didn't know what to do. I was hospitalized several times over the course of a year, but my mood wouldn't respond to medication. Eventually the doctors resorted to electroshock therapy. During the course of the treatments, I was unable to work or go to school. The procedure required heavy sedation that left me groggy, and the side effects impaired my thinking and my memory. I could barely get to the grocery store, let alone wield a paintbrush or read a book.

With no job and no income, the small amount of savings I had quickly dwindled. It was a struggle just to keep gas in my car, but there was one miracle that kept me from total financial ruin: I was covered under my mother's health insurance at the time, which allowed me to seek treatment without incurring debt. But I was nearing my twenty-sixth birthday, and I was scheduled to age out of the insurance in the midst of the electroshock therapy treatments. As always, my mother sprang into action. She helped me navigate the painstaking application for Social Security Disability, and she used the pending application to petition her company for an insurance extension, explaining that I was in no condition to provide coverage for myself. After a great deal of fighting, the company relented. They agreed to continue my coverage temporarily, so long as the Disability claim came through.

As we waited for news from the Social Security office, I continued with the treatments and medications. The doctors kept telling me that I needed to see a psychologist, and while I had never experienced much success with therapists before, I gathered up my pennies and scheduled an appointment. The therapist was a middle-aged woman with wire-rimmed glasses and sleek brown hair. She was the only clinician available on short notice, and she seemed out of her element with the types of problems I was presenting. Even so, I continued to see her for a few weeks. I wasn't well enough to advocate for anything different.

During our sessions, I often talked about the stress of being poor. The therapist nodded and wrote things in her notebook until I came to her office with a more pressing problem. I told her that I had made a few bad decisions with a fellow house painter. The man had bought me a few drinks while I was out of work, and now I was worried that I had gotten pregnant. The therapist put down her pen and rolled her eyes.

"Why didn't you just go buy Plan B?" she asked, her voice heavy with condescension.

The therapist's tone hit me hard. It exemplified what I had experienced so often in my life. Risky behavior is a hallmark of bipolar disorder, but people usually interpret it as a character flaw. Admittedly, I shouldn't have gone drinking when my brain was in such a precarious state, but my decisions were also influenced by my disease. I suffered from racing thoughts and obsessive thinking, and alcohol was a quick way to ease my frenetic mind. I was also horribly depressed, which made me crave sex to lift my spirits with a tiny hit of dopamine. It's always hard to say where personal culpability ends and psychiatric illness begins, but one-night stands weren't a normal occurrence for me. I was awkward around men and painfully insecure in my body, which meant that I rarely slept with people I wasn't dating, but the worst impulses of my disease had turned me into someone I no longer recognized.

"Well," the therapist said, "why didn't you do something to prevent this problem?"

I stared at her for a moment. She knew that I was on food stamps, and she knew that my application for Social Security Disability was pending. Even though I had talked at length with her about the state of my finances, this middle-class professional woman heard the word *poor* and defined it by her own middle-class standards. Maybe she thought that I was dipping too far into my savings. Maybe she thought that I was a little over budget at the time, or maybe she thought that I had to forgo some of life's niceties. That wasn't my reality. After writing a check for the copay that day, I had a total of thirty-two dollars in my bank account. I had no income, and I had no idea what I was going to do when the rent came due again. I also knew that Plan B cost forty-five dollars, which meant that the pill was a luxury I couldn't afford.

At the time, I didn't have enough mental clarity to realize that Planned Parenthood may have offered me the pill at a discount. I didn't have access to credit, and I didn't want to ask my parents for money to use on contraception. They were practicing Catholics, and Plan B was strictly forbidden by the Church. Even though I was reeling from the symptoms of my disease, I was still their daughter. I didn't want to do anything that would merit disapproval, and I didn't want to use their money in a way that belittled their deeply held beliefs. In my mind, it felt like I was being forced into an impossible choice. Pay the therapist in the hopes of feeling well again, or buy the pill that would prevent an unwanted pregnancy.

"Well?" the therapist said, tapping her pen on her knee.

"Haven't you heard me?" I asked. "I'm too broke to buy Plan B. There's no money. I'm fucking poor."

The therapist wrote something down on her notepad and stared at me from her seat across the room. I muddled through the rest of the session and silently decided that I wasn't going to waste any more money on her services. Thankfully, I didn't turn up pregnant. I didn't have to make the impossible choice between adoption and abortion and a child I couldn't raise. The government approved my Disability claim a few weeks later, and my first SSI check felt like salvation. That check meant that I could keep my apartment and my insurance. It meant gas in my car and food on my table. That check was my independence and my self-esteem. It allowed me to move forward.

When the worst of the episode was behind me, I reenrolled in graduate school and finished my thesis. My mind was still foggy from the electroshock therapy, and I found it difficult to get out of bed on most mornings. The thesis I wrote wasn't very good, but it was passable. After a successful defense, the college notified me that I had filled out one of the graduation forms incorrectly. *It's just a small problem*, they assured me, but I had already been through so much. The form felt like one more mountain I was too exhausted to climb, so I ignored it.

I went back to painting houses, which offered the same safety net as academia. I always painted for small mom-and-pop companies. My bosses knew that I had a very strong work ethic, and they also knew that my bipolar disorder could make me act in uncharacteristic ways. They didn't think twice about giving me the space I needed. I could take sick days and extended absences without question. No matter how long it took me to recover, my job was always waiting for me.

In the back of my mind, I knew that a full-time position wouldn't be quite so forgiving. It felt easier to paint houses than to risk failure elsewhere, so I spent years putting half-hearted applications into the job market with the secret hope that I would be turned down. The ailing economy never failed to disappoint, and potential employers either ignored me or told me that I wasn't right for the job. The years rolled on, and I never got the diploma I had worked so hard to achieve. My bipolar disorder had scared me into apathy. I was afraid that the symptoms would return with debilitating intensity, creating havoc in the life I wanted to build for myself. It was safer to stand on the sidelines. It was safer to pine after everything I *could have* been. That way I never had to lose anything to a fickle disease that felt impossible to control.

Now, as I sped toward the mill in the growing dawn, it seemed that bipolar disorder was the least of my worries. My chronic tardiness was going to get me fired long before I had a chance to see if I could manage full-time work with my illness, so I pushed the hatchback to go faster. If I could just give it a little more gas, I might arrive on the job with a few minutes to spare.

I checked the clock for good measure. Then I checked it again. In fact, I checked the clock so often that I forgot to look at the road. By the time I finally tore my attention away from the glowing green numbers on the dashboard, I was about to pass my exit. If I had to double back, then I would surely be late.

In a split second, I decided to aim for the exit ramp. I slammed on the brakes and cut sharply across two lanes of traffic. Almost immediately, my tires began to screech. They rumbled over grass and gravel, and I felt myself losing control. My backend fishtailed, so I jerked the wheel to the side. Just as quickly as I had gotten onto the exit ramp, I careened off. The hatchback went spinning across the highway, and the brakes did nothing to stop its momentum.

The hatchback spun around once, and I saw the headlights of oncoming traffic.

I can't stop this, I thought, gripping the steering wheel.

I spun around again, and two pairs of headlights flew past me.

Everything moved in slow motion, and I took note of a concrete median that divided the highway. I was heading straight for it.

Just when everything in my life was going right, I thought.

The concrete median grew closer. I could clearly distinguish every stone, every crack, every pockmark. I felt weightless inside the spinning car—my mind surprisingly clear. I thought back to one of my first days in the mill.

Be careful, the older employee had said to me. *These machines will eat you up.*

The man had been talking about a very different kind of machine, but the warning now landed like a prophecy. I was stuck inside a renegade machine, about to be devoured. The median was nearly upon me, so I closed my eyes and tightened my fists on the steering wheel. The hatchback crashed into concrete, and everything stopped spinning.

Shocked from the impact, I sat in the hatchback and caught my breath. My glasses had been thrown from my face, and I couldn't find them anywhere. I was nearly blind without them, but I tried to survey my body anyway. Nothing seemed to be bleeding. I couldn't tell if anything was broken. With shaking hands, I fumbled through my purse and pulled out my cell phone. I didn't call an ambulance. I didn't call the police. I didn't even call my family. Instead I called my union representative and told him that I'd just crashed my car.

"I can't lose this job," I said through my tears.

He assured me that my job was safe and asked if I had called an ambulance.

"No," I told him, "but I see lights."

Thankfully, a stranger in one of the passing cars had called 911 for me. The police pulled up beside my rear bumper, and an ambulance followed shortly after.

"Do you need to go to the hospital?" an EMT asked.

"I don't know," I said, still shaking from the adrenaline. "I can't find my glasses."

My brain felt too fuzzy to make a decision. I needed someone to tell me what to do, so I tried calling my parents. Neither of them answered their phones. My mom was already at work, and my dad probably hadn't gotten out of bed to start his day. The EMT rummaged through my car in search of the lost glasses, and I tried calling Tony. He answered after a few rings.

"I got into an accident," I said, my voice trembling slightly.

I mumbled an explanation of what had happened. The spinning car. The concrete median.

"How fast were you going?" Tony asked.

"Fast."

"Did you call the police?"

"No," I told him, "but somebody did. The ambulance is here. They're asking me if I want to go to the emergency room."

The EMT came over to me and held out his empty hands, indicating that my glasses were nowhere to be found.

"Are you hurt?" Tony asked.

"I don't know."

"Do you need to go to the hospital?"

"I don't know. What should I do?"

The line went silent for a few moments. As much as I loved Tony, he wasn't always the best at making decisions. Normally, this didn't cause much of an issue. I could usually make up my mind quickly and confidently, and I could easily direct Tony whenever he was torn between two choices. Now, as I sat shaking in my car, I just wanted him to tell me what to do.

"I don't know what you should do," Tony said at last. "If you feel like you need to go, then go."

I looked over at the EMT, who was pacing near the front of my car. Tony's advice left a pit in my stomach. He wasn't helpful when I needed him, so I pulled myself together long enough to decide on my own.

"Okay," I said. "I guess I'll go."

"Do you want me to meet you there?" Tony asked.

"I don't know."

The line went silent again. I could tell that Tony wanted me to be the one to make the decision again, but I couldn't possibly do that on top of everything else.

"Well," Tony said after a long pause, "I guess I'll go in to work for a few hours. I'll try to find a substitute teacher, and then I'll come out to see you."

I desperately wanted Tony to rush to my aid, but I didn't have the wherewithal to tell him that. We both said our goodbyes, and I promised to call him later in the day. The EMT walked me to the ambulance, and we arrived at the hospital a few minutes later.

A nurse ushered me to an open bed, barking orders in the rushed tone of someone who's overworked. A woman from financial counseling took my insurance information and gave me a few documents to read, and then I was left alone. While I waited to see the doctor, I stared up at a clock that was fixed to one of the walls inside the room. The clock was fairly large, but I couldn't read the time. Without my glasses, the world looked fuzzy and indistinct. Faces were a blur, and objects blended into one another. The sharp edges of a countertop fused with the blood pressure cuff that was hanging beside it. A green tank of oxygen merged into the beige arms of a nearby chair, and the words on the insurance documents looked like sweeping smears of gray.

Nurses walked past my bed, seemingly oblivious to my presence, and I started to feel like I was stuck in one of those dreams where you try to scream but nothing comes out. I had gotten into the worst car accident of my life, and no one was coming to meet me at the hospital. To top it all off, I was too blind to read the clock on the wall. I pulled a thin white blanket over my knees and started to cry.

My mind turned to my bipolar disorder. I couldn't shake the feeling that my disease was the cause of my loneliness, even though there wasn't a tangible reason for my thoughts to twist in this way. Bipolar disorder hadn't caused the accident. It wasn't the reason my parents hadn't answered their phones. It wasn't the reason Tony hadn't come to meet me at the hospital, and it wasn't the reason my glasses had flown from my face. I equated bipolar disorder with loneliness out of habit. After years of dealing with the disease, I had experienced the heartbreak that comes when people see you in your worst times.

Friends are lost. Parents grow angry. Lovers call you a crazy bitch. I often felt isolated as a result of my symptoms, and I had unwittingly taught myself to blame any form of isolation on my disease.

As I sat and cried in the hospital bed, I couldn't shake one fear in particular. I was afraid that my bipolar disorder would eventually drive Tony away. The disease was cyclical in nature. My episodes came and went, and they were often interspersed with periods of complete normalcy. Sometimes I went months or years without any symptoms whatsoever. During those times, I was competent and productive. I was able to work toward goals and build relationships just as well as anyone else.

Tony and I had started dating during one of these asymptomatic periods, and I wasn't sure he really understood what it meant to be in a relationship with someone who had bipolar disorder. I told him about the disease while we strolled the streets of downtown Willoughby, the suburb where Tony lived. The old-fashioned storefronts had been revitalized with modern businesses, and it was our Saturday ritual to get breakfast at Kleifeld's Restaurant before grabbing a cup of coffee and poking into a few of the shops.

My nerves buzzed as we headed to a little antique store in the center of town. Tony and I had been dating for several weeks, and things were beginning to turn serious. It was the moment I dreaded in every relationship, when I would have to lay out my baggage before the word *girlfriend* came into play.

"I have to tell you something," I said, preparing to make my confession.

"What's that?" Tony asked. He took a sip of coffee and admired a plate of cupcakes that had been placed in the window of a bakery.

"It might change the way you feel about me."

I was trying my best to sound serious, but the cupcakes were winning the battle. Tony stared longingly at the chocolate icing and the caramel swirls. He wasn't a man of many addictions, but he had a fondness for cigarettes and sweets.

"What would change the way I feel about you?" he said, his eyes still fixed on the bakery.

If I wanted his full attention, I would have to up the ante. "I have a health condition you should know about," I said more sternly.

Tony turned to me with a puzzled look in his eyes. The top of my head barely came to his chin, and I suddenly felt too short in his presence. I usually liked looking up at him. My head fit perfectly against his shoulder whenever we embraced, but now his eyes felt like a spotlight shining down on me.

"What health condition?" he said.

I ran my thumb over the cardboard sleeve on my coffee cup, picking at one of the edges until it frayed.

"I have bipolar disorder."

I searched Tony's expression for some kind of reaction, and the only thing I found was relief. He had probably expected some kind of physical ailment—cancer, hepatitis, herpes—and he was thankful to know it was all in my mind.

"Oh," he said. We both turned forward and continued walking down the street. "Like depression?"

"No," I told him slowly, "not depression. Bipolar disorder. Sometimes I have symptoms of depression, but there are other times when I get manic."

"What do you mean by 'manic'?"

I took a long sip of coffee and watched a few cars roll down the street. Willoughby had a cozy feel, as if you'd just stepped back in time. The two-story brick buildings had arched windows and elaborate friezes. There were kitschy cloth overhangs above some of the storefronts, and the doorways had been decorated with molding. It was the kind of place where a horse and buggy would have fit in just as well as an SUV.

"My mania can come out in different ways," I told Tony. We were still facing forward, navigating down the sidewalk. "Sometimes it's not very severe. I just get hyper, or I sleep less. But sometimes it's much worse. I can get delusions and hallucinations."

"What kind of hallucinations?" he said.

We passed a crepe shop, and the smell of powdered sugar wafted through the air.

"Sometimes I hear things that aren't there," I explained. "Sometimes I see shadows out of the corner of my eye."

Tony looked over at me. His relief had turned to fear. "You hear voices?"

"I've only heard voices a few times," I said, regretting that I'd even mentioned it. I could tell that Tony was getting spooked, and I didn't want him to run for the hills. "The hallucinations only happen during an episode. Even then, it's pretty rare."

"How often do you have an episode?"

I shrugged and took another sip of coffee. "It's hard to say. Sometimes it takes months for a new episode to start. Sometimes it takes years."

"But you're okay now?" he asked.

"I'm doing well at the moment, but there's no saying what will happen in the future."

We walked in silence for a while, dodging another couple who was coming down the street. Tony drew in a long breath and exhaled loudly.

"You know, I got really depressed after my divorce," he said. "It felt like the whole world was crashing down on me. I didn't want to do anything except work and smoke cigarettes. I didn't think I'd ever shake that feeling. I even went to see a doctor, who prescribed some pills. I don't think the pills worked, though. Eventually I just decided to get up off the couch and do all the things I never got to do when I was married. I went hiking. I went to the beach. I reconnected with old friends. It took a lot of effort, but I just had to work my way through it."

I didn't know what to say, so I continued to pick at the sleeve of my coffee cup until we reached the antique store, which was packed with trash and treasures. Once we were inside, the mood lifted. We left the conversation about bipolar disorder at the door and turned our attention to the curiosities in front of us.

Every wall was covered with old pictures, old movie posters, and old beer signs. A row of typewriters lined a few shelves near the entrance, and several cases of estate jewelry dominated the middle of the room. The store reminded me of the pawnshop where my father had once worked. It was full of gems just waiting to be unearthed.

Tony and I explored the shelves, eventually stumbling on a pair of old telephones like the ones we had used in the nineties.

"You know you're getting old when the stuff you used as a kid ends up in an antique store," Tony said.

I smiled. I understood what he was trying to do. He had used the experience of his own depression to build a bridge. He wanted to show that he empathized and understood. Now he was changing the subject to show that he accepted my disease. He continued with our Saturday morning routine as if nothing had happened, insinuating that my diagnosis didn't change things between us.

While I was glad that I hadn't scared him away, I wasn't sure he really understood the gravity of what I'd told him. His own depression, which sounded largely situational, wasn't the same as a mixed episode, and he had favored willpower over medication in his recovery. I worried that he saw bipolar disorder as a purely psychological illness, not a physical one caused by abnormalities in the structure and chemistry of my brain, and I feared that in the future he would expect me to use self-discipline to overcome my symptoms. I could already envision how our relationship would end. One day, when I could no longer curb my delusions, Tony would assume that I was weak and obstinate. He would see my symptoms as flaws, and he would throw his hands up in the air in frustration. Then, after much turmoil, he would leave me.

Tony and I continued to rummage through the oddities in the antique store, and we never talked about my mental health again. Our relationship continued to progress, and bipolar disorder remained the skeleton in the closet. Now, as I sat in the hospital after the accident, I worried that the skeleton would eventually drive a wedge between us. The next episode was coming. It always came—even if I didn't know exactly *when*—and every passing moment brought me closer and closer to that collapse.

When the doctor eventually came to see me in the exam room, I did my best to pretend that I hadn't been crying. She performed a quick examination and declared that I hadn't broken anything. I had strained my neck slightly, but it was nothing that muscle relaxers and a chiropractor couldn't fix. She wrote up a few prescriptions and told me that I was free to leave, which was easier said than done. I swallowed my tears and got dressed. Then I stumbled through the halls of the hospital, unable to read the signs directing me to the waiting room. After I'd gone in the wrong direction a few times, a kindly aide finally took pity on me. He escorted me to the exit and called a cab, which made me feel even lonelier than I had before. The cabdriver was nice enough, but I was never so happy to get back to my tiny mouse-infested apartment. Inside its walls, I could at least be lonely in private.

I kicked off my shoes and headed straight for bed. One of the nurses at the hospital had given me a painkiller before I left, and I was already tired and loopy. Just as I started to nod off, my phone rang. It was Tony.

"Hello," I said, barely raising my head from the pillow.

"Hey, I'm heading over to your place now. It'll take me a while to get there, though, because I'm just leaving work."

Tony had spoken with a fellow teacher after arriving at work that morning. The teacher was dumbfounded when Tony told him about my accident. *Um, you should probably go check on her*, the teacher had said.

It was just the push Tony had needed to make a decision, and I was extremely grateful to the coworker for his advice. But Tony's impending arrival made my anxiety rear its head again. My apartment was a mess. There was laundry that needed to be done, and there were dishes in the sink, and the bathroom floor was in need of a good scrubbing. I only had forty-five minutes to make everything look presentable, so I climbed out of bed and started on the dishes. I was exhausted, but I vacuumed the burgundy carpeting and washed the bathroom floor. I changed the sheets on the mattress. I picked up the mousetraps in the foyer and the kitchen, and I buried them behind some books in the closet.

I wanted Tony to see me a certain way. I wanted him to think that I had it all together, and the state of my apartment was only one part of a larger equation. The fresh sheets and the squeaky-clean floors were emblematic of the real thing I was hiding from Tony: I didn't want him to get a whiff of my bipolar disorder. If I could hide the marks of poverty with lemon-fresh disinfectant, then maybe I could do the same with my disease.

Tony knocked on my door just as I finished cleaning. He gave me a look of concern as he stepped inside.

"How are you doing?" he asked, putting his hands on my shoulders.

"Okay," I said. "Just a little dazed."

"What did the doctors say?"

"They said that I'm basically fine. I'll just be sore for a few days, but it's nothing to worry about."

"Come here," he said, drawing me close.

He put his arms around me, and I rested my head against his chest. His warmth radiated through me, and I could hear his heart beating lightly. I smelled the detergent on his T-shirt. I ran my fingers along the muscles in his back, milking every bit of sweetness from the moment. In his arms, I felt safe. I felt cared for. I closed my eyes and exhaled deeply. The tiny sigh that escaped from me was heavenly, because he was there to hear it.

When we finally sat down on the couch, I did my best to act chipper. I betrayed no hint of the tears that had afflicted me at the hospital. Deep down, I believed that Tony liked happy things. He owned two geriatric cats and a middle-aged dog named Scout, and he far preferred the spirited pit bull over the misanthropic cats. Both cats had grown difficult with age. They puked on the carpeting and missed the litter box, and they spent their afternoons growling under the bed. More important, the cats no longer showed much affection. The dog was a different story. She licked. She played. She curled up beside you on the couch.

From what I could tell, Tony would have done anything for that dog. When she tore her meniscus, he paid thousands of dollars for a surgery that would repair the injury. A year later she tore the meniscus on her *other* leg. Tony shelled out more money for more surgery, and he did so without hesitation. The cats, however, were met with his frustration. They mewed and hissed, and Tony just rolled his eyes.

In my mind, he cared most for the animal that was easy to love. He showed deference to the dog that wagged her tail at the door when he got home from work every afternoon, but he was far less enthusiastic about the animals that didn't immediately make him feel good about himself.

When Tony came to visit me after the accident, he saw what I wanted him to see. I looked like I had it all together. My apartment was in order, and my tears had been replaced by an exhausted smile.

"Do you want to do something fun while you're here?" I said. "We could play a game. We could go to lunch."

I could pretend to be like the dog. I could be excited and loving and affectionate. I could bottle up my sadness long enough to make Tony feel good about himself for a few hours. Then, when he left, I would crumble into a woman who was afraid of losing everything at the hands of a disease. The mice would come out from under the sink, searching for crumbs in the darkness, and I would desperately try to ignore my demons. I knew that there would come a day when I wouldn't have the sense or the sanity to smile anymore. I would grow into a cloying, ravenous thing who arched her back and bared her claws. I would spew and hiss. I would rage at anyone who got too close, because I wasn't the dog. Not by a long shot.

6

I returned to work shortly after the accident, and I found that the union official who answered my panicked call had been right. I didn't lose my job, although the HR Department gave me grief over my excuse. The note from the emergency room had been signed by a nurse, not a doctor, which was unacceptable in the eyes of the company. It wasn't until I produced a time-stamped police report that a woman from HR finally gave me a pass. The incident was one more reminder that absence wasn't tolerated in the mill, especially when it came to Orange Hats.

Once the matter was cleared up, Jeremy notified me that I would no longer be sweeping floors or cleaning rail docks. He wanted me to start training on a more involved job inside the mill, while Sam and Charlie continued wielding brooms and moving dumpsters. They were stuck on cleaning duty indefinitely. Apparently I had more seniority than both of them.

As in most union shops, seniority in the mill was based on the day when you were hired. If, however, you happened to be hired on the same day—like Sam, Charlie, and I had been—then seniority was a crapshoot. No one really knew how the company determined who ranked above whom, but everyone had their theories. Maybe it had to do with your birthday or your Social Security number or your mother's astrological sign. Whatever it was, I was lucky enough to rank above the two other Orange Hats. They were both a little jealous that

I would be ditching our cleanup crew, but mostly they just accepted their fate. In the mill, seniority was sacred. You welcomed your place without protest.

On my first day of training, I was directed to a tiny shanty in the middle of the Shipping Department and told to ask for Gunner. I remembered the quirky middle-aged man from my first buggy ride in the mill, and I found the shanty easily enough. I stood awkwardly in the doorway while Gunner flipped through the pages of a magazine. He didn't seem to notice me, so I cleared my throat and tried to introduce myself.

"What?" Gunner said, looking startled. He held up the magazine, which featured a cherry-red hot rod on its cover. "I was just reading my model car magazine," he told me.

"Oh," I said, unsure how to respond. "Jeremy told me to find you. I think you're supposed to train me or something."

"Okay." He nodded before looking back down at his magazine.

I leaned against the door frame, hoping for more instruction. "Do you want me to do anything right now?"

"No, no," Gunner said. "I'm on a break. Have a seat."

He motioned to an empty chair on the other side of the shanty. The shanty itself was barely big enough for two people to fit inside, and I had to squeeze past him to get to the chair. My knees grazed his knees, and he had to dodge my lunch box as I shimmied around him. When I finally got myself settled, Gunner handed me the model car magazine. I wasn't quite sure what to do with it, so I leafed through the pages and feigned interest.

"I like these model cars," he explained. "I've always liked them. Ever since I was a kid, I've been building model cars. Other kids would make fun of me, but I didn't care."

Gunner smiled at me. His front teeth had been worn down to nubs, and his gray hair stood on end, but there was something bright and guileless about his gray eyes. Gunner had been making steel for upward of forty years. He was the kind of guy who laughed at his own jokes, and he often got so lost in his thoughts that he barely noticed the world around him. While this trait might have been endearing in some contexts, it was downright dangerous inside the mill. I often saw Gunner wandering beneath the cranes that carried the coils overhead. The cranes would blow their sirens as a warning, and Gunner would glance up as if he'd just been roused from a dream.

I stared at the pictures in Gunner's model car magazine, admiring the craftsmanship of the tiny trucks and the tiny convertibles. Fruit flies buzzed around my face, no doubt attracted by the crumbs that littered the floor.

"I don't just do model cars," Gunner continued, growing more animated with every word. "I also modify real cars."

"Yeah?" I said.

I was a little taken aback by the sudden friendship that Gunner seemed to be forging with me, but I welcomed any camaraderie I could find. Time sometimes passed slowly in the mill, and it was always nice to have someone to talk to during a twelve-hour shift.

"Right now I'm painting flames on the hood of my car," Gunner told me. "The flames are purple, but I outlined them in black to make them pop, and I found this spray paint that has glitter in it, and I used the glitter on some of the flames, so everything kind of sparkles. I'm not done yet, but it's looking really good."

"That's cool," I said, even though I wasn't the kind of person who'd ever drive anything covered in flames. "What kind of car is it?"

Gunner shrugged. "It's a Dodge minivan."

I had to keep myself from laughing.

"That's an interesting choice."

"Yeah, my wife says we can't afford a sports car, so I just work on the minivan. I don't mind it. You can still do a lot of stuff to a minivan."

I could only imagine what that minivan looked like, and I could only imagine the sneers Gunner got from passersby. For a moment I pitied him in the way you might pity a three-legged dog in a kennel. The dog doesn't seem to notice the missing leg, which makes his wagging, panting enthusiasm all the more endearing.

"Are you sure there's not any work I need to be doing?" I asked again.

"Nope," he said. "Not yet."

There was an awkward pause. Gunner just smiled at me.

"I don't just do body work on the minivan," he continued. "I also work on the engine. I really souped it up last year. It's got about five hundred horsepower now. It could probably outrun a Corvette."

Gunner hesitated, as if waiting for my approval.

"Is that a lot of horsepower?" I asked.

Gunner cocked his head. "You don't know much about cars, do you?"

"I know where the windshield-washer fluid goes."

"Well," he said, reclining in his chair. "I'll tell you the basics."

With that, Gunner gave me an explanation of horsepower that was anything but basic. He told me about hoses and pistons and valves, most of which I didn't fully understand.

I'd heard whispers about Gunner from the Rumor Mill. He'd found himself in the Finishing Department after a serious brush with the company. He had worked for years in the Blast Furnace, where he operated a series of cart-like contraptions known as larry cars, which dumped coke and limestone into the furnace. When you operated the larry cars, you followed a predetermined recipe that appeared on a computer screen. *Put in this much limestone, this much coke.* You filled the larry cars accordingly and sent them to the furnace.

Every once in a while, the person in charge of the Blast Furnace would radio up to the person working the larry cars and ask for an extra load of coke. An extra load of coke would ensure a complete reaction— the carbon in the coke would rid the iron oxide of its oxygen—but it also slowed down the process. It meant that it would take longer to produce the iron, which meant that the person working the larry cars could catch a break. Since you could add extra coke to iron without ruining it, Gunner had an idea. He would just put an extra load into *every* batch of iron. He did this for years before anyone caught on, and it's rumored that he wasted millions of dollars of coke in the furnace. When the company asked him why he did it, there wasn't an ounce of subterfuge in him. He stared at the people from Human Resources, his bright eyes probably looking a bit stunned. *I just wanted a decent break*, he said. The union took care of the rest. They cut a deal with the company. Gunner wouldn't lose his job, but he also wouldn't be allowed to return to the Blast Furnace. They forced him into the Finishing Department, where he eventually found his way to Shipping.

"So," Gunner said after finishing a lecture about engines that left me completely lost, "that's pretty much how horsepower works. Do you get it?"

"Um, yeah. I guess."

There was another long pause. Gunner stared at me, and I got the sense that he wanted me to prove that I understood what he had been talking about.

"Hey," I said, trying to deflect. "You know a lot about cars. Do you know anything about boxer engines? Are those good engines?"

While I had escaped from the car accident unscathed, my little hatchback hadn't fared so well. It was completely totaled, and I was in the market for another car. Tony and I had been going around to dealership lots for test-drives, and I had all but decided to buy a car with a boxer engine.

"A boxer engine?" Gunner said. "That's different. Do you want me to tell you how it works?"

"No, that's okay," I told him, not getting the one-word validation I'd hoped for. I was desperate to avoid more talk about cylinders and torque, so I tried again to steer the conversation in another direction.

"Tell me more about these model cars."

Gunner took a long breath and smiled. "Well," he said, "a lot of people buy kits that come with all the parts. Most of those guys just follow the instructions and build the same car that anybody could build, but I don't think that's much fun. Anybody can follow instructions, so I always try to do something different. I've made a few models from scratch, and I make my own modifications whenever I use the kits. That way I end up with something that no one's ever seen before."

Gunner pulled out his phone and showed me a few pictures of his work while explaining the meticulous processes involved in the construction of the models. He talked about mixing paints and building bucket seats. He told me about the tiny hoses that had been rigged to the tiny engines. Many of his modifications took a good deal of ingenuity, and the results were impressive. Some of the cars had been displayed at conferences geared toward model car enthusiasts, and one had even made it into the pages of a magazine like the one I held in my hand.

Many of my coworkers possessed a creative side, which intrigued me. There was a man who made stained-glass windows, and there was a woman who made jewelry out of animal bones. Some people built furniture and gazebos for their families, and there was one crane operator who made elaborate sculptures out of recycled silverware. The man once showed me pictures of the sculptures, and I was floored. There was an eagle with butter knives for feathers and an alligator with spoons for scales. Each was large enough to decorate the lobby of an art school, and each one was perfectly proportioned and expertly designed. I wouldn't have been surprised to see them in a gallery somewhere, and the crane operator's talent didn't end with silverware. When he wasn't making his sculptures, he was crafting hand-carved rocking horses.

On one quiet afternoon in the mill, I ate lunch in the Social Shanty while leafing through a few pictures the crane operator had taken of the rocking horses. They were stunningly detailed and beautifully painted. Each horse looked whimsical, yet lifelike. I figured they would fetch a handsome price at an art fair.

"You should sell these," I said to the crane operator before taking a bite of my sandwich.

"I don't know," the man said. He picked at a casserole, moving his fork as if it were the bow of a violin. "I get too attached to sell them."

I nodded. I could almost imagine him working on a rocking horse, his hands sanding gingerly, his nose covered in sawdust. A single horse probably took him many months to complete.

"Actually," the man continued, "I did sell a rocking horse once. It was a long time ago. One of the guys who worked down here begged me to make one for his daughter. I usually don't do that kind of thing, but it was Christmastime and the guy really had his heart set on a rocking horse. So, I made a special one just for him. He was so excited to give it to his daughter, but he never got around to it."

The man paused and stared down at the noodles in his bowl, while I wiped a glob of peanut butter off my pants.

"Why didn't he give it to her?" I asked.

The crane operator looked at me and shook his head.

"The guy died right before Christmas," he said.

"Really? What happened?"

"No one really knows for sure," he told me, setting his fork down on the table. "They found him in the slag pit, but he was already dead. There was a walkway that ran above the pit, so people think that he probably slipped off it. Maybe the grating gave out from under him, or maybe he just took a bad step. He might have lived if someone had found him in time, but that slag is so hot. It just cooked him alive."

I put my sandwich on the table and thought back to the apocalyptic trucks I had seen during orientation, which carried the smoldering slag to the pits. Even though the slag inside those trucks had cooled enough to harden, it still contained a kind of heat that most people never know. Slag wasn't hot like an oven or a pot of boiling water. It was hot like a furnace, which is a decimating kind of heat.

"That's horrible," I said to the crane operator.

"Yeah," the man agreed. "It was the damnedest thing. It could've happened to anyone, I guess. But why him? He had that daughter. He'd bought that rocking horse."

A few other old-timers had also been listening to the story. They all chimed in with their own memories of the incident, and I looked again at the pictures of the rocking horses. I studied their arched necks and their suspended hooves. They all appeared to be frozen in mid-stride.

I often wondered whether the stories told by the older employees were meant to scare me. Their stories certainly had that effect, but I was beginning to sense that they were motivated by more than a blatant attempt at hazing. I started seeing the stories as a type of memorial. Death graced the strangest places in the mill. In the corner of the Social Shanty, there was a bulletin board filled with the obituaries of past employees. Notices for upcoming funerals could be found on doorways and lunch tables, and people often took collections for the families of those who had passed away. It didn't matter if someone died from a heart attack or old age or cancer. Everyone was remembered with enthusiasm, like family. The gruesome stories weren't told for shock value. They were a way to remember all of the men and women who had given their lives to make a living. Perhaps more important, those stories were a way to speak a hard truth: *It could have happened to anyone. It could have happened to me.*

Back when I was a little girl whose father drove her past the mill, I only saw the ugliness. I saw the smokestacks and the ominous orange flame. The mill was nothing more than the remnant of a decayed, dying industry, and the rust that decorated so many of its buildings seemed like a fitting shade. Back then I didn't realize that the mill was sacred ground. It was a memorial and a monument. For some, it had been a deathbed. For most, it was an identity. Lives were spent down in Cleveland's industrial valley. Breakfasts were made on electric skillets inside shanties, Thanksgiving dinners were eaten out of Styrofoam containers, and drinks were had after work at the little dive bar down the road. There were more than a few old-timers who worked well past retirement. They told everyone that they kept working for the money, but I knew better. Being a steelworker was who they were, and making steel was what they knew. Leaving it all behind would have felt like losing a religion, because the mill was more than the rust that everyone else saw. It was a moving piece of history, and within its borders we were all connected to something larger than ourselves.

Even though Pittsburgh had come to be known as Steel City, Cleveland was once a steel capital in its own right. The present-day mill had its beginnings in the early twentieth century, when two different companies set up shop on the banks of the Cuyahoga River. Corrigan-McKinney Steel built a plant on the east side of the river in 1913. The following year, Otis Iron and Steel built one on the west. Eventually those two plants would merge into one. For many decades, however, the east-side and west-side plants were two separate entities with their own evolutions, and each contributed to the industry in its own ways.

The legacy of the west-side plant began long before anyone broke ground for construction. It was in the late 1800s when a Cleveland-based businessman known as Charles Augustus Otis decided to revolutionize the way America made steel. At the time, commercial steel was primarily made with the Bessemer method, in which blasts of air were forced directly into huge vats of molten iron. This kept the temperature of the metal high, and it refined the iron into steel. While the Bessemer method was rather efficient, it also had a fatal flaw. Trace amounts of nitrogen and phosphorus could often be found in the finished products. Both of those chemicals made the steel brittle, and brittle steel could shatter and split.

After studying advanced steelmaking concepts in Europe, Otis came to the shores of Lake Erie and did something that no one else was doing. He built an open-hearth furnace that refined iron in a shallow bowl that was heated with a mixture of hot air and fuel. The open-hearth process took more time than the Bessemer method, but it also allowed nitrogen and phosphorus to be controlled by adding fluxes that would draw the impurities to the metal's hot surface. The resulting slag could be easily scooped away, reducing the nitrogen and phosphorus that plagued the Bessemer-produced steels.

While Otis certainly didn't invent the open-hearth method of steelmaking—it was actually devised by Carl Wilhelm Siemens in the mid-nineteenth century—he was the first to prove its commercial viability. A better, more reliable product could be generated by the open-hearth furnaces, and it wasn't long before Otis's Cleveland-based operation led an industry-wide trend. Other steelmakers followed suit, and for the first half of the twentieth century the open-hearth process became the preferred method of steelmaking in the United States.

After the success of Otis's lakeside plant, the company expanded its operations. In 1914 they built a steel mill on the west side of Cleveland's Cuyahoga River. A small portion of that very same mill, which was born of Otis's ingenuity, continued to chug along after more than a century. While Otis's open-hearth furnaces had long been replaced by Basic Oxygen Furnaces, the mill on the Cuyahoga River was still a living, breathing reminder of the enterprising spirt of the Rust Belt.

The portion of the mill that sat on the east side of the river boasted a different kind of history—though no less important in the evolution of steel in America. A year before Otis Iron and Steel built a plant on the west side of the river, Corrigan-McKinney Steel set up shop on the east. At the beginning of the twentieth century, the Corrigan-McKinney plant produced a variety of crude products, such as billets and sheet bars, but they expanded their operations in 1927 to include rolling mills like the ones in use today. The company stayed in business for roughly two decades. Then, in 1935, Corrigan-McKinney was bought out by the Republic Steel Company. The company invested heavily in the east-side mill, and although they had holdings across the country, management quickly decided to move Republic's headquarters to Cleveland. The move was made in 1936. The following year, the company would be involved in one of the biggest labor disputes in US history.

The steel industry was primed for a strike in the spring of 1937. The Wagner Act, which created the National Labor Relations Board, had been passed two years prior. Workers in the auto industry had formed the United Automobile Workers (UAW), which won recognition from General Motors in February of '37. At the time, the U.S. Steel Corporation—colloquially known as Big Steel—was the industry leader in American steel. When the company saw that the winds were shifting toward unionization, they quickly signed a contract with the Steel Workers Organizing Committee to avoid a strike. Not all steel companies followed Big Steel's example, though. A coalition of four companies—Bethlehem Steel, Inland Steel, Republic Steel, and Youngstown Sheet & Tube, which were collectively known as Little Steel—refused to recognize a worker's right to unionize. By and large, Republic Steel led this effort. The company used violence to intimidate union sympathizers, and the company's chairman, Tom Girdler, was rumored to have said that he would rather turn the mills into farmland than recognize a union. The antagonism came to a head in May of 1937, when workers rallied together in a strike against Republic and the other Little Steel companies.

While strikers sat on the picket line, Republic tried to keep its Ohio plants in operation. The company airlifted supplies—and scab labor—to its plants on the eastern side of the state. When strikers tried to prevent trains from getting materials onto Republic's properties, violence and vandalism resulted. Only one death occurred at the Cleveland mill—a man on the picket line was struck by a passing car—but the Ohio strikes inspired protesters to march on a Republic-owned mill in Chicago. The Chicago mill was still in operation at the time, and it was heavily guarded by police. Tensions rose quickly, and a riot broke out. Demonstrators were beaten with truncheons. Others were shot. The riot, which later became known as the Memorial Day Massacre, left ten people dead and nearly a hundred injured, ten of whom were permanently disabled. Later, coroners discovered that some of the people who had lost their lives had been shot in the back.

A few weeks later, in Youngstown, Ohio, a similarly ugly scene played out. The wives and children of striking workers had joined their husbands and fathers on the picket line. Choice words were reportedly exchanged between a few female picketers and police, which prompted the officers to release tear gas into the crowd. Women and children suffered the effects of the gas. Many of the men rushed the police in response, making matters worse. The tear gas turned to bullets, and at least one man died after being shot in the neck.

When all was said and done, sixteen people lost their lives as a result of the Little Steel Strike of 1937. Hundreds more were injured. Nearly a month after the violence in Youngstown, people began returning to work. Nothing seemed to have been accomplished. Little Steel hadn't recognized the union's negotiating power. No contract had been signed. No demands had been met. It wasn't until 1942, after a wave of walkouts in New York, Pennsylvania, and Ohio, that the Little Steel companies finally ratified contracts with the union.

With this long history of hard-won—and hard-lost—battles, it's no wonder that the mill represents something nearly holy to the people who work within its borders. It's a memorial to the people who have lost their lives on the job. It's a shrine to the men and women who have been killed or injured in the fight for better pay and safer working conditions. It's a testament to the sacrifice and ingenuity that built a nation, but that's not the story that people usually remember.

In 1942, J&L acquired Otis Iron and Steel on the west side of the Cuyahoga River. In 1968, Ling-Temco-Vought, which would later become known as the LTV Corporation, bought a majority interest in J&L. In 1984, the LVT-owned J&L merged with Republic Steel— the east-side and west-side plants became one. In 1986, LTV declared bankruptcy, but the Cleveland plant continued steel production on a limited basis. In 2000, LTV declared bankruptcy again. In 2001, the Cleveland plant laid off its remaining workers.

That's the story people remember. They remember the downfall of LTV. They remember the slow decline of Cleveland's prominence as a producer. They think of a Rust Belt that's bleeding jobs and money overseas.

I was in high school when LTV went under, and for many years I thought that the old mills were forever doomed. Steel had left Cleveland for good, at least in large part. I was told time and again that the industry had packed its bags and headed for China. In college, I noticed that the orange flame still shot from the stacks of the old mills, but I figured that Cleveland couldn't possibly be a competitive producer in the market. If anything, the flames from the mill symbolized a breed of stagnation that typified the Rust Belt. We weren't innovating. We weren't moving forward. We weren't embracing the booming tech industry. Cleveland was a city built on sad stories, or so I thought. I didn't yet realize that we were also a city of comebacks.

Long before Wilbur Ross became Secretary of Commerce for the Trump Administration, he bought LTV's assets and restarted Cleveland's east-side plant under the name International Steel Group (ISG). A small section of the west-side plant reopened a few years later. The mill changed hands again in 2005, becoming Mittal Steel. Mittal Steel eventually became ArcelorMittal Steel, which is the largest steel-producing company in the world. While the Cleveland mill has gone through some rough patches since then, especially during the Great Recession, its doors remain open. It has a reputation for making the innovative high-strength steels used in the auto industry, and it also has a reputation for making steel more quickly and efficiently than other American mills. We might have been down and out, but we did what we do best. We kept chugging quietly along.

Gunner was still talking about model cars when a crane began setting steel coils in an open area right outside our shanty. The area was lined with long pallets, each of which contained thin strips of cardboard, and there were stacks of black plastic rings nearby. Gunner and I could monitor the space through a pair of large windows, so I watched as the crane did its work, lowering each coil slowly and methodically. While the cranes caught me off guard when I first started in the mill, I had quickly grown accustomed to them. Now I probably could have deciphered their movements with my eyes closed. I knew the clicking noise they made when lifting a coil. I knew the whirring, screeching sound they made when traveling quickly, and I knew the groans they made when coming to a stop.

"Okay," Gunner said, interrupting his talk of model cars mid-sentence. "It's almost time for us to work."

The coils that the crane placed on the ground had just come from the Hot Dip Galvanizing Line, where they had been coated in a layer of zinc. It was Gunner's job—and now my job—to package these finished coils for sale. But inside the mill, we never used the word *package*. We called it *banding*, because the job involved wrapping thin metal straps—which were known as *bands*—around each coil to pre-vent it from unraveling. Since Gunner and I were the people who banded coils, we were both known throughout the mill as Banders. Many of the unofficial job titles in the mill operated under the same logic—you simply added *er* to whatever it was you did on a daily basis. There were Stockers who stocked, and Catchers who caught, and Rollers who rolled.

From the window of our shanty, Gunner and I waited as the crane placed the last coil onto the ground. Eight coils had been spaced a few feet apart, and each coil was upright. There were two different ways in which a coil could sit: eye to the sky or upright. An eye-to-the-sky coil looked somewhat like a washer lying flush on a table. Such a coil rested on its flat edge, and the hole in the center of its diameter—the *eye* that had been created by the spool that rotated the coil in the mill—pointed toward the ceiling. Hence the name, eye to the sky. An upright coil, on the other hand, looked more like a washer that was balanced on its circular edge, as if someone were trying to spin it on a tabletop. A twenty-ton coil was far more stable than a dinky washer, though, and the majority of coils were four or five feet wide, allowing them to sit steadily upright. The eight coils lined up in front of Gunner and me were all oriented in this way—their eyes pointed in our direction.

"Okay," Gunner said as the crane whirred away. "Let's get out there."

He handed me a pair of soft, flexible gloves that were as strong as Kevlar, and we both emerged from the shanty. Gunner went up to the first coil and demonstrated our task. It was simple, really. A coil was just a large cylinder, and the outer edges of this cylinder needed to be protected from any potential damage that might occur during shipping. To accomplish this feat, Gunner wrapped one of the long, thin pieces of cardboard around the edges of a coil. He then placed plastic rings in either side of its eye; these rings would likewise protect the interior of the coil from damage. After the cardboard and plastic were in place, he added the bands. Two bands were threaded through the eye. One band was wrapped around the right side of the coil; the other band was wrapped around the left. When the bands were in place, Gunner handed me a metal tool that was attached to an air hose.

"You ratchet the bands," he instructed, "and I'll crimp."

The tool in my hands vaguely resembled the bill of a platypus, except it had a circular appendage that could grab the bands and pull them tight. Gunner wielded another tool, which looked more like the mouth of a spider. After my platypus ratcheted a band as far as it would go, Gunner's spider crimped a steel fastener to the band. The fastener kept the band secure, and the band kept the coil tightly wound. We performed this process on the row of eight coils, which turned out to be more difficult than it looked.

"Try doing a cardboard," Gunner said, pointing to the long pallet on the edge of our work area.

I picked up one of the strips, which was twenty feet long and impossible to maneuver. I dragged it through the oil on the ground, trying to get a good grip on it.

"Hold it up like a U," Gunner told me.

I grabbed each end of the cardboard and stretched my arms up as far as they would go, but I kept stepping on the bottom of the U.

"Hold it up higher," Gunner said, but I wasn't tall enough. "And don't forget your tape gun."

Gunner slipped a tape gun between my fingers and walked over to the coil with me. In order to get the cardboard around the steel, you had to hold the bottom of the U next to the coil with your foot while wrapping the rest of the cardboard snugly around the edge. Once tight, you taped the cardboard down with the tape gun before moving on to the next coil. It was an awkward balancing act, and I didn't get the hang of it on the first try. The coil was taller than me, and I lost my grip on the cardboard, which landed in a puddle of oil.

"Now it's too slick to hold the tape," Gunner explained. "You'll have to get a new one."

I set the cardboard aside and tried again. This time, the tape gun flew out of my hands, clattering to the ground. The cardboard fell in the same puddle, so I went to get another one.

At last, Gunner took mercy on me. He helped me apply the cardboard, which finally stayed put. Then I watched as he banded most of the other coils in the row.

Every coil was the same. *Cardboard, plastic, bands. Ratchet. Crimp. Repeat.*

And repeat. And repeat.

Like most workers in the steel mill, a Bander performed the same task over and over again. We did the same motion until its memory was burned into our fingertips. It would only take a few shifts before I was banding coils in my sleep, but Gunner took the lead on my first morning on the job.

When we finished the task in front of us, we went back to the shanty and waited. A crane picked up the coils and took them to a worker known as the Wrapper, who wrapped each coil in plastic.

After a few minutes inside the shanty, Gunner began to grow restless. He stood up, then sat down, then stood up again. He swatted some fruit flies and fiddled with the computer screen that tracked the progress of the coils.

"We have a lot of time till the next round," he said. "Do you mind if I leave you here for a while?"

"Um, I guess not," I said, even though I still didn't feel very comfortable in my new job as a Bander.

"Okay, good," he told me. "Just stay put. I'm going to look for pop cans."

"Pop cans?"

"Yeah. You can find a lot of 'em around here."

Gunner walked quickly out of the shanty, scanning the ground for anything aluminum. He was something of a scavenger. He took old pallets home to use as firewood, and he had gotten himself into a few precarious situations in the pursuit of renegade pop cans. He sold these cans as scrap metal, which struck me as odd. None of us were hurting for money in the mill. Still, Gunner's scavenging was strangely refreshing. I had already given up my recycling campaign with the water bottles, and it was nice to see that someone still had a feverish desire to reuse and repurpose the mill's waste.

With Gunner gone, I reached for my phone and distracted myself with the news. There was one particular story buzzing around Cleveland at the time. Our city had been chosen to host the Republican National Convention, and we were making last-minute preparations for the event. Reporters and politicians would soon flock to our underdog city, and it seemed very likely that Donald Trump, reality-star billionaire, would be named the presidential candidate for the Republican Party.

In the months leading up to the convention, I had already watched my hometown change before my eyes. Fifty million dollars had been spent to renovate Public Square. Fancy hotels had sprung up across the city, and national security catchphrases now graced the billboards that once held advertisements for local businesses and universities. *If you see something, say something.* Buildings were being sized up as vantage points, and the police presence was increasing by the day.

It seemed that fear had come to our little city, and it wasn't just the caution that attends an event of national importance. The whole country was on edge, and Trump was fanning the flames: *Be afraid of immigrants, who rape your women and steal your jobs. Be afraid of minorities, who want to bring everyone down. Be afraid of the men and women who practice Islam; they will kill you in a heartbeat. Be afraid of the globalists, the feminists, the socialists, the Democrats.*

It seemed that Trump sensed the anxiety in the Rust Belt, so he gave its people a few places to point their fingers. In reality, however, the source of our anxiety was far more elusive than we allowed ourselves to believe.

Even though the Cleveland mill was still in operation, it had suffered a major blow in the early 2000s. Several years after LTV laid off the last of its workers, a local real estate developer created a plan to repurpose a 125-acre section of land on the west side of the Cuyahoga River. The entire area, which once housed the #2 Finishing Department of the west-side mill, was slated to become an open-air shopping mall complete with corporate stores and chain restaurants. There was going to be a Target, a Chipotle, a Home Depot. Eventually there would even be a Walmart.

The plan was meant to revitalize a small swath of Cleveland with jobs and commerce, but it was met with initial outrage. All of those big-name stores, whose goods came from China, rubbed salt in the wound of an already flailing economy. We had traded the high-paying full-time jobs of the mill for the low-paying part-time positions of retail stores and restaurants. We had shipped our livelihoods off to China, and now we couldn't afford more than the cheap Chinese crap sold to us at Walmart. Some of the people in the community recognized the troubling symbolism of a shopping complex built on steel mill soil, but their tiny cries of dissent didn't echo very far. The shopping center opened anyway. It had its own momentum. There were parking lots and strip malls. It was a cold corporate landscape filled with things to buy and no one to buy them.

Behind the brightly colored signs for beauty stores and record shops, the mill loomed with its huge furnaces and its rust-colored warehouses. The mill churned and chugged. It threw steam into the air. It spat steel from its jaws. The mill looked menacing behind the cold, sanitized facades of those corporate chains, but at least it felt alive. The people inside the mill's boundaries weren't handing out fake smiles and fake corporate concern. They were tapping heats and swinging rolls and stirring vats of molten zinc. They were hoping that they wouldn't get caught in the mill's deadly teeth, and they were remembering the ones who hadn't been so lucky. *A man once bought a rocking horse, but he died in a pile of slag.*

I began to see the shopping center from a steelworker's perspective. The corporate stores sat at the edge of the mill, taunting: *You're being forgotten. You're becoming obsolete.* All while a bunch of cold, sanitized politicians in Washington kept promising change, but the change only ever came for someone else. Those politicians seemed no better than the boxy buildings that housed the Walmarts and the Home Depots. They were just another reminder: *You're powerless. You're getting left behind.* They claimed to have your best interests in mind, but they had no idea what it was like inside the mill.

The real problem was more than just globalization and automation. It went beyond the seeming indifference of a few out-of-touch politicians. When you worked at the mill, you felt owned by the mill. The lack of sick days meant that you slogged through your shift with a fever. The absence of paid time off meant that you might miss your daughter's birthday or your son's graduation. There was very little vacation time, especially for newer employees, and you couldn't request a day off. That wasn't even the worst of it, though. I had only been working at the mill for a couple months, but I already got the sense that the rich, powerful people who ran the company thought we should be grateful for being owned. That was the kicker. We sensed it from the bosses, who said they could replace us in a heartbeat. We sensed it from the HR Department, who scanned the footage from CCTV cameras for people to punish. We sensed it from the corporate types, who always wheedled their way out of paying us a profit sharing bonus.

According to the union contract, the steelworkers at the Cleveland mill were entitled to a quarterly bonus that was based on the company's net profits. But every quarter the company did some fancy accounting. They would declare massive profits to investors on Wall Street, and then they would turn around and tell us that there were no profits to be had. Steelworkers usually came up empty-handed. If we complained, the company types would roll their eyes. *You guys make enough money as it is*, they would say. They were right. We did make good money, but we were also the ones risking our lives on the floor. If the company did well, then we should do well too.

It was common knowledge throughout the mill that the man who owned the company wasn't hurting for much. He was already one of the richest men in the world. His net worth was in the billions, and he wasn't shy about flaunting it. When his daughter got married, he spent $60 million on a weeklong wedding celebration that included dinner at the Palace of Versailles and fireworks from the Eiffel Tower. If he had taken the wedding money and divided it up among the two thousand odd employees who worked at the Cleveland mill, each person would have been given a bonus of approximately thirty thousand dollars. The steelworkers I knew didn't want or expect the man to sacrifice that much, though. We were capitalists at heart, and we knew that the higher-ups deserved to make more money. They had more invested, and they had more responsibilities. We just wanted to feel like we were getting more than scraps, and we wanted the people at the top of the ladder to value us as more than a bottom line.

When I first started at the mill, the company was in the midst of negotiating a new contract with the union, and it wasn't going well. Their interest in the bottom line became even more apparent as they vied to downgrade our health insurance and curtail the pensions of new employees. The union was fighting tooth and nail to keep the hard-earned benefits that would have come as a matter of course if the people at the top of the food chain really saw their workers as living, breathing human beings. Luckily, the union was able to spare the majority of our benefits by sacrificing a pay increase, but the company's opinion of its workers resonated long after the contract was signed. *Let them eat cake*, they seemed to say, and we were supposed to welcome the insult.

Of course, it's not just steelworkers and auto workers and miners who feel this way. The problem isn't sequestered to the Rust Belt. So many of us spend our lives working for corporate America, where we're subtly told that we don't matter all that much. We feel impotent, and there's nowhere to point the finger. Corporate culture isn't as obvious as a drug dealer on a street corner, and the wage gap can't be cuffed by police. The real enemies bringing us down aren't easy to isolate, so Trump gave people a few targets to blame: *It's the immigrants, the Democrats, the Muslims. It's Black Lives Matter. It's Hillary Clinton. It's an enemy with a name and a face.*

People clung to Trump's message with vigor.

"I want him to blow up the system," they said. "I want him to tear everything down. Build the wall! Put Crooked Hillary in jail!"

My father was one of the people who said such things. He believed that Obama hadn't been born in America. He thought that many of the people in politics, especially the Democrats, were part of a larger conspiracy to destroy the country, and he thought that journalists and reporters were coconspirators in the plot. He still listened to talk radio and Fox News, and we both knew better than to discuss politics at Thanksgiving and Christmas. It always devolved into an angry mess, even though I had once shared the same beliefs that still had a hold on my father. His views were rooted in more than just politics and ideology. They revolved around a very particular kind of fear, which I experienced best when I was fifteen years old.

At the time, I was a sophomore at a Catholic all-girls academy. As I sat in third-period French, a September breeze blew through the cracked windows at the edge of the classroom. A handful of other girls were working quietly alongside me.

Je suis, I wrote on a piece of paper. *Tu es.*

"Attention, ladies," the principal's voice said over the PA system.

Everyone in the room looked up at a wooden speaker, which was situated next to a wooden crucifix.

"I want to inform you all that two planes have flown into the World Trade Center," the principal said. "Another has crashed into the Pentagon. Please, stay in your classrooms. I will update you about the situation soon."

Most of the girls in the room paused for a moment. Then we all went back to our work. *Il/elle est*, I wrote on my paper. *Nous sommes. Vous êtes.* We didn't quite comprehend what we had just heard. The World Trade Center. The Pentagon. Had the pilots not see the buildings? Had the planes gone haywire? It didn't cross my mind that anyone would intentionally attack America. It didn't occur to me that anyone *could* attack us. We weren't at war. We weren't a target. Most of all, we weren't supposed to be vulnerable.

"The Pentagon?" a girl asked from across the room. "Isn't that, like, serious?"

It took some convincing, but our teacher eventually let us watch the news. We stared at the replayed footage of the planes crashing into the towers, and the magnitude finally hit us. This was an attack and a violation, and it undermined everything we had been taught about the strength and safety of our country.

As I sat and watched, I couldn't help feeling the same apocalyptic fears I had experienced as a child. Maybe this was the beginning of the end. Maybe the writing was on the wall. Later in the day, I searched the Internet and found various websites dedicated to apocalyptic predictions. The Devil's face could be seen in the smoke rising from the towers. Biblical passages from the book of Revelation were said to have predicted the event. The World Trade Center was Babylon, and Babylon would be punished. *Seventy years after* Roe v. Wade, *God will destroy America.*

Deep down, I knew that it was very unlikely that the end of the world was upon us. I was rational enough to understand my own irrationality, and yet I couldn't help myself from obsessing over something that probably wouldn't happen. For years I had heard priests say that the end of the world would come suddenly. Many people would

Gunner sighed. "I guess so."

We sat in silence for a moment, and I imagined the kid he must have been back then. I imagined a young, slightly drunk teenager sinking to his knees amid a pile of tiny broken cars. *Grow the fuck up*, his friends must have said while they drank his beers and laughed. *Grow the fuck up*, they must have said, these friends he'd invited into his home. On the floor, the wreckage sat in splinters. It was everything a teenage boy had created. Everything he'd loved. Engines and hubcaps and hoods so small, they could've fit in the palm of your hand.

Gunner looked at me and smiled his cockeyed smile.

"You know what?" he said. "A lot of those guys are dead now. They got into drugs and shit. Some of them overdosed. So, you know, the joke's on them."

His sudden shift toward vengeance caught me off guard. Perhaps it shouldn't have. He was trying to make sense of something that was senseless. He had thrown his whole heart into making those cars—he had spent hours toiling over the tiny tires and the tiny engines—and yet the people he trusted had smashed his hard work to bits.

A few days after hearing this story, I ate lunch with Sam and Charlie in a tiny shanty on the outskirts of the Shipping Department. We all sipped from ice-cold bottles of water and picked at our sandwiches.

"How do you like banding?" Charlie asked me.

"It's all right," I said. "The job itself is really easy."

Sam opened a bag of chips and leaned back in his chair. "What's it like working with that Gunner guy? He seems like a character."

"Oh." I smiled. "He is."

"Yeah," Charlie said. "I've talked to him a couple of times. He told me this crazy story about a few guys who pissed him off. At the end of it, all of the guys ended up dying in a car crash or something."

I perked up at Charlie's anecdote, nearly spilling the bottle of water in my hand.

"Oh my gosh," I said. "He told me the same kind of story."

"I wouldn't want to mess with him." Charlie laughed. "You just might end up dead."

I screwed the cap onto my water and thought of the innocence and awe that Gunner exuded whenever he talked about model cars.

"I don't know," I said. "I think he's harmless. I kind of like him, actually. There's something about him that reminds me of Cleveland. Like, Gunner *is* Cleveland in some weird way."

The two men chewed their sandwiches and grew silent. I was afraid that my assessment was way off base.

"I never really thought about him that way," Charlie said, breaking the silence. "I don't really know how to explain it, but I think I know what you mean."

I didn't know how to explain it either, so I let the thought slip from my mind for several weeks. Then I happened to park next to the Dodge minivan that Gunner had been working on for so long, and something clicked.

I had been wrong to pity Gunner when he told me about his minivan. The thing was a goddamned work of art. The curling flames were the color of muddied lilacs. A few strategically placed black shadows provided just the right amount of depth, and each flame appeared to be hovering gently above the metal. A pale shade of green, which accented the purple perfectly, had been skillfully blended throughout. Even the sparkling spray paint provided a subtle shimmer reminiscent of some holy, ethereal fire.

Hell, I thought, *I'd rock that minivan any day of the week.*

Through my conversations with other employees, I also learned a bit about Gunner's financial situation. When he first told me that his wife didn't think they could afford anything more than a minivan, I was confused. For an old-timer in the mill, sports cars weren't out of reach. Mustangs and Camaros peppered the lots, and fully loaded Harley-Davidsons were ubiquitous. Some old-timers even kept vintage Corvettes and antique Jeepsters in their garages. So what happened with Gunner? Rumor had it that most of his money flowed to other people. He helped foot the bills for his grown children, for his in-laws, for his distant relatives. Whenever someone needed money to make ends meet, Gunner provided relief. He bolstered the people who were down on their luck, and he still found contentment in everything he had left.

When I told Sam and Charlie that Gunner reminded me of Cleveland, I wasn't thinking about the vengeful part of his story. Deep down, I knew that Gunner was more than that. He was the kind of guy who didn't let a devastating loss defeat him. He continued to create. He continued to give. He continued to make models and move forward. More important, he didn't let a few bullies take his passion. That's what made him Cleveland. That's what it meant to live and work in the Rust Belt, and that's the thing that Trump got wrong about us. He didn't see our resilience, and he boiled us down to our worst parts. He viewed industrial workers as a down-and-out people, and he let us believe that being down-and-out was our only identity. He offered us scapegoats and outrage to mask our anxieties, which blinded us to the fact that he was just another rich, powerful man who wanted to gain more power on our backs. He fed us vengeance, and he stoked our anger. He crippled the good in us, which meant that he never really understood the delicate beauty of everything we were fighting to defend.

7

When I was a little kid growing up in the Catholic Church, I was well versed in biblical metaphors. Christ was a lamb. Mary was a star. People were metal, and God was a furnace.

"He will sit as a refiner and purifier of silver," it said in the book of Malachi.

"For you, oh God, have tested us; you have tried us as silver is tried," it said in the Psalms.

"I will smelt away your dross as with lye and remove all your alloy," God said in the book of Isaiah.

Back then, there was no doubt in my mind that liberals were the dross of America. Those nasty liberals wanted to curb our freedoms by putting limits on our right to bear arms, and they wanted to play God by popping birth control pills and procuring abortions. Liberals wanted to tax us heavily and force hardworking Americans to pay for the lazy, deceitful welfare queens who just wanted to mooch off the system. They didn't believe in trickle-down economics, which was the only kind of economics that worked. They scoffed at the mention of Ronald Reagan, who was one of the best presidents in the modern era. They wanted to put an end to capitalism, and they thought that Christians were just a bunch of unfortunate, naive fools.

As a child, I believed that America was supposed to be one nation under God—with an emphasis on *God*—but the liberals wanted to erase every mention of the religious tradition that had helped give birth to our country. I thought of myself as a soldier for Jesus and a champion of the faith, which also meant that I was a defender of American freedom and democracy. The two went hand in hand, and the fight against the Devil was just as important as the fight against the Democrats.

As I grew deeper into my political and religious beliefs, my childhood dreams of the convent continued to solidify. I still thought fondly of the sign that the Virgin Mary had given to me when I was nine years old, and I started calling convents halfway through my senior year of high school. I would be seventeen when I got my diploma, and I didn't want to waste my time with college. I hoped to become a novitiate before my eighteenth birthday, but all of the Mothers Superior said some version of the same thing: *Go to college. Get a degree. See if this is really the path you want to take.*

I reluctantly followed their advice. I applied to a few Catholic colleges that were known for incorporating faith into academia, but there was one place that stood out above the rest. It was a little college in southern Ohio known as the Franciscan University of Steubenville. To Catholics, it was considered the gold standard of holiness. People flocked from far and wide to its gates for faith retreats and youth conferences, and the priest who served as chancellor was rumored to be a saintly man. My application was accepted, and I enrolled without hesitation. I viewed my college career as the first step on my path toward the convent. Someday I would don a habit and rid the world of dross in God's name.

Now I found myself contemplating a very different kind of dross. I stood beside a fellow steelworker on a raised platform in the Hot Dip Galvanizing Line, which was the pristine area I had once toured during orientation. The platform was suspended a few feet above a vat of molten zinc, and the noise coming from the nearby machines whined at deafening levels.

"Do you see it?" the man shouted over the noise, pointing down at the zinc. "There's the dross."

It was a few weeks after I'd finished my training with Gunner, and the young man who was standing beside me had become my new teacher. His name was Mike, and he looked to be in his early thirties. While Mike had been a steelworker for only a few years, much of his time in the mill had been spent managing the vat of molten zinc. Now he was showing me the ropes.

For the most part, everyone in the mill referred to the vat as the Pot, even though the word *pot* didn't do it justice. It was the size of a small swimming pool—big enough to swallow you up if you fell inside—and a sheet of razor-sharp steel shot up through the middle of it at speeds that could slice you in half. Drowning and dismemberment weren't the only dangers, though. The zinc was kept at a balmy 850 degrees Fahrenheit, which was hot enough to cook you alive.

A few days before I started training with Mike, I had asked the Godfather what would happen if I fell into the zinc.

"If Jesus loves you," he said, "he'll just let you die."

The Godfather told me about a man who had fallen into the zinc at another mill. The third-degree burns were the least of the man's worries. When he fell into the zinc, he aspirated the liquid metal, which hardened in his lungs. Doctors couldn't remove it. The man survived, but he probably wished he hadn't.

"You're never the same after something like that," the Godfather said. "But don't worry. They'll give you a harness. It will catch you if you fall."

But when I got to the Pot, there wasn't a harness. Or, more accurate, there *was* a harness, but Mike scoffed when I asked about it.

"You don't want to use that harness," he said. "If you fall, it'll just bob you up and down in the zinc. You're better off just going all the way under and dying right away."

As I stared down at the zinc, I felt very much like a frog suspended above a pot of boiling water, except the Pot didn't boil or bubble. In fact, the zinc was so silvery and smooth that it looked fake. The metal could have been a villain's elixir or an alchemist's failed attempt to find the fountain of youth, and the only thing separating me from its depths was a small fence-like barrier that I wouldn't have trusted around an herb garden. I probably would have gotten lost in my fear if not for the pungent odor emanating from the zinc. The smell was a cross between dirty armpits and fertilizer, and it was so strong that I could think of little else.

"See the dross?" Mike said again. He had the broad, muscled shoulders of someone who enjoyed working out, but he didn't seem like the type to flaunt it.

I took a closer look at the Pot and saw a series of small silvery clumps floating around the edges. Some drifted like islands on the surface of the zinc, but others bunched together, forming ridges that looked like alligator scales.

"Yeah," I said. "I see it."

"This is your job," Mike told me, still yelling over the noise. "Every thirty minutes, you have to scoop the dross out of the Pot."

I nodded, and Mike beckoned me to a pulpit a few feet away. The air-conditioning raised goosebumps on my arms as I walked inside, providing a welcome relief from the heat, and an old-timer waved at us from his chair. The man was sitting in front of a long table that held a variety of computer screens, all of which were positioned below a huge window looking out at the Pot. The screens blipped all sorts of information to him. There were bars and graphs and calculations. One computer showed real-time footage of the steel moving through the zinc, and another looked like a control board for a nuclear reactor.

"This is our SOT," Mike said, gesturing toward the old-timer. "He controls the line."

An SOT, or Senior Operating Technician, was considered a top dog among union workers. Most lines and mills had an SOT assigned to each shift, and they controlled all of the equipment involved in processing the steel.

The SOT quickly said hello before turning back to his computers, while Mike and I took off our personal protective equipment. In addition to our uniforms and hard hats, we had to wear face visors, aluminized gloves, and itchy green jumpsuits whenever we worked near the Pot. The visors kept the zinc out of our eyes, the aluminized gloves kept our hands from burning, and the green jumpsuits prevented us from catching on fire. All of it together made the sweat drip down your back, so Mike and I each grabbed a bottle of water from a nearby refrigerator before sitting down in the corner of the room.

"This job isn't rocket science," Mike told me. "You're mostly just removing dross."

I drained half of my water bottle and wiped my mouth unceremoniously. "Where does the dross come from?" I said, always eager to learn more about the whys and hows of steelmaking.

Mike shrugged and leaned back in his chair. "I'm not sure. It just happens."

"The dross gets blown off the steel," the SOT interrupted, turning away from his computers for a moment. He had a friendly smile and thinning hair, and he seemed genuinely excited to explain the process to someone who had an interest.

"Blown?" I asked.

"See that big box?" the SOT said, pointing to a contraption that was hovering just above the zinc. "Those are air knives. The knives blow any excess zinc off the steel to make sure it's coated evenly, and all of that excess zinc hardens in the air and becomes dross."

I stood up to get a better view of what he was talking about, but the steel was moving so fast that I could barely tell what the knives were doing. The way I imagined it, a piece of dross was like an ice cube floating in a glass of water. It was made of the same substance as the liquid zinc, but it had taken on a different form in the cool air.

"Why doesn't the dross just melt back down once it hits the molten zinc?" I asked the SOT.

He paused for a moment. I had asked a question he'd never heard before.

"I don't know the chemistry of it," he told me, "but I think it has something to do with the heat of the Pot. It's just not hot enough to melt the dross."

Behind me, Mike finished his water and crumpled the bottle before throwing it in the trash. He had popped a piece of gum into his mouth, and the motions he made with his jaw accentuated a pair of well-defined cheekbones that sat beneath his deep brown eyes.

"All I know is that you don't want the dross to touch the steel," Mike said.

"Yeah," the SOT agreed, "you don't want to be on the hook for ruining thousands of dollars of steel, especially when you're an Orange Hat."

As it turned out, dross was less like an ice cube and more like gravel in a can of paint. If it got onto the steel during the galvanizing process, the dross would leave specks and imperfections on the surface. There was nothing you could do with steel that had been hit with dross. It couldn't be sold, and it couldn't be mended.

I sat back down next to Mike, worried about the responsibility I was suddenly carrying on my shoulders. Old-timers in the Shipping Department had told me rumors about the Hot Dip Galvanizing Line. *The bosses down there are a bunch of assholes*, everyone said. *Be careful when you're an Orange Hat. They won't think twice about firing you.* In the Hot Dip, the bosses were far more involved than Jeremy. They didn't send messages over the fax machine, which was its own kind of curse. The bosses knew your business. They knew your habits. They rode your ass hard, and they acted like hawks whenever you screwed up. The SOT's warning stuck with me like an omen. I didn't want to get fired for ruining tons of steel during the last step in its evolution, and I cursed myself a little as I finished the rest of my water. I had gotten myself into this mess.

A few weeks prior I had signed my name on a bunch of bids for various departments in the mill. These "bids" were intra-company job applications. They were posted sporadically throughout the year, and they allowed workers to move between the many departments that existed within the mill. If you didn't like the job you were doing, you could sign a bid to work somewhere else. If you hated the Tandem Mill, you could sign your name on a bid for the Pickle Line. If you were sick of running a crane, you could sign a bid to the Roll Shop. You were never guaranteed to get a bid, because they were based solely on seniority. The most senior worker who signed a bid was always given first dibs on taking the job. If that worker had a change of heart, then the position would go to the next senior worker, and so on.

While most people used the bidding system to escape jobs they no longer wanted, it wasn't a hatred of the Shipping Department that caused me to sign a bid to the Hot Dip. If anything, banding coils was a dream job. It was safe, relaxed, and hassle-free, but there was no guarantee that I would stay in Shipping. New employees started in the mill without a bid. While the company had placed me in the Shipping Department, I wasn't considered a permanent, or *bidded*, resident there. Until I won a bid into a particular area, my job would be subject to a certain level of unpredictability. The company could force me to work anywhere within the Finishing Department—they could send me to the Tandem Mill or the Pickle Line or the cranes—and they could do so at a moment's notice. That wasn't true for bidded employees. The company couldn't jostle them around on a whim. More important, workers who had bids generally had set schedules. They could predict when they would be working, and they could take advantage of their days off. As an un-bidded employee, I didn't have that luxury.

My schedule varied drastically from one week to the next, especially after I finished my training as a Bander. The company had started using me as a fill-in for other workers. I covered for vacation time, and I was asked to work extra if someone got sick. It wasn't unusual for me to work more than fifty hours a week, and my twelve-hour shifts were always a mixture of days and nights. I might work two days in the beginning of the week, followed by two nights in the middle, followed by another day at the end of the week with barely any time to recover from the changing shifts. I rarely knew if I was coming or going, and it was difficult to do anything other than work and sleep.

Desperate for consistency, I signed my name on every bid that came out. I knew it was a long shot. I barely had any seniority in the mill, so it came as quite a surprise when the company told me that I qualified for a bid in the Hot Dip.

One of the managers from the Finishing Department called me with the offer, and I was eager to accept. I remembered the Hot Dip from orientation. I thought fondly of its clean floors and freshly painted walkways, and I drooled at the prospect of a set schedule. The one caveat was that if I accepted the offer, I would have to start out by working the Pot.

"It's a really difficult job," the company man said over the phone. I was speaking to him during one of my shifts at the mill. There weren't any vacations for me to cover that day, so Sam, Charlie, and I had been scheduled to do cleanup together. We were painting walkways in a warehouse when I received a message from the company man, so I had stepped outside to return the call.

"Don't worry," I told him, "I've done difficult jobs before."

"I mean, it's really physical," the man warned. I could tell that he was trying to choose his words carefully.

"That doesn't bother me," I said. "I used to paint houses, so I'm used to physical labor."

The man paused for a few moments, and a bead of sweat trickled from beneath my hard hat. The weather in Cleveland had made the abrupt shift into summer, and the air felt humid and oppressive. I was standing in a lonely section of the mill that wasn't often trafficked by buggies and semis. A few rusty warehouses loomed nearby, making the space look like a derelict courtyard. Weeds struggled through the cracked pavement. Heaps of trash littered the street, even though there was an empty dumpster a few feet away. There were old take-out containers, old water bottles, and old pallets with broken boards.

"I guess I'm trying to say that a lot of women don't seem to like the Pot very much," the company man said. "Most women don't stay on the job for long."

I bristled. I had signed the bid in search of a predictable schedule, but now the man had given me a new reason to accept. He was telling me that women weren't cut out for the job, and I wanted to prove him wrong.

"I'll take the bid," I said without hesitation.

Later that day I talked to my fellow union workers about the Pot. They all warned me that the job was hot and dangerous, and I started to wonder if I had made a rash decision. I tried my best to ignore the thought. Steelworkers were prone to hyperbole and the Pot couldn't possibly be as awful as everyone made it seem. Besides, the job came with a grace period. Whenever you accepted a bid within the Finishing Department, the company gave you fourteen days to decide whether or not you wanted to stay in the new position. If I discovered that the awful rumors were true, then I could give up the bid and go back to banding coils. If I decided to keep the bid, however, I would be stuck in the Hot Dip for at least a year.

During those twelve months, I would be ineligible to sign any other bids. The company had established the policy to maintain continuity in the workforce, and it raised the stakes for every newly bidded employee. I only had a short time to decide whether I liked the Pot well enough to give up my cushy job in the Shipping Department. If I made the wrong decision, I might be kicking myself for a year—or more. With my low seniority, there was no guarantee that I'd find another bid so easily, even after completing twelve months on the Pot. One year could easily turn into several years, which was exactly what had happened to Mike.

"Mike wants to get you trained as fast as possible so he can get off the Pot," the SOT told me during my first day of training. "You're his ticket out of here."

Of all the people who worked with the zinc, Mike had the most seniority. Once I was trained, he would be allowed to move into the other positions in the Hot Dip, all of which were far more desirable than stirring molten metal. For most of the day, Mike had been looking at me with hungry eyes. There was nothing flirtatious or sexual in his gaze; he was a desperate man, and I was his salvation.

"I've done my time," Mike told me. "I want to get off this job."

"How long have you been on the Pot?" I asked.

"About three years now."

"*Three?*" I said. I couldn't imagine stirring zinc for that long.

"Yes." Mike shuddered. "Three."

After my first shift in the Hot Dip, I called Tony from my apartment to tell him about the new job. My hair was still wet from the long cool shower I'd taken to wash away the day's dirt and sweat, and I sat cross-legged on the ground in front of a box fan. I was still living in the mouse-infested apartment, although the mice no longer pestered me. They had been eradicated with the poison, and I was reluctant to move. While I wanted a nicer apartment, I didn't want to jump into a new lease before I amassed some healthy savings.

"Hi," Tony said after the phone rang a few times. "How was your first day?"

The fan hummed into my ear, and I lifted my shirt to get the cool air onto my skin.

"It was pretty crazy," I told him. "The Pot was bigger than I thought it'd be, and I was just standing on this little platform right above the molten metal. It freaked me out. I mean, there's not much to catch you if you fall. And it was so hot. I was dripping sweat all day."

"Yeah," Tony told me, "it *was* really hot today. I went to the beach this afternoon, and I think I got a little touch of heatstroke."

I stretched out on the burgundy carpeting, letting the air from the fan wash over me like water. Tony was enjoying one of the coveted benefits of being a teacher—summer vacation—and I didn't want him to forget that his version of *hot* wasn't the same as mine.

"Sure," I said, "but it was ridiculous inside the mill. The Pot is, like, eight hundred and something degrees Fahrenheit. *Plus*, the mill is already warm because it's summertime. *And* you have to wear all of these layers of protective equipment. I had to wear this jumpsuit and these aluminum gloves. So I was literally drenched with sweat the whole day. I mean, drenched. I must've drank seven or eight bottles of water, and I didn't pee once."

"That's a lot of water," Tony agreed, but he didn't sound impressed. "I think I got a really bad sunburn today. I put on sunscreen, but it must have rubbed off."

I ran my hand across the carpeting and sighed. I wanted Tony to be excited and intrigued by my new job. I wanted him to ask questions and prod me for more information, but the conversation was always turning away from the mill.

"Sunburns suck," I said after a long pause.

"Do you think aloe will help?" he asked.

"Yeah," I said, "aloe would probably help."

There was a yawning gap between our daily experiences, and it showed. When we went for hikes together, I would be in the middle of a monologue about the mill only to find that Tony was staring at a flock of birds. During the school year, Tony would go into detail about his students and curriculum, but I would only give him the cursory information about my job because I sensed that he was bored by anything more. Sometimes it felt like my part of the conversation was just filler—his sunburn mattered, the aloe mattered—but Tony wasn't trying to be aloof or distant to hurt my feelings. He shrank back when he was out of his element, and talking to a girlfriend who stirred molten zinc was certainly out of his element. Perhaps more important, though, Tony had already begun to resent the mill. If he didn't press me for more information about my job, it was because my job was already affecting our relationship.

We hadn't seen much of each other since I'd completed orientation. My erratic schedule made it hard to find time together, and I still wasn't comfortable letting him spend the night on the used mattress in my crappy apartment. When I did get a chance to go over to his house for a day or two, I just wanted to sleep and watch TV. For Tony's sake, I tried my best to be active, but the swinging schedule was taking a toll on my body and my mind. I couldn't seem to recover as quickly as my coworkers, and no amount of caffeine put a dent in my exhaustion.

In the weeks before I started on the Pot, all of our time together had been spent searching for a new hatchback to replace the one I'd totaled. Romance had been replaced by test-drives, and dinner dates had taken a back seat to dealership visits. Our relationship became a matter of practicality and time management, and Tony was helpful through it all. He let me use his convertible to get to work, and he did most of the research on new cars, which wasn't something I had the time or inclination to do. I would have bought something on a whim, but Tony kept me grounded, insisting that it was best to know the facts before pulling the trigger. He may not have been good at asking about my job, but he was the type of person who showed his affection by comparing engines and exploring trim packages. For him, love was composed of actions, especially when those actions were necessary and mundane.

After test-driving every hatchback in the city, Tony and I went to a dealership intent on buying. We sat across from a portly young salesman in a lobby that was decorated with a palette of grays and blues.

I stared down at the tile floor while Tony negotiated the price with the salesman. The two men talked about discounts and bottom lines. They haggled over floor mats and cargo nets.

"I think you can throw in six oil changes," Tony said, driving a hard bargain.

The salesman put his hands behind his neck, knitting his fingers together and exhaling loudly. "Hey, man, I can't do six oil changes at this price. You're already getting an insane deal. It's the best I can do, I swear. But I'll let you guys talk about it for a few minutes."

The salesman walked away to get a cup of coffee, and I conferred with Tony. We both agreed that it was a good price—better than other dealerships had offered us—so I nodded in approval when the salesman returned.

"I'll take it," I told him.

The salesman smiled and sat down in triumph. Then he began explaining how he would get the car for me. He would have to weasel it away from another dealership with a few white lies, essentially stealing it out from under another salesman. Tony and I had already met the salesman who this guy was about to swindle. We had taken a few test-drives with him, and he seemed like a nice enough man. He walked with a slight limp, and he had the watery eyes of an injured puppy. While the man hadn't been able to give us a great price, I didn't want to deceive him.

The mechanics of the deal were starting to make me uncomfortable, so I turned to Tony when the portly salesman walked away to find some paperwork.

"I think this guy's being sleazy," I said. "I want to go back to the other dealership."

I knew that we could get the car for a higher price from the puppy-dog salesman without all of the dishonesty.

"So you're going to pay more for a car just because the guy's being sleazy?" Tony asked.

"Yeah," I told him. "I don't like sleazy."

Tony shrugged. After bidding our goodbyes to the portly salesman, who looked at us in desperation, Tony and I hopped in the car and left.

Within minutes, my cell phone rang in my purse.

"Okay," the portly salesman said on the other end of the line, his voice crackling over the bad reception, "I'll cut four hundred dollars off the price, and I'll throw in six oil changes and an extra cargo net."

I relayed the message to Tony, who looked at me in surprise.

"Holy shit," he said, "that's a good deal."

"Should we go back?" I asked.

"You should do what you want," Tony told me, "but I wouldn't pass up that price."

Sleazy or not, Tony was right. It was a killer deal, so I pushed the memory of the puppy-dog salesman from my mind. Money was money, and business was business.

"I can't believe you haggled them down," Tony said as we drove back to the dealership. A look of defeat had spread across his face. "I guess you're a better man than I am."

I shook my head and smiled. "Not true," I told him, even though I liked being called a better man. I was always glad when people recognized me as masculine, so long as the comments were aimed at my personality and not my body.

Tony glanced over at me and wrinkled his brow. "You certainly didn't need me to help you negotiate."

I could tell that he was spiraling into self-deprecation, so I tried to lighten the mood.

"Lies and fabrications," I told him. It was a term we'd coined together, reserved for times when one of us said something ridiculous, and I was using it now to bolster his ego. "If I didn't have your help, I would have paid full price for the first car that caught my eye. We're teammates, remember?"

Tony liked the word *teammates*. He always used it to describe us, and I could feel his tension easing as we stopped at a red light. The word lingered in the air, softening the scowl that had spread across his face.

The company man who'd offered me the Hot Dip bid had set me down the path toward molten zinc when he insinuated that women weren't cut out for the job, and the demographics of the Hot Dip only solidified my goal. Of the forty odd people who worked in the department, only one other than myself was a woman. I was struck by the desire to prove that I was just as good as any man.

Before I started on the Pot, the old-timers in Shipping had told me stories about the other lone woman. Her name was Miss Joyce, and she was one of the SOTs who ran the line. Like all SOTs, Miss Joyce carried a good deal of responsibility on her shoulders. She controlled the galvanizing process and delegated tasks to other workers, and she also had to answer for any mistakes or mess-ups that occurred on her shift. Bosses always went to SOTs looking for answers. *What went wrong? Why was this batch of steel damaged? Why didn't you correct the problem sooner?*

Given their responsibility, the SOTs in the mill occupied the highest pay bracket among union workers, and it wasn't easy to move into these well-paid positions. Like most promotions in the mill, one's ability to become an SOT was based solely on seniority. It took many years to qualify for the job, but Miss Joyce didn't have to worry. She had been making steel for decades, earning her right to occupy the best positions that the mill had to offer. Or so she thought. When Miss Joyce finally amassed enough seniority to become an SOT in the Hot Dip, the bosses overlooked her. They started training a less-seasoned worker—a man—in a job that was rightfully hers. Miss Joyce quickly contacted the union, which came to her aid. Union officials complained to the company, and the company relented. They trained Miss Joyce as an SOT, but the fight she had to endure spoke for itself.

The story lingered in the back of my mind during those first days on the Hot Dip. I wondered if the company's actions had been an accident or not, and I felt very aware of my place as the only other woman in the department.

On my second day of training, I arrived at the Pot early and grabbed a bottle of water in the pulpit. Mike walked in a few minutes later and greeted me quickly.

"It's going to be hectic today," he said. "Let's get to work."

The dross stopped for nothing, so we fitted ourselves in our visors and jumpsuits. Before we stepped out into the heat, Mike gave me a warning. He pulled down the collar of his shirt and revealed a network of scars on his chest.

"See these?" he said. The scars looked like old pockmarks, and there were quite a few of them scattered across his skin. "These are from the zinc." Splatters of molten metal had landed on Mike's green jumpsuit at various times during his three-year tenure as Pot Worker.

"Just be careful," he told me. "Don't trust these jumpsuits to protect you against the heat. They're flame retardant, but they aren't heat resistant. If the zinc lands on you, you'll still get burned. The jumpsuit just prevents you from bursting into flames."

With that, Mike pulled up his collar and walked onto the platform that surrounded the Pot. I followed quickly behind.

It was nearly impossible for us to speak more than a few words to one another over the sound that the steel made as it moved through the zinc, so we spoke with wild hand gestures. Mike grabbed a tool that looked like a long garden hoe and pointed to the Pot.

Watch me, he motioned.

Mike stood upright and coaxed the garden hoe through the metal with quick sweeps, as if he were using a push broom. The dross broke apart under the weight of his movements and drifted into a channel on the far side of the Pot. Once inside the channel, the lumps of hardened zinc moved slowly toward a robot, named Robbie, that stood a few feet away.

In the simplest of terms, Robbie's body was a jointed arm that could dip down into the zinc, and his head was a sieve that could scoop the dross from the channel. Every time Robbie scooped a bit of dross, he turned around and dumped it onto a piece of bent rebar. The hot dross solidified onto the rebar, forming a silvery network of clumps and creases. At the end of each shift, the Pot Worker hooked the tongs of a forklift into the rebar and carried the dross to a disposal site.

"When you work the Pot," Mike had told me, "Robbie is your best friend. If Robbie breaks, you're out of luck. You'll have to scoop all of the dross by yourself. Believe me, you don't want to do that. It's hell."

I looked over at Robbie while Mike pushed the garden hoe through the zinc. The robot and I were both on opposite sides of the Pot, but I could already tell that he was aptly named. Robbie had the air of a self-conscious eighth grader navigating a school dance. His arm jerked awkwardly whenever he scooped the dross, and the sieve made him look downright goofy.

Robbie was the kind of robot that got his ass whooped by the other robots on the playground, and I immediately took a liking to him. The base of his body was burnt orange, my favorite color, and he didn't fit with the crisp blue machines that churned around him. Like me, Robbie knew what it was like to be an awkward outsider in a world of perfect robots.

Mike tapped me on the shoulder, drawing my attention back to the task at hand. He pointed again to the garden hoe. Then he pointed to me.

Now you try.

Mike had pushed the dross effortlessly, but as I mimicked his movements, I was amazed at how difficult it was. The zinc was heavier than it looked, and it took every ounce of energy I had to break up the thick alligators that had formed around the Pot. The zinc kept sucking the hoe under the surface, and I couldn't help pushing the dross closer and closer to the center of the Pot, where a sheet of steel was in the process of being galvanized.

"Don't push it toward the steel!" Mike shouted, grabbing the garden hoe from my hands and redirecting the dross toward Robbie. He was able to create a current with his shoulders, working the hoe with rhythmic movements that carried the dross into the channel. Later, the SOT would tell me that Mike hadn't intervened in time; my lack of precision had marred a sheet of steel with dross. I blushed with embarrassment. Only one coil had been ruined, but one coil was worth more than I had paid for my car. *You're still in training, so you won't take the fall for it this time,* the SOT later warned, *but don't make a habit of it.*

When Mike got the dross under control, he gave me the garden hoe and once again motioned toward the zinc.

Try again.

I made every effort to be more careful with my movements, but my arms quickly tired as I pushed the dross around the Pot. I could feel myself losing control of the garden hoe, so I leaned forward and braced myself against the little barrier at the edge of the platform. In that position, I could use my lower body to move the dross with more precision.

Mike lifted the plastic visor covering his face and drew close to my ear, the deafening noise thundering around us.

"No, don't do it like that," he said. "Use your shoulders. It'll be easier."

I wanted to tell him that he was wrong. I couldn't push the metal with my shoulders like he did—my power was in my legs—but the noise of the steel was too loud to explain this to him. I stood up straight and tried again to use my shoulders, but it didn't take long before I was leaning forward and pushing with my thighs. When I finally managed to clear the rest of the dross from the Pot, Mike and I went back to the pulpit for a short break.

"You should really use your shoulders next time," he said before taking a swig of water. "It's easier that way."

"Really?" I said. "I found it more difficult."

"No," he told me. "Trust me. People are stronger in their shoulders."

I politely agreed to tend the dross differently next time, even though I knew that I would still use my legs. As I sat down and drank a bottle of water, I couldn't help but think of an adage I had heard from my family. *Men and women are just different. They have different bodies and different hormones. Why can't feminists just accept that fact and move on? Why are they so obsessed with being equal?*

It was an argument that always tripped me up. It seemed intuitive and inarguable, and my father always sat back in triumph whenever he made the claim. It was his trump card when we talked about feminism. Was I really going to argue that a penis and a vagina were the same thing? I usually sat back, defeated. I knew from years of painting houses that my body *was* different from that of a man. The men were usually taller, which meant that they could reach farther. They were heavier, so they could lift more weight. But equality wasn't an argument about hormones. It wasn't a debate about breasts or genitalia.

So often, a woman's perception of her own body was discredited. We were more likely than men to be given antianxiety pills for physical symptoms, and we were less likely to be given a stress test when experiencing symptoms of a heart attack. When we went to the emergency room with acute abdominal pain, we waited longer than our male counterparts to receive pain medication, if we received any at all. Many of us tended to bring our boyfriends, husbands, or sons to doctor visits to help verify our symptoms, and we were more likely to be misdiagnosed for serious conditions like heart disease or stroke. But equality wasn't the debate my father wanted to have. It wasn't about whether a penis was the same as a vagina. It was about making sure that all bodies, regardless of sex or gender, mattered in an equivalent way.

Of all people, my father should have understood the biases that existed, at least as they related to health care. He had been present at my birth, which was supposed to be a routine cesarean section. My mother wasn't worried about the procedure. She had delivered my sister in the same way without any complications, but things didn't go so well on the day that I was born. The doctor performed a spinal block. Then he probed my mother's legs and stomach to make sure that they were numb.

"I can still feel that," my mother told him.

"No," the doctor said, "you can't feel that."

"Yes, I can," she said.

"No. It's all in your head. You're just sensing the pressure."

Meanwhile, the nurses prepared for surgery. They checked vital signs and laid out instruments. My father stood next to my mother and held her hand, which was sitting on a padded armrest. There were two of these armrests, one on each side of the operating table, and my mother's arms had been securely fastened to them.

The doctor readied the scalpel and put his hand on my mother's stomach.

"I can still feel that," she said.

"No," the doctor said. "It's just in your head."

He slid the scalpel into my mother's skin with a single, decisive stroke, and my mother let out a chilling scream. She instinctively flexed her arms with such force that she broke the armrests. My father fainted. The nurses scrambled for drugs. Someone put my mother under, and the doctor attended to the wound in her belly. In the midst of that chaos, I was born.

My mother didn't sue the doctor who failed to listen to her. She didn't receive compensation from the hospital, and she never once hinted that the oversight had anything to do with sexism. *Sexism* was a word that feminists used, and feminism was taboo in my family. It was the worst insult my parents could hurl at a woman, which was an odd position for my mother to hold. She came from a line of strong women, all of whom passed along their wisdom and resolve.

Artie, my mother's grandmother, raised seven children in the tiny city of Chester, West Virginia, during the Great Depression. For years, Artie supplemented her husband's income by painting pottery at a local mill on the Ohio River. Day after day she drew delicate flowers on porcelain dinnerware. She painted plates and teacups, while her husband, the local barber, gambled and made bathtub gin. In my family, it was rumored that Artie's name came from a gravestone. Her own mother, Alice, had walked into a cemetery and closed her eyes. Then, with her head tilted back among the graves, Alice stretched out her arms and spun around in a circle, eventually landing on the marker of some guy named Art, which meant *champion*. It suited my great-grandmother perfectly.

Artie's oldest daughter, Peggy, was known to run the numbers for her father from time to time, but she found that small-town life didn't suit her. Peggy wanted out. She wanted to see the world. During

World War II, the government initiated the Women's Reserve of the United States Coast Guard, known as SPARS, and Peggy joined the ranks. She spent most of the war stationed in Washington, D.C., and when her service was up, she met and married a handsome Army Air Forces navigator from Ohio. Together, they bought a tiny house in a Cleveland suburb, where they started a family. Peggy would give birth to three children—two sons and my mother—but she wasn't content as a housewife. When her children were old enough, she got a job at General Motors, where she worked with some of the first computers ever used in the auto industry. For a while, Peggy's salary surpassed that of her husband. In an era of housewives and kept women, she was both mother and breadwinner.

Even though my own mother told me that men and women were just *different*, she was far more similar to Artie and Peggy than she realized. She didn't believe that a woman's place was in the kitchen. She had more education than my father, and she earned a higher hourly wage at her job. My mother didn't care that I preferred toy horses over dolls. She didn't mind that I hated dresses. She expected that Laurel and I would go to college, and she was relieved when my sister ditched a deadbeat boyfriend to pursue a career as a pharmacist.

In our household, there was no limit on what my sister and I could accomplish, and my mother made a rule for both of us. If we wanted to get married, we weren't allowed to do so before the age of twenty-five. My mother wanted us to finish college and establish careers before we started thinking about husbands and babies, and I assumed the rest of the world operated in the same way.

While I had more interest in nuns than nuptials when I enrolled as a freshman at the Franciscan University of Steubenville, I expected to meet like-minded women aspiring to do great things in the world. Maybe there were women who wanted to become famous inventors, doctors, or scientists. Maybe there were others who wanted to be on the cover of *Time* magazine.

During the first week of classes, my RA requested that all of the new students write a few facts about themselves on note cards that were later posted near the dorm's main entrance. The cards asked for our names, our hometowns, our majors. The bulk of each card, however, was dedicated to a single question: *What are your goals for the future?* I stood beside the doorway and read the note cards, excited to see how many women had goals and interests that were similar to my own. On most of the cards, the same refrain repeated itself over and over: *I want to become a loving wife and mother.* A few other women wanted to become nuns too, and nearly all of the women mentioned their faith. *I want to pray the rosary every day. I want to grow deeper in my relationship with Christ. I want to go to daily Mass.*

My card stuck out like a sore thumb: *Get at least one PhD. Write a book. Write a treatise on moral philosophy. Climb a mountain. Scuba dive. Skydive. Travel to Africa. Become a nun.*

Early in the semester, I met a fellow freshman at an event designed to help new students build friendships and connections. The woman had flawless skin and silky blond hair that fell to her shoulders. She was neatly dressed, but she wore no makeup. She had excellent posture, but she wasn't pompous.

We sat across from each other in the school cafeteria, sipping the punch that the school had provided for us.

"So," I said to the woman, "what's your major?"

She brushed a strand of blond hair away from her cheek. "Oh, I'm here for my MRS degree," she said proudly.

I leaned forward in curiosity. The woman had answered with such conviction that I assumed she must be studying something very complex, and I was excited to learn more about it.

"I've never heard of an MRS degree before," I told her. "Does it have to do with the sciences?"

The woman cocked her head and stared at me. Her worried expression seemed to suggest that I was missing something obvious.

"An MRS degree," she said. "A missus degree."

I shook my head. I figured that a *missus* was a physics term I hadn't yet learned.

The woman finally spelled it out for me. "I'm here to find a husband." She spoke the words slowly, as if relaying them to a child.

"Oh," I said. "But you have to study *something* while you're here. Don't you have any interests?"

The woman shrugged. "I don't know. I guess I'll just pick an easy major. Do you know any easy majors?"

While it wasn't awful that the woman's college career revolved around her future husband, it certainly meant that we had very little in common. The all-girls school I had attended for high school was filled with a feistier type. We had high goals and high ideals. We were serious in our studies and crass in our jokes. We had five-year plans, and we believed that women weren't born only to be homemakers. The people I found at Franciscan University seemed to think otherwise. They didn't flinch when a woman said that she wanted her MRS degree, and they all carried their faith with ease.

Like most college freshmen, I wanted to blend seamlessly into the student body. I wanted everyone to accept me with open arms, but most of the women on campus could tell that I was different. They rarely talked to me. They didn't invite me to pray with them. They didn't extend invitations to dinner. I felt like an outsider in their presence, but I desperately wanted to be like them. I tried to find student organizations and activities that might bring me into their fold, and something political caught my eye during the first few weeks of school. George W. Bush was running for reelection against John Kerry at the time, and Kerry had scheduled a rally in Steubenville. Some of the students on campus had decided to take action. They were going to protest abortion rights while Kerry spoke, so I signed up to join them. I wanted to endear myself to the faith-filled women who otherwise ignored me.

The event drew a large group of student activists. We were all young, white, and Catholic, and we mostly came from middle-class households that could afford to foot the bill at Franciscan University. We armed ourselves with rosaries and antiabortion signs before driving to the center of the city, where the streets were already congested with Kerry supporters. Most people gave us funny looks as we passed, but I didn't care. There was a holy adrenaline surging through my veins. I had only been at the college for a few weeks, and I was already doing the Lord's work. I was standing beside the other holy women, ready to do battle against the Kerry supporters who heckled us from the crowd. We were the righteous ones—God's sacred people—and we would show those Democrats the error of their ways.

I followed my fellow protesters through the throngs of people, needling my way between the tightly packed bodies. Some of the students in my group were praying the Our Father or reciting a litany of saints, but their words were swallowed up by the noise of the crowd. If our prayers were going to be heard, we would have to recite them together. So that's exactly what we did. Once we fought our way into the heart of the rally, we kneeled on the ground and prayed the rosary.

"I believe in God, the Father Almighty, Creator of Heaven and Earth," we prayed while Kerry spoke. I focused so intently on my prayers that I barely listened to what he said. I directed all of my attention toward abortion, ignoring his words on racial diversity, economic opportunity, and the end of the war on terror.

"I believe in the Holy Spirit, the holy Catholic Church, the communion of saints, the forgiveness of sins," the prayer continued.

We went through the entire rosary, which contained a series of sixty-seven individual prayers. My legs went numb halfway through the recitation, but I relished the gravel that dug into my knees. I was taking a stand. I was doing something holy, as I'd been called to do. At the time, I believed that praying rosaries on street corners was an adequate form of activism, and my world wasn't wide enough to show me otherwise. I hadn't experienced poverty, as I would in years to come. I didn't yet understand the privilege of being white. I hadn't met any women who had exercised their right to choose, and I hadn't been faced with the issue myself.

I left the rally with an air of self-righteousness, but I didn't leave with any meaningful female friendships. Only a few of the other women had talked to me, and they only seemed interested in talking about God and marriage.

As the semester progressed, I began to gravitate more toward the men on campus. I had always been something of a tomboy, so my newfound friendships with men came naturally. We could talk about philosophy and joke about Ovid. We could discuss our aspirations for the future and go on adventures in the woods. If I walked around campus, I was usually accompanied by a platonic male friend. Of course, this posed its own difficulties.

Franciscan University was the kind of place where men and women weren't allowed into each other's dorm rooms. You could socialize with a man in one of the common areas, but you had to keep your feet on the floor. I used to joke about the rule. *Surely desperate lovers can find a way to consummate their desires while keeping all feet firmly planted!* Most people at Franciscan University didn't appreciate those kinds of jokes, and the ones who did weren't always models of Christian piety. By the middle of the semester, I spent most of my time smoking pot in a local cemetery with two men who were both majoring in philosophy. They would get me high and talk about the writings of Thomas Aquinas, C.S. Lewis, and Saint Augustine. Saint Augustine had famously said, "Lord, make me chaste, but not yet." Maybe the Mothers Superior were right. I felt destined for the convent, but I still had some wild oats to sow before God refined me into the right kind of woman. Until then, I was just one of the boys.

After a few days of working in the Hot Dip, Mike gave me a better taste of what the job entailed. I donned my jumpsuit, my hard hat, my visor, and my gloves. With my garden hoe in hand, I began pushing the dross to Robbie. The newly galvanized steel rose out of the zinc, glistening under the bright lights, and I started to develop a rhythm with the dross. I found just the right balance of shoulders and legs to create a current that swept the hardened zinc into the channel, and Mike gave me a thumbs-up when he saw that I hadn't marred a single piece of steel.

"We have to go clean Robbie!" he yelled over the noise.

Every time Robbie scooped a load of dross from the Pot, a small amount of zinc hardened on his arm. After a while, the zinc built up to the size of a baseball. If you didn't clear it away, Robbie would break. Mechanics would have to be called in to fix him, and you would have to scoop away all the dross by yourself.

Mike and I walked over to the little platform where Robbie did his work. We pushed a few buttons on a control panel and cut Robbie's power when his sieve-like head dipped below the surface of the zinc.

"I want you to try it by yourself," Mike said as he handed me a harness. I strapped it tightly around my waist.

Even though harnesses weren't required while pushing the dross, you had to wear one whenever you got close to Robbie. The tiny platform was difficult to navigate, and there wasn't a barrier around the metal. If you slipped, you'd land straight in the zinc. Whatever confidence I was developing with the dross quickly dwindled.

I double-checked my harness as Mike handed me a long, thin lance that was attached to a tank of nitrogen. After he showed me how to turn it on, I looked at Robbie and hesitated. I didn't want to get close to the molten metal, and I would have given anything to unbuckle the harness and run back to my old job with Gunner. Mike nodded toward Robbie.

"Go on," he said. "Robbie won't bite."

There was no way I could unbuckle the harness and save face, so I edged toward the Pot. I told myself that it would be over in a few minutes, but that didn't put a dent in the fear. My heart raced and a bead of sweat dripped off the tip of my nose. The zinc was so close that I could feel the heat emanating from its depths. I inched forward like a toddler afraid of water, and I stopped when I was still a few feet away from the edge. Even with my arm fully extended at the end of the nitrogen lance, I couldn't quite reach the big lump of zinc that had grown on Robbie's arm.

"You have to get closer," Mike called to me.

I took a tiny step forward.

"Closer."

I took a bigger step.

"A little closer."

I took one more step, which put me within inches of the zinc. My hands were shaking as I turned on the nitrogen and stretched the lance toward Robbie. His lump was situated on the surface of the molten metal, and the nitrogen bubbled in the silvery liquid as I probed Robbie's arm with the tip of the lance. A few pieces of hardened zinc began to fall away in chunks, but I wasn't willing to make any quick movements to speed the process along. I shifted the lance slowly and delicately, and I rejoiced to myself when a big piece of the lump finally dropped down into the molten zinc.

I turned off the nitrogen and quickly surveyed my work. There were still a few sizable globs of zinc on Robbie's arm. While the perfectionist in me wanted to clean the robot further, my fear of the zinc overcame my best intentions. I couldn't bear to stand on the platform any longer, so I backed away from the Pot and set the nitrogen lance aside.

A wave of relief passed over me as I reached safety, but it quickly evaporated. Much to my disappointment, Mike wanted to double-check what I had just done. He strapped on a harness and grabbed the nitrogen lance. With steady hands, he leaned out over the zinc and cleaned away the remaining globs that I had left on Robbie's arm. My face flushed with embarrassment. I didn't want him to think that I was the type of person who did second-rate work, even though I would have left anything half finished in order to get away from the molten metal.

When Mike came back, he flipped on Robbie's power and critiqued my work.

"You'll have to clean Robbie a little better next time," he shouted over the noise. "And you'll have to be quicker too."

He was right. I had done a poor job slowly, and a thick layer of dross had already built up around the Pot by the time Robbie was ready to go again. Mike and I each grabbed a garden hoe and went to work. The dross was so abundant that it had coagulated into logs, which I had to break apart with the end of my hoe. My arms felt like rubber as I leaned against the barrier around the Pot. The zinc was hot enough to send sweat dripping down my back, and it was only amplified by the summer heat that baked every inch of the mill. I was completely drenched beneath my green jumpsuit, and I wanted nothing more than a few minutes of air-conditioning. When the dross was clear and I had set my garden hoe aside, Mike pointed toward a forklift that was sitting nearby.

"Get more zinc!" he yelled.

The steel was constantly being galvanized and the zinc needed to be replenished often. It was the Pot Worker's responsibility to make sure that there was always enough. I reluctantly forced my aching body to climb into the forklift. With great caution, I drove to a little nook at the end of the Hot Dip Galvanizing Line, where rows of zinc ingots lined the gray floors.

The ingots themselves weren't particularly large. Each one stood roughly two feet high and three feet across, but a single ingot weighed more than a ton. All of the ingots had been stacked in rows that were four high, but the forklift could handle only two at a time.

I pulled up to the zinc and surveyed my options. If I couldn't find a pair of two neatly stacked ingots, then I would have to lift two from the top of a stack. I didn't want to do this for one simple reason: The forklift terrified me, especially after the incident with the train tracks. The brakes felt squishy and unreliable. The vehicle had rear-wheel drive, which meant that it didn't turn like a car. Everything felt wonky and backward, and the view through the front window was partially obstructed by the chains and gears that were attached to the forks. To make matters worse, the forklift could flip. If you didn't center the weight on the forks—or if you tried to carry too much weight—you risked a disaster that just might crush your skull.

I had gone through forklift training during my job orientation, but I was still nervous every time I turned the key. The training itself had lasted only a few hours. A young instructor brought a group of Orange Hats to one of the mill's huge warehouses, and Amelia and I were the only two women in the class that day. We watched men climb aboard the forklift with a certain level of self-assurance. They approached the driver's seat with square shoulders and bright eyes, and they maneuvered the vehicle with ease. When it was Amelia's turn to take a stab, the spunky single mother exuded her usual air of self-confidence. Like the men, she approached the forklift with square shoulders and bright eyes.

"Okay," the instructor told her, "show the boys how it's done."

Amelia climbed into the forklift, but her confidence faltered when she started working the controls. She drove slowly and fitfully, and she nearly backed over the instructor. While she eventually completed the tasks that were given to her, she did so with greater difficulty than the men.

When my turn came to drive the forklift in front of the class, I was determined to outperform everyone. I buckled myself into the vehicle and put it into gear. Then I glanced out of the window. The men stood around and watched, and I read volumes in their crossed arms and bored eyes. Even though these men didn't harbor any ill will toward me, their very presence shook my resolve. In an instant my confidence disappeared. I had trouble getting the forks into the base of a pallet, and I almost crashed into a toolbox when I put the forklift into reverse.

I did well enough to pass the course, but I still felt defeated. A few of the men made snide comments about female drivers, to which Amelia and I could only smile. We were both Millennials who had grown up in an era of female empowerment. We had been taught that women could do whatever men could do, and yet the old stereotypes still weighed heavily upon us. This awareness produced a deep anxiety that crippled our confidence and impeded our performance. Then, when we floundered with the forklift as a result, it chipped away at our confidence even more.

I drove slowly past the rows of zinc ingots near the Pot, fearing the same outcome as my training run. If I was going to stay on the job, then I would have to use the forklift on a daily basis. The thought made my stomach drop, but I tried my best to focus on my work. After giving myself a silent pep talk, I found two lonely ingots that were sitting at the front of a nearby row. It looked like I could pick them up easily, so I slipped my forks under the bottom ingot. When the forks were set, I pressed the lever that would raise the load. Nothing happened. I pressed harder on the lever. Still nothing. I kept pressing on the lever when everything suddenly pitched forward. The cab of the forklift shook, and the entire back end lifted into the air. I was thrown toward the steering wheel. My heart beat wildly, and my mind raced through all the warnings I had heard in orientation. *Forklifts can tip over. Forklifts can kill you.*

When the adrenaline settled, I took stock of the situation. The vehicle was still upright, but the back end was hovering above the ground. I had put the forks too far under the ingots. Instead of picking up the two ingots at the front of the row, I had been trying to pick up those two ingots *and* the four ingots stacked behind them. The little forklift had nearly buckled under the pressure. I slowly lowered the forks, and the back end crashed to the ground.

"Screw this," I huffed under my breath. Hands still shaking, I threw the forklift into reverse and headed back to the Pot without any ingots to show for it. I told Mike that there was something wrong with the engine, and he was too busy with the dross to argue.

When I finally finished my first week in the Hot Dip, I packed a bag and went to Tony's house for the weekend. I arrived late on a Friday night, and Tony was already dressed in a pair of plaid pajama pants. He greeted me at the door, a cup of tea in his hand, while Scout wagged her tail behind him.

"You're so late," he said, heading into the living room as I dropped my bag onto the floor.

"I know." I sighed. Scout twisted her body between my legs in excitement, so I scratched her behind the ear. "I had to do the laundry. And clean. And go grocery shopping."

"But you missed a good sunset," Tony said. His disappointment was palpable. I had told him that I would be able to make it to his house by dinner, but life had gotten the best of me. The twelve-hour shifts at the mill made it difficult to manage a household, and there were more chores than I had expected.

I followed Tony to the couch and plopped down beside a pillow.

"I'm sorry." I smiled, nestling close to him. "I'm here now. Let's watch a *Star Trek*."

Tony shrugged and turned on the television, but I was asleep before the opening credits played. The mill brought on a type of exhaustion I had never known. I could barely catch up on the sleep missed during the swing shifts, which made it feel like I was slogging through life. I couldn't give my full attention to anything. I forgot chicken at the grocery store. I neglected to do a load of whites. I looked down at the bathtub I was scrubbing only to realize that I had already scrubbed it earlier in the day. My mind had grown dull and foggy. My diet was quickly changing from home-cooked food to energy drinks and take-out meals. It always felt like I was barely catching my breath.

Tony eventually roused me off the couch and into bed, and I tossed and turned for the rest of the night. As usual, Tony woke early and made a pot of coffee. He loved summer mornings spent reading or playing the ukulele on the patio, but I wasn't quite as eager to start the day. My head ached from fatigue, but I forced myself out of bed. I knew that Tony was falling to the wayside like so many other things in my life, and I didn't want him to feel neglected.

I joined him on the patio, and we both sipped our coffees as the summer sun climbed above the trees. Scout trotted around the small yard with her nose to the ground, occasionally biting at a piece of grass that caught her eye.

"So," Tony said, "are you liking the stuff with the molten metal?"

I wrinkled my brow and shrugged. "Not really. It's kind of scary, and it smells like armpits."

"I thought you liked armpits." Tony laughed. In a fit of silliness, I had once told him that I found the smell of his body odor attractive. He never let me live it down.

"I like your armpits," I crooned, "but zinc armpits are different."

"You're weird," Tony said, blushing beneath his thick beard.

I raised my coffee, as if making a toast. "But you love me."

"Yep, I do." Tony paused to pet Scout, who had placed her head in his lap, and then he returned to our conversation about the Pot. "Do you think you're going to keep the job?"

"I don't know yet," I said, fiddling with the rim of my coffee cup. "I'm kind of torn."

"But doesn't it come with a regular schedule?" Tony asked. I sensed that he was partly asking for himself. A set schedule might mean that I would be less tired and more available.

"It does," I told him, "but I don't know if it's worth it."

In reality, I hated the Pot. The job was hot and hectic, and my old position in the Shipping Department looked more enticing by the day. Even so, I hadn't yet made up my mind to leave. Every decision felt like the wrong decision. If I stayed on the Pot, I'd be giving up the easy life of a Bander just to prove that I was a good as any man. If I left the Pot, I would be admitting defeat to the company man who insinuated that I couldn't do the job. If I stayed, I might have to fight the types of battles that Miss Joyce had already encountered. If I left, the skewed demographics of the Hot Dip would remain unchallenged. Staying meant a set schedule, which would help my relationship with Tony. Leaving meant that Tony might continue to feel ignored.

When we finished our morning coffee, Tony and I got dressed and headed to downtown Willoughby for our usual Saturday morning ritual. We got coffee and did some window-shopping before ending up at a locally owned toy store that specialized in collectible action figures and movie memorabilia. The owner of the toy store had come to recognize us, even if he didn't know us by name, and we often spent hours slipping quarters into the four brightly lit pinball machines that were nestled behind shelves of tiny posable superheroes.

On that particular morning, Tony gave me a pocketful of quarters and headed to the *NBA Hoops* machine, even though it drove him crazy. It took only a few minutes before he was cursing at the ball, and I wasn't faring much better. I wasted a few dollars on a game called *FunHouse*, the goal of which was to shoot the ball into the mouth of a ventriloquist's dummy named Rudy. Rudy's head sat in the back of the playfield. He had rosy cheeks and a cocked eyebrow, and he talked incessantly while your ball pinged on bumpers or cruised along ramps.

"No way," Rudy taunted as the lights flashed on the game.

Almost immediately my ball drained past my flippers, as if confirming the dummy's prediction. My mind was focused on the mill, not the game, which made following the ball nearly impossible. I needed to make a decision to stay in the Hot Dip or go back to Shipping, and I wasn't sure which way to lean.

I launched another ball in Rudy's direction, aiming it into a little void behind his head.

"*I'm watching you,*" the dummy exclaimed, his shifty eyes panning from left to right.

No matter what I decided about the Hot Dip, it felt like men were in the middle of everything. I was measuring myself against men, trying to live up to men, trying to be one of the boys. I was overly conscious of what men wanted me to be. When the old crane operator with the lazy eye wrapped his arm around my shoulders and told me that I was too pretty for the mill, I didn't wiggle out of his embrace. Deep down, I was flattered that he thought me pretty. When the old-timers blamed me for getting the forklift stuck on the train tracks, I offered no protest. I didn't want to be seen as *one of those women* who lectured people about sexism.

"*I'm not happy with you now,*" Rudy said as I shot my ball up a ramp. The lights on the machine flickered, and Rudy blinked.

For so much of my life, it felt like I was caught between who I was, who I wanted to be, who men thought I should be, and who I hoped to be in relation to men. In all of that mess, it was easy to lose sight of what I wanted for myself. Sometimes the effects of sexism weren't as obvious as harassment and abuse; sometimes it was a matter of the conflicting expectations that felt impossible to satisfy.

"*You're making me very unhappy,*" Rudy told me as my ball hit another bumper.

I knew that I could learn how to do the job on the Pot. I had accomplished more difficult feats in my life, and the Pot was like any of them. With a little time, my confidence would grow and stirring zinc would feel like second nature, but I didn't want to end up like Mike. I didn't want to be stuck on the Pot for years, thirsting for an opportunity to leave. I didn't want to be surrounded by trigger-happy bosses when I was still an Orange Hat. No schedule was worth stirring zinc, especially when I could just as easily be a Bander, and no amount of pressure could change what I felt in my gut.

"*Big deal*," Rudy said from the corner of the machine. The words had barely escaped his lips when my last ball rolled past the flippers, ending the game. I hadn't gotten the ball into his mouth to shut him up, but I knew what I had to do about the Pot.

On Monday morning I called the company man and turned down the bid. Several men had already done the same, and none of them questioned themselves. They put their own needs above all else, which seemed like the best symbolism I could coax from a rock and a hard place.

"No problem," the company man told me. "But you'll have to finish out your time in the Hot Dip before I can place you back in Shipping."

I reluctantly agreed, but when I suited up in my green jumpsuit with Mike, another boss beckoned me away. He had gotten wind of my intention to leave, so he put me on cleaning duty instead.

I spent the rest of the day scrubbing a staircase that led into a dank, dirty basement. The handrails were coated in black oil, and the company wanted them to sparkle like new. I scoured those handrails until the greasy water from my rag seeped into my gloves and drenched my shirt. Dust clung to my neck, and oil streaked my sweaty cheeks. I could taste the grime on my tongue, but like any good Orange Hat, I kneeled on the staircase and scrubbed. I was a far cry from the seventeen-year-old girl who had prayed rosaries at a John Kerry rally. Back then I thought that I knew how to scoop away the dross of the world. I thought that I had everything figured out. I was so convinced that God would forge me into a saintly sort of silver, but he had humbled me with steel instead.

8

Well after I started at the mill, I went back to see my friend in Washington, D.C. We drank whiskey with the same lawyers who had once asked me what Cleveland produces. Now that I finally had an answer for them, they started asking different questions.

"Remind me," one of the lawyers said as he poured another round of whiskey, "what do you do for a living?"

"I'm a steelworker," I told him.

The lawyers raised their eyebrows and nodded slowly. I was a curiosity they had never seen before.

"That's interesting," the second lawyer said.

The condescension in his voice made me cringe. I had seen the video bytes that news stations used of industrial workers, and it always seemed as if the reporters chose the most bumbling, inarticulate people from the crowd. The blue-collar worker was less educated and less intelligent in the eyes of coastal America, and I assumed that the lawyers thought the same thing about me.

The first lawyer rolled a swig of whiskey around in his mouth before swallowing loudly. "Let me ask you a question," he said. "How do you feel about Chinese steel?"

I stared down at the coffee table that was positioned between us, where a plate of Brie sat beside two bottles of whiskey. The cheese was the only thing I had eaten in hours, and I was craving a piece of bread to soak up the booze.

"Chinese steel?" I said, my mind reeling for a good answer. "I don't like it, I guess."

The lawyer laughed and turned to his friend.

"She doesn't like it," he scoffed. Now both of the men were laughing.

My body tightened and my shoulders tensed. I didn't like being the butt of the joke, so I tried to come up with a more nuanced view that was colored by my experiences in the mill.

"Even with all of that Chinese steel, I don't think my mill will go under," I said. "I'll likely keep my job. We make a higher grade of steel than the stuff dumped into the market by China."

"Are you saying that Chinese steel doesn't affect you?" the first lawyer asked. He had the polished air of someone who went yachting on the weekends, and he handled his whiskey like someone who kept a flask in his desk.

"No, that's not what I mean," I told him. The alcohol was making me slur my words. "I'm just saying that I don't think I'll get laid off as a result of Chinese steel."

My words jumbled into one another. I was trying to make some kind of observation about innovation and competitiveness, but I couldn't think of the right way to articulate it.

"How can you say Chinese steel doesn't affect you?" one of the lawyers pressed.

"I don't mean it doesn't affect me. Obviously, Chinese steel lowers prices across the board. I was just trying to—I don't know. I was just trying to put it into context or something."

Everyone sipped their whiskey in silence. I cut a big piece of Brie from the plate.

"You know, I never paid much attention to the news when I was young," the first lawyer said to me. He seemed to be suggesting that he was old and wise, even though we were both the same age. "Now that I'm an adult, I understand the importance of staying informed. Now I realize how all of these things affect our lives. Chinese steel, for instance."

The lawyers began talking with each other. They spoke with great pride, and I listened. Maybe they would give me some insight into economics. Maybe they had some numbers up their sleeves. Maybe they had a creative solution to the problem of Chinese steel, but the men didn't talk about economics. They didn't even talk about Chinese steel. Instead they spent several minutes bragging about all of the ways they stayed abreast of the latest news. They talked about the websites they frequented. They talked about the newspaper subscriptions they carried. They spoke with great poise and bravado. They articulated perfectly, and they said absolutely nothing. After a long conversation, the lawyers didn't offer a more nuanced view of Chinese steel than I had: *Chinese steel? I don't like it, I guess.*

I sat quietly and drank my whiskey. The men didn't ask me any more questions. My stumbling, whiskey-laden words had confirmed their assumptions. I was an ignorant blue-collar worker.

I ate another piece of Brie and started to grow sour. Despite my deep insecurities about the mill, I was developing a complicated love for it. I felt a fierce protectiveness for its people, and there was a part of me that actually preferred the life of a steelworker to that of an academic. The mill didn't have the cutthroat sense of competition that sometimes existed in academia, and steelworkers weren't worried about impressing one another with their knowledge. We were a people of grit and substance. We valued authenticity and sincerity, and we saw right through those lawyers in D.C. They were just pathetic social climbers whose daddies had probably footed their college bills. They were out of touch, and they certainly enjoyed too much privilege. Those lawyers were nothing more than elite assholes who didn't know jack about the real world, and they couldn't understand steel if they tried.

Shortly after turning down the bid in the Hot Dip, I walked toward the Shipping Department to start another day as a Bander. The sun was just beginning to rise, and the rusty buildings stretched far into the distance, nearly glowing in the rosy dawn. The steam rising from the Hot Mill bled into the sunrise, and the white tower above the Hot Dip took on a crimson hue. Everything was sepia tones and faded edges, like the portrait of a coiffed and corseted woman from some bygone era that was now on sale at a thrift shop. It was the kind of thing that made you wonder who would ever let something so intimate slip through their fingers.

As I headed slowly toward the long hours that lay ahead, a buggy stopped beside me.

"Hey, baby girl," the driver said with a smile. It was a fellow Bander named Sleepy Bear, who never seemed to be in a bad mood. "Want a ride?"

"Absolutely," I said, squeezing beside him in the front seat. Sleepy Bear was a particularly large man with broad shoulders and a bit of a gut, but he had these large brown eyes that were downright jolly.

Once I settled into the buggy, Sleepy Bear sped down the street without stopping to brake for corners. The wind felt warm and dewy on my face, and I smiled at the picture-perfect mill as we rolled past.

I was glad to be back in the Shipping Department after my brief stint with the zinc. The company had even given me a promotion, of sorts, when I returned from the Hot Dip. They officially placed me on a crew, meaning that I now had the predictable schedule I'd been hoping for all along. From what I could tell, I would be allowed to work on the same crew for months. I was serving as the semipermanent fill-in for a Bander who was out with a knee injury, and the whispers in the Rumor Mill predicted that the recovery would take a while. Tony and I rejoiced at our luck. I would be better able to manage my life and our relationship, and I didn't even have to stir zinc for it.

In the terms of the mill, Sleepy Bear had become my new partner. We spent all of our shifts together in the same shanty I had once shared with Gunner. When Sleepy Bear worked, I worked. When he was off, I was off. I hadn't seen much of anyone else since I was placed on Sleepy Bear's crew. Sam had been next in line for the bid that I turned down in the Hot Dip. He took it gladly and decided to stay, which meant that we rarely had an opportunity to cross paths. Charlie and Gunner still worked in Shipping, but we almost never worked on the same days. Gunner was on a different crew, and Charlie had assumed my old role as floater. He mostly filled in for old-timers who were out on vacation, and he was usually scheduled in the building across the road from mine.

Sleepy Bear and I generally got along well together. Sometimes he shared his wife's cooking with me, and I always brought him a fresh bottle of water whenever I stopped in the Social Shanty. There was only one thing that irked me about him. Several times during every shift, Sleepy Bear would prop his feet on a milk crate and take a nap. I didn't understand how he could fall asleep so easily. One moment, he would be engaged in a lively conversation. The next, he'd be out cold. Nearly every time we had a break—even if it was only for ten or fifteen minutes—he would be back in his chair, sleeping.

When we arrived at our shanty that morning, Sleepy Bear and I both hunkered down for our shift. I slouched into a chair with a cup of coffee, and Sleepy Bear assumed his usual position. It wasn't long before he was snoring, even though it was almost time for us to work. A fresh coil was already coasting through the air, firmly grasped in the claws of a crane that clicked and screeched as Crazy Joe, the crane operator, soared wildly through the air. While I waited for Crazy Joe to do his job, I pulled out my phone and wasted a few minutes on the daily news.

The RNC was drawing closer by the day, and reporters couldn't get enough of it. Clevelanders were getting excited—and nervous—about their moment in the spotlight. The convention was our chance to show the rest of the country that we were just as competent and beautiful as any other city in America. Maybe the people in New York and LA would finally realize that Clevelanders weren't a bunch of Midwestern bumpkins. Maybe the people from Washington, D.C., would see that our hometown was more than a heap of rusted remains.

To help achieve this goal, city officials had erected white signs with *Cleveland* written on them in three different locations across town. One sign was placed in North Coast Harbor, near the Rock & Roll Hall of Fame. Another was built at Edgewater Beach, on the coast of Lake Erie. The third was situated in Tremont, which is a stone's throw from the mill. The signs were intended to draw visitors to picture-worthy destinations, but they also showcased the things that had built us. A lake, an industry, and rock 'n' roll.

I skimmed through an article about the signs, but I barely had enough time to finish before Crazy Joe lined up seven of our eight coils in front of the shanty. There were a lot of things you could say about Crazy Joe—he was gruff, he was miserly, and he guzzled energy drinks until his vision blurred—but at least he was fast. I put my phone aside and began the delicate ritual of rousing Sleepy Bear from his slumbers.

"Hey," I said loudly.

Sleepy Bear didn't open his eyes. I sighed.

"Hey, wake up."

Nothing. I was growing more annoyed with each new snore, so I banged my hand against the wall.

"I heard you the first time," Sleepy Bear huffed.

"Sorry," I said. "I just wanted to make sure you were awake."

Sleepy Bear kept his eyes closed until Crazy Joe brought us the last coil. Then he sat up slowly and put on his hard hat, which was oily and scuffed after twenty years in the mill.

"Okay, let's band these coils," he said with a wide grin.

My irritation quickly melted away. I was a sucker for Sleepy Bear's smiles. His big, boyish brown eyes could soften me up in an instant. They didn't quite fit with the rest of his tall, imposing body, and they made it impossible for me to stay mad at him for long.

Sleepy Bear and I lumbered out of the shanty and walked toward the coils, but the Godfather sauntered over before we had time to put on our gloves. He always looked bright-eyed and cheery beneath his yellow hard hat, and I wondered how he did it. The Godfather often worked eighty or ninety hours a week, but he never betrayed a hint of exhaustion.

"What do you have there?" Sleepy Bear asked, pointing to a piece of paper in the Godfather's hand.

"A memo from Jeremy." He laughed. "What else?"

Sleepy Bear rolled his eyes. "Oh boy, what does he want?"

"Hey now, don't shoot the messenger." The Godfather smiled,

handing us each two pieces of fabric that looked like a pair of long yellow socks. "They're Kevlar sleeves for your arms. Jeremy says we have to wear them from now on. Company policy."

Sleepy Bear took the sleeves in his hand and eyed them with disgust. "These things look hot as hell."

"Yep," the Godfather agreed. He was already sporting a pair, which extended from his wrists to his biceps. "I'm gonna wear mine, though. You know they've got cameras all over this place." The Godfather looked down at me and nodded to my orange hard hat. "You better wear them too. You don't want to give the bosses any reason to fire you."

I obediently pulled the sleeves over my arms and went to work while Sleepy Bear talked with the Godfather for a few minutes. They gestured passionately and shook their heads. The sleeves had inspired their outrage, and now they were lamenting the indignity of being forced to wear the itchy Kevlar. It wasn't unusual for steelworkers to make mountains out of molehills. We spent so much time in that valley, doing the same jobs over and over again, that we latched on to anything that would break up the monotony.

Even I had to admit that the sleeves were uncomfortable—my skin was already starting to sweat beneath them—but I tried to ignore the problem and focus on the job, putting one cardboard strip after another around each gleaming coil. I was halfway done with the round by the time Sleepy Bear joined me.

"Boy, it's hot," he said as he picked up a cardboard.

Together, we finished in minutes, working like a well-oiled machine. *Cardboard, plastic, bands. Ratchet. Crimp. Repeat.* When Sleepy Bear threaded the bands through the eyes of the coils, I caught them. When he ratcheted, I crimped. We could have done it with our eyes closed.

After the steel was neatly packaged, we shuffled back to the shanty so that another crane could bring the banded coils to the Godfather, who was working as the Wrapper. Sleepy Bear sat down and stretched his legs. We both took off our sleeves and tossed them aside while an air conditioner rattled between us. My sweat dried quickly, and it wasn't long before I was shivering. I didn't want to turn the air condi-tioner down, though. It wouldn't be long before we were back out in the heat, banding more coils, and I wanted to get as much cool air as possible.

"The Godfather was telling me the story behind these sleeves we have to wear," Sleepy Bear said.

I leaned forward in my chair, excited to hear the latest bit of gossip. No matter what I told myself, I wasn't immune to the molehills either.

"Apparently, someone in the Temper Mill cut his arm on the edge of a coil," Sleepy Bear continued. "And you know how the company is. Once someone hurts themselves, they start making changes. Now everyone has to pay the price with these sleeves."

"Wait a second," I said. "How in the hell did someone get hurt on a coil?"

I tried to imagine the mechanics of it. For the most part, the sharp edges of the steel were layered on top of one another, rendering them harmless. You would have to actively rub on the side of the coil in order for it to cut you.

"I don't even know," Sleepy Bear said. "It takes all types around this place."

I sipped my coffee, and we talked about this piece of news like a couple of old ladies in a quilting circle. Did we know the man who'd cut himself? How bad was the gash? Sleepy Bear was always good at seeking out rumors, and I was always eager to hear them. It became a ritual of sorts: Sleepy Bear would stay awake long enough to catch me up on the gossip. It rarely took longer than an hour, but it was my favorite part of the day. Even though I had been working at the mill for months, I still felt awkward and shy around my new coworkers. Most people were older than me, and many shared a long history of inside jokes and distant memories. I wasn't quite sure where I fit in, but Sleepy Bear's gossip pulled me into the fold.

When we exhausted the rumors about the sleeves, Sleepy Bear closed his eyes and fell asleep again. Dozing off in the workplace might be sacrilegious in other jobs, but it wasn't uncommon for work-ers to catch a catnap here and there in the mill. This was especially true of the old-timers, most of whom had spent many years in a state of chronic sleep deprivation caused by the swing shifts. After two decades in the mill, Sleepy Bear had simply learned to find rest wherever he could, and I envied him.

I had assumed that a predictable schedule was what I wanted. I would finally be able to get into a rhythm with my job, but it turned out that I was wrong. Since there were only four crews that rotated between nights and days, the resulting schedules were ridiculous. My crew worked like dogs for three weeks, during which time we were on for a stretch of days, then a stretch of nights, then another stretch of days that were followed by another stretch of nights. It was difficult to get your body acclimated to a different shift once a month, let alone four times in the span of twenty-one days. Our schedule even included a dreaded twenty-four-hour turnaround, which meant that we got off work at 6:00 A.M. on one morning and we had to be back to work by 6:00 A.M. the following day, giving us only twenty-four hours to adjust our bodies to the new shift. While the permanent schedule might have been predictable, it was no less grueling than it had been when I was working as a floater.

There was supposed to be a silver lining to all of it, though. At the end of those three weeks, we were given six days off. At first I jumped at the chance for a week's vacation every month, but I quickly learned that those six days weren't all they were cracked up to be. Since I was the low guy on the totem pole, I was given the extra shifts that no one else wanted. It wasn't unusual for the company to schedule me to work on my days off, which meant that I barely had a chance to recover from the strenuous schedule, and I was too green to imagine falling asleep within the mill's walls. There was never a silent moment. Cranes were always moving overhead and buggies were speeding past. Maybe twenty years on the job would teach me how to nap, but twenty years sounded like an eternity. The crazy shifts had already made me feel like I'd aged five years.

While Sleepy Bear napped in the corner, a host of fruit flies buzzed around a Styrofoam cup of vinegar that someone had left on the window ledge. A handful of dead fruit flies floated inside, and a few others balanced on the edge and tempted their fates. I pulled out my phone to read more articles, but I strayed from the news. The RNC wasn't the only issue weighing on my mind at the time. In my sleep-deprived state, I had become convinced that I had cancer of the belly button.

It didn't matter that cancer of the belly button didn't technically exist, and it didn't matter that there was no reason for me to suspect that I had any form of cancer whatsoever. Something inside me felt untamed and off-kilter, as if part of my body had turned against itself, so I figured that a tumor was to blame. Once the thought latched onto my mind, I couldn't stop it from consuming me.

I had already spent hours toggling between various scientific studies about belly buttons and malignant cells. In my frantic research, I came across something called urachal cancer, which fit my obsession well enough. Apparently, some adults retained the remnants of a canal that once drained urine from their bladders to their belly buttons during fetal development. This remnant was called the urachus, and every so often it developed a tumor. People with this type of cancer sometimes had symptoms in their belly buttons, so I became fixated on urachal cancer as the reason for my malaise.

On the other side of the shanty, Sleepy Bear's snores grew louder. Each stuttering breath resonated off the walls in the tiny space, competing for attention against the rickety air conditioner and the rumble of the cranes. I tried my best to ignore the distractions and keep after my research. I looked up information about the prevalence of urachal cancer. *Extremely rare.* I looked up information about the prognosis. *Poor.* I looked up obscure stories of people who had survived urachal cancer, and I prodded my stomach in search of lumps.

Most psychiatrists will tell you that swing shifts and sleep deprivation greatly increase the risk of relapse for patients with bipolar disorder, and my sudden obsession with urachal cancer was prime evidence that I was becoming unhinged. The delusions of a mixed episode had begun to creep up on me, but I didn't have the wherewithal to recognize it. I had just spent more than twelve months in a healthy frame of mind, and I didn't want to believe that I was sinking into another episode. When you spend such a long time without any symptoms whatsoever, it's easy to blind yourself. *Maybe the diagnosis was wrong. Maybe the doctors were quacks. Maybe I never had an illness in the first place.* When you start to feel unwell, it's difficult to see reality for what it is. After all, reality involves the admission of a painful fact: You are not as well as you thought, and the sickness you've inherited can never be fully fixed. In that situation, it's far easier to believe that your belly button is to blame.

I learned about bipolar disorder when I was just a child. The disease was in my blood, and I occasionally heard my parents talking about it with hushed tones and exhausted sighs. My father's mother, Monica, had long been afflicted with the manic highs and the depressive lows, and the disease had been poorly managed for most of her life. My grandfather divorced her before I had a chance to know them as a couple, and my family rarely visited the little apartment that Monica called home. My father wanted to keep his distance. Monica had struggled with alcoholism throughout her life, often using liquor to dull the symptoms of her disease. As a result, she was an absent parent who had left my father and his two sisters to fend for themselves. Even as a child, I understood that he resented her for it. We sometimes saw Monica on holidays, and she always sent birthday cards in the mail. But mostly she existed like a ghost at the edge of the family.

I knew my grandmother by her handwriting, which was unsteady and cramped. Every birthday card looked like it had been written in the midst of an earthquake.

"That's from the lithium," my mother told me. "It gives her tremors."

I knew my grandmother by her ailments, which she didn't hesitate to disclose. On the rare occasions that my family did visit Monica, she talked about the dysfunctions of her body. We learned about urinary tract infections, loose teeth, and indigestion. Every pain and twinge was described in excruciating detail.

"I think the urinary tract infections are psychosomatic," my mother told me. "I'm pretty sure she was sexually abused as a child."

In my mind, Monica was a woman falling apart.

At some point in my childhood, I asked my parents more about my grandmother's illness, and they told me a story that would haunt me throughout my life.

In the midst of a manic episode, Monica went to the mall and bought dozens of pairs of shoes. She packed her car full of them. Loafers. Sneakers. High heels. Then she went and bought a pack of cigarettes, even though she didn't smoke. On the car ride home, Monica puffed away at the cigarettes, flicking the butts out the window. One of the embers floated back into the car, landing on the boxes of shoes in the back seat. Later that evening, Monica called my father.

"I had a little fire," she said.

My parents drove to her apartment, expecting a burnt spot on the passenger seat, but they found the smoldering remains of my grandmother's sedan. The shoes were in the back seat, a mess of scorched leather and melted soles.

When I was eventually diagnosed with her disease, I was terrified that I would suffer the same loneliness. Maybe I would be relegated to the fringes of my family. Maybe I would be ignored, divorced, and isolated. Maybe, like Monica, I would one day burn through my father's love.

Years later, after my politics had turned liberal, I went over to my parents' house for dinner. Obama had been recently sworn in for his first term, and the weather was making the slow turn toward spring. With the change in seasons came the risk of a mixed episode, and I could already feel the symptoms niggling at my shoulder. I cried more easily. I flew off the handle at my boyfriend. I had grown more paranoid, believing that he was about to leave me, and I had stopped taking my medications. As usual, I ignored the warning signs. Maybe the episode would go away on its own.

I sat at the table with my parents, eating salmon and mashed potatoes. Just as I was digging a spoon into a bowl of green beans, my parents approached me with an offer.

"Your mother and I think you should take the concealed-carry course," my father said. His fascination with guns was just beginning to solidify, although he hadn't yet amassed his apocalyptic stockpile in the basement.

"What kind of course?" I asked. I had graduated from college a few months earlier, and I didn't have any courses on my mind.

"The concealed-carry course," my mother repeated. "It's a class you have to take if you want to carry a concealed weapon. Your father and I both got our licenses already."

"Like, you guys carry guns?" I asked, a little taken aback. My mother was a short woman who startled easily, and she had never expressed an interest in weaponry before.

"Sometimes," my mother said, adjusting a pair of rectangular glasses that sat atop her sharply pointed nose. "The important thing is that we *can* carry guns if we want to. It's important that you take the course too."

I spooned through my mashed potatoes. "I don't know. I've never shot a gun before."

"That doesn't matter," my father said with his fork poised in front of his mouth. He had a little piece of salmon dangling from his chin. "They'll make sure you know how to handle yourself by the end of the class."

My mother nodded in agreement. "We'll pay for you to take it," she added.

None of us mentioned my mental health as our forks clicked on our plates. I had tried to kill myself several times before, and my bipolar disorder was barely contained. Any gun in my possession would greatly increase my risk of committing suicide, but my parents wanted me to complete the course anyway.

"Now that Obama's president, he's going to make it difficult to get these licenses," my father explained. "He's going to threaten our right to bear arms, so it's best to take the course. That way, you won't have to worry when Obama takes our freedom away."

Up until that point, I had no interest in guns. I was frankly afraid of them. I'd never wanted to hold one, let alone carry one on my person, and yet my father's warning infected me. An old fear cropped up again. I was afraid of not being afraid. The feeling was a reflex that would take years to unlearn. It was like looking through a kaleidoscope, where everything appeared fractured and distorted. I had voted for Obama—in fact, I had dressed as Sarah Palin as a joke on Halloween, completing the costume with a big button that said, *I can see Russia from my house!*—but now I was afraid Obama would take away my right to bear arms. I had no interest in guns, and yet I wanted to be able to carry one anyway. If I didn't remain vigilant, someone would take away the rights I never knew I cared about.

"Okay," I said, adding a bit of salt to my potatoes. "I'll take the class."

A few weeks later I sat in a room with other gun enthusiasts while a potbellied instructor lectured beside a whiteboard. We all had cups of coffee and sleepy eyes, but the instructor did his best to keep us awake.

"If you carry a gun," he told us in a booming voice, "you have to be ready to use it. You have to shoot to kill. If not, someone can take the gun and use it against you."

I stared down at the packet of papers I'd been given earlier that morning. It was filled with laws and advice about wielding weapons, but the words blurred as I looked at them. I imagined turning a gun on another human being. Maybe a robber would try to steal my wallet. Maybe a man with a knife would try to lead me down a back alley. I would probably feel threatened and on edge, but I didn't think I could shoot to kill.

The class went on for several hours, and I started to wonder if I had made a mistake in coming. I didn't want to be the type of person who knew how to kill another person. I didn't want to carry a gun in my pocket, worrying that it would go off, but the old fear kept nagging in the back of my mind. I was just exercising my rights. I was just maintaining my freedoms. Of course, I was also slipping slowly into a mixed episode, which often made me act on impulse, but the instructor didn't talk about mental health as he led us to a shooting range for our final test. In order to pass the course, we would have to use our guns to hit a paper target.

I walked into a tiny black booth and put a .38 Special down on the shelf in front of me. My father had let me borrow the gun, giving me a quick tutorial on how to load it and shoot it. *The bullets go here. Squeeze the trigger, don't pull.* The barrel of the gun frightened me, and I stared down at it with the same intensity an animal warden would use when cornering a rabid dog.

The instructor sauntered over with a hand on his big gut.

"That's a good gun," he said, nodding in approval. "Very reliable. Go on, give it a try."

We each donned a pair of noise-canceling headphones, and I picked up the gun from the shelf. It was a small silvery thing that was heavier than it looked, and my hands shook as I aimed it at the piece of paper on the far side of the range. There was a body-shaped target on the paper, and I was supposed to land a shot in the center of it, near the heart. I squeezed the gun like my father had shown me, and a shot reverberated through my forearms. The headphones muddled the noise, making the blast sound like a wardrobe falling from a window. There was a loud thud, then eerie silence.

I put the gun back on the shelf and surveyed the target with the instructor. My bullet had barely grazed the edge of the paper.

"That's okay," the instructor told me. "Keep trying."

It took a few attempts, but I eventually made a hole several inches from the center.

"Good enough," the instructor said, and that was it. The man moved on to the next person, and I was officially considered competent enough to carry a concealed weapon.

At the end of the day, I received a certificate that said I had been through the proper training. In order to get the actual license, I would still have to get fingerprinted and pay a fee to the county, but I had other plans for the evening. My roommates were throwing a party at the house we shared.

The party was already in full swing by the time I arrived, so I did my best to catch up. I drank vodka straight from the bottle and downed a beer for good measure. I shot whiskey and tequila. I wasn't drinking for the taste, and I wasn't drinking to be social. I was drinking to forget. My bipolar disorder was making me more depressed and anxious by the day, and every sip of liquor made me less aware of the symptoms that were starting to overtake me. In twenty minutes' time, I accomplished what I'd set out to do. I was far more hammered than anyone else in the house.

Some of the other partygoers were sitting around the dining room table, carrying on a quiet, civil conversation. I fell into a chair with the certificate from the concealed-carry course in my hand.

"The government thinks I can carry a gun in my belt," I told everyone, waving the certificate with one hand and sipping from a glass of spiked punch with the other.

"Do you know how to shoot a gun?" one of the men at the party asked. His curly brown hair was pulled back in a man-bun, and he had been trying to ingratiate himself with my roommate all night.

"Nope," I told him.

"Do you want to own a gun?" he asked.

"Nope."

I reached for the vodka, which was making its rounds, but I knocked over an uncapped bottle of cranberry juice in the process. The liquid flooded the table, covering the concealed-carry license in a sticky film.

I leapt up and tried to mop up the cranberry juice with the sleeve of my shirt, and one of my roommates looked at me in confusion.

"Why in the hell did you take the concealed-carry course?" she said.

I looked up from the puddle of cranberry juice, my shirt soaking wet. "Beats me," I told her before landing in my seat and taking another swig of vodka.

I was too drunk to realize that whatever had possessed me to take the course was similar to the thing that had caused my father to stockpile guns. By championing our rights, we gave ourselves the illusion of control in lives that had very little. My father's budding business was just beginning to fail, and I was sinking back into the throes of a disease that often left me paralyzed. We both felt invisible, each in our own ways, but our God-given constitutional rights made it seem like we still had power in the world. Those rights weren't just guarantees given by our government, which were subject to revision and interpretation; in our vision of America, those rights were intimately connected with what and who we were. The slightest adjustment to those rights was a threat against the individual, which made it easy to pacify any feelings of invisibility and neglect—whether in our lives, in our families, or in our relationships—by turning our personal battles into political crusades. Our rights gave us a voice when it felt like we had none. Our rights gave us a way to fight back against the things that were bringing us down, even though most of those things were too intangible to be stopped by bullets.

The morning after the concealed-carry course, I awoke with one of the worst hangovers of my life. Between bouts of vomiting, I looked at the concealed-carry certificate, which had dried into a wrinkled mess, and I recalled the words that the instructor had said during our lesson: *You have to shoot to kill.* The thought sickened me more than the alcohol. I didn't want a gun. I didn't want to hold something lethal in my hands, and I sensed that the certificate carried with it a danger that I didn't want to bring into my life. What scared me most was the ease with which I'd passed the course. I wasn't equipped to own a weapon. I had no experience, no knowledge, and no skill, and yet I had the right to buy a weapon that could be hidden beneath my belt. Fear had pushed me to take the course, and now I was struck by the reality of what that fear implied. If I turned into the type of person who could shoot to kill, then there would always be a part of me that would view the world as a target. I didn't want that for myself, so I put the certificate in a filing cabinet that was stowed in my closet. A few months later I was hospitalized in a psychiatric ward for a full-blown mixed episode. At the time, I desperately wanted to take my own life, and when I made a full recovery, I was thankful that the concealed-carry certificate was exactly where it needed to be—safely forgotten and covered in cranberry juice.

I was standing in the shanty, getting myself situated for the start of my shift, when Sleepy Bear walked in with a piece of paper in his hand.

"Look what I've got," he said, waving the paper in the air.

I used a wet napkin to wipe the little table next to my chair. Its surface was chipped and scratched, and a layer of black dirt had formed around its edges.

"Let me guess," I said, barely looking up. "It's a memo from Jeremy."

"Yep," Sleepy Bear told me as I threw the napkin in the trash.

"What does he want now?" I asked.

I put a stale cup of gas station coffee on the newly cleaned table. A few fruit flies were already buzzing around the top of the cup, craving the sugary creamer I had poured in to disguise the taste.

"Oh, you'll love this," Sleepy Bear said. "He wants us to clean the pads in the coil field."

My shoulders slumped when I heard the news. The coil field contained rows and rows of finished coils, all of which were waiting to be picked up by customers, and it was probably a half acre in size. Sometimes people flung garbage into the aisles of the coil field—old bottles, old pieces of cardboard, old bands—but the worst part was the oil. Before the coils arrived in the Shipping Department, they were coated in oil to prevent rust, but the oil tended to leak out of the coils as they sat in the field. Absorbent pads had been placed in each aisle to help contain the mess, and they were both heavy and nasty when saturated. If you tried to lift the pads from the ground, the oil would get everywhere—on your clothes, on your boots, on your hard hat—and it was rumored that the mixture contained hexavalent chromium, a known carcinogen.

"Motherfucking Jeremy," I said with a sigh.

"I'm not doing that crap," Sleepy Bear told me as he took a seat. "That should be overtime work. Besides, we're Banders. If there's a coil that needs banded, we'll band it. But we're not doing housekeeping too. That's some bullshit."

I sank into my chair and fiddled with the cuffs of my blue uniform. I might have been able to bad-mouth Jeremy, but I wasn't hardened enough to ignore his request completely. I was still the little perfectionist who didn't want to let anyone down, and Jeremy's warning rang in the back of my mind. *Don't let this place change you. Don't grow obstinate.*

"Maybe we can just do a little bit of cleaning," I said to Sleepy Bear, trying not to sound like too much of a kiss-ass. "That way, Jeremy can't bitch at us."

Sleepy Bear shook his head and rolled his big brown eyes. "Oh, you're such an Orange Hat."

I smiled and shrugged, as if to say I couldn't help it.

"Fine," Sleepy Bear told me, "we'll go out and do a few aisles if it makes you feel better."

Later that afternoon, when we had a break from banding, Sleepy Bear and I placed a dumpster beside the coil field and went to work. The absorbent pads looked like long pieces of carpet padding, except they were coated in yellow-green oil and dirt. Puddles of oil sat in some places where the pads had been soaked all the way through, and it didn't take long before the oil seeped through our leather gloves. Sleepy Bear and I worked as a team, pulling up the pads together and dragging the heavy blobs along the ground. Every time we threw one into the dumpster, little splatters of oil hit our necks and our cheeks.

We worked tirelessly for a while, but then Sleepy Bear started wheezing. He rested his weight against a coil, and I saw that a black film of dirt and oil had formed on the sleeves of his shirt.

"I just need to take a breather," he said.

"Take your time," I told him, but I didn't stop to rest. There was no sense in dragging out the task any longer than we needed to, so I went down an aisle and started pulling up a pad by myself.

The pad was as long as the aisle, about fifty feet, and it was particularly heavy. I wadded it up into a sizable ball, lugging it slowly along the slippery floor. My back hurt from bending up and down to throw each pad in the dumpster, and my arms were shaky from all the work Sleepy Bear and I had already done. Just as I was nearing the end of the aisle, my boots slid out from under me. My arms flailed, searching wildly for something to break my fall, but I landed right in a puddle of oil, which began soaking through my pants.

"Oh my gosh," Sleepy Bear said as he rushed over to me. "Are you okay?"

I kicked at the oily ball of padding, which was sitting at my feet. Nothing was hurt but my pride.

"I'm all right," I told him, struggling to get up.

Sleepy Bear extended his hand and pulled me from the ground. Then, still wheezing slightly, he helped me throw the big ball into the dumpster.

"Let's give it a rest for today," he said, wiping his brow with his dirty forearm. "We've done a lot. The other crews can handle everything else."

"Okay," I said, grateful that Sleepy Bear had enough sense to call it quits.

He headed back to the shanty to wait for some coils to band, and I stopped by the locker room to change my pants. Dirt and oil had gathered along the sides of my neck. It sat in the dips above my clavicle bones. It formed a mustache above my lip. There were still a few hours left in our shift, and I wanted nothing more than a shower and a good meal. The coil field had put a damper on the entire day, but I tried to console myself. At least Jeremy would see that we had given it our best try. Or so I thought.

Sleepy Bear and I wouldn't get a gold star for slogging the oily pads all afternoon. In fact, Jeremy wouldn't notice any of the work that we had done. The other crews, all of which were composed of old-timers, would crumple up the memo and throw it in the trash, leaving the rest of the coil field untouched. That's the thing Jeremy noticed. Eventually all of the Banders in Shipping would receive another memo, which passive-aggressively hinted at our collective insubordination, and the task of cleaning the coil field would be given out to other workers as overtime.

"Screw this," I told Sleepy Bear when I read the second memo. "Jeremy's just gonna yell at everyone, even though we were the ones who actually did the fucking job?"

Sleepy Bear smiled and shook his head. "You're starting to see how things work around here."

I tossed the memo onto the ground and furrowed my brow.

"You know what?" I said to Sleepy Bear.

"What?"

"Fuck Jeremy."

Sleepy Bear laughed, and I smiled along with him. He was like a proud parent watching a child ride without training wheels, and I was a little kid wobbling to the end of the drive.

After cleaning the coil field, Sleepy Bear and I finished our shift in the usual way. *Cardboard, plastic, bands. Ratchet. Crimp. Repeat.* When it was finally time for us to leave, I showered in the locker room and went to Tony's house for dinner. I drank a beer on his back porch while he grilled a few burgers. His summer vacation was still in full swing, and he had spent his afternoon playing the ukulele on a Lake Erie beach.

"How was your day?" he asked.

"Hot," I told him. "And long."

The sun slowly crept toward the horizon, but the waning daylight did nothing to ease the humidity. My shirt stuck to the sweat on my sides, and I had to wipe my forehead every few minutes to keep the beads of moisture from dripping into my eyes. I had just spent the whole day toiling in the dirty mill, and I craved the sweet relief of central air-conditioning.

"Do you mind if we eat inside?" I asked.

Tony turned around and gave me a look of disappointment. In the summers, he had a compulsion to be outside during every hour of daylight. It didn't matter if the heat was oppressive and unbearable. He thought that any moment spent inside was wasted.

"I thought it'd be nice to eat outside," he said.

"I know. I'm just sick of sweating."

Tony pleaded at me with his eyes. "But it's such a nice night."

I looked down and picked at the label on my beer bottle. If I insisted on eating inside, then Tony's disappointment would last for the duration of the meal. He would probably mention the nice night that we were missing. Later he might even make it clear that he had graciously sacrificed a wonderful outdoor dinner for my benefit.

Ever since I'd started working swing shifts, little situations like this one had been cropping up more and more often. When I came over to his house after working the night shift, I sensed that he was put out by my need to sleep. When I just wanted to relax with him after working a twelve-hour shift, I noticed that he was frustrated by the fact that I couldn't do more. It seemed like he expected me to work my schedule and still have the time and energy to keep pace with someone who was on summer vacation. I had started feeling like a constant disappointment, but the truth of the situation was far more complicated. Every time a mixed episode starts creeping up on me, I grow paranoid and reactive. I see anger where none exists. I interpret people's actions as something other than what they are. I start weaving my own, myopic world, where I am a victim under threat.

In reality, Tony was doing everything possible to accommodate me. He was cooking the dinners. He was letting me rest. He was sacrificing his own desires to suit my needs, and all he wanted was a nice meal in the fresh air. My disease wouldn't let me see it that way, though.

"Okay," I said to Tony when dinner was nearly ready. I didn't want to be the object of his disappointment yet again. "I guess we can eat outside."

Tony brought the burgers to the table, and I filled some water glasses. Then, when we sat down to eat, I started to stew. In my mind, I was trying my best to be what he wanted me to be. I made the trek to his house whenever I could. I went on walks with him, even when I was exhausted. I went to his family gatherings, even if I would have rather been sleeping. I tried to be chipper and agreeable, even though it was becoming difficult to keep up that facade. Tony didn't appreciate the demanding nature of my job, and now I was sweating through dinner for his benefit. I saw myself as the target of some great injustice, and the feeling worsened with every passing moment. I picked at my vegetables until I was positively irate, and I let out a deep sigh to make my anger known.

"What's wrong?" Tony asked.

"Nothing," I said, staring down at my plate.

"Something's wrong. Just tell me what it is."

I skewered a piece of broccoli with my fork, unsure how to articulate my anger. My mind was spinning in a thousand directions, and I didn't know how to stop it.

"Fine," I said after a long pause. "I just spent the whole day sweating at work, and then I drove all the way out here to see you, and you can't just let me eat in the fucking air-conditioning. But we always have to do what you want to do. It's always your way or no way."

Tony clenched his jaw and looked up at the sky.

"Let's just go inside," he said, picking up his plate.

"No," I argued. "If we go inside, you're just going to make me feel guilty about it. We'll just finish dinner out here."

Tony set his plate down and took a deep breath.

"What do you want me to do?" he asked. "You're mad at me if we eat outside, and you're mad at me if we eat inside. I can't do anything right."

"I just want you to be more understanding."

Tony bit his lip to keep himself from yelling. "How can I be more understanding? I try to give you time to rest. I try to give you space. I try to be considerate when you don't have the energy to do anything."

"Yeah, but you always have to be a martyr about it."

Tony shook his head and shrugged. He wasn't privy to my warped reality, where he was the villain.

"I don't know what else I can do to make you happy," he said with resignation. "I really don't know what else I can do."

We argued for a while longer, hurling resentments at one another. I eventually went inside to finish my dinner while he sat outside until the sun set. We spent the rest of the night in silence, and we both went to bed angry.

In retrospect, I realize that the mill was hard on both of us. It's difficult to lose your partner to a job, and it's even more confusing to watch her slip slowly into the throes of her disease. At the time, however, I only saw things from my own perspective. With every passing day, I was finding it more and more difficult to notice anything—or anyone—outside of myself. I couldn't control my thinking. I couldn't stop myself from brooding obsessively. I couldn't ease my irritability or temper my moods, and my anger could escalate in an instant. It felt like the mill was consuming me, and I was helpless to stop it.

Shortly after the fight, I sat with Sleepy Bear in the Social Shanty and watched Trump give his RNC acceptance speech on a big-screen television that was supposed to be reserved for safety videos. Flies buzzed around a box of old Danishes that was sitting on the fake mahogany table, and Sleepy Bear and I sipped at ice-cold bottles of water. The reception on the television cut out whenever a crane rumbled overhead, but we got the gist of what Trump had to say.

"I have a message for all of you," he boomed through the screen. "The crime and violence that today afflicts our nation will soon—and I mean very soon—come to an end."

He outlined the affliction for his listeners: murderous criminals, murderous immigrants, murderous terrorists. Everyone was out to get us, and we should be afraid. Of course, *everyone* meant anyone who was different. *Us* primarily meant disgruntled whites, particularly men.

Sleepy Bear and I both shook our heads together during the speech. Trump showed antipathy toward anyone who was different. His was a hatred born of prejudices and assumptions. Such hatred takes the best parts of our humanity—our goodness, our charity, our diversity—and tries to squelch them.

"I've had about enough of this," Sleepy Bear said, waving his hand in dismissal. "You wanna help me get some cardboards?"

"Absolutely," I told him, even though I knew what *getting some cardboards* meant. One of us would have to drive the forklift, and I prayed it wouldn't be me.

"You wanna get them this time?" Sleepy Bear asked.

"No way," I told him. I had watched Sleepy Bear get cardboards before, and the task looked daunting. Each pallet was roughly twenty feet long, and it was amazingly difficult to navigate something that large around the tight corners in the mill.

"Don't tell me you're afraid of the forklift," Sleepy Bear teased.

"No," I said with a shrug. "I'm just not good at driving it."

Sleepy Bear smiled. "All the more reason for you to practice. Go get the forklift. I'll meet you by the pallets."

I reluctantly obeyed Sleepy Bear's direction. There was a communal forklift behind the Social Shanty, so I hopped inside and shifted it into gear, driving to the far side of the Shipping Department where the pallets of cardboard had been stacked on top of one another.

Sleepy Bear must have sensed my concern when he met me by the pallets. He signaled for me to open the window with a flick of his fingers.

"Don't worry," he told me, resting his arm on the forklift. "I'll guide you through the process. Start by spreading your forks as wide as they'll go."

The vehicle shuddered a little as I pulled the lever that changed the width of the forks.

"Good," Sleepy Bear said. "Now center yourself on the pallet."

He took a step back to give me space. Then I drove the forklift slowly toward the cardboards, slipping the forks right in the middle.

Sleepy Bear nodded in approval. "Now tilt your forks back, lift up, and throw her into reverse."

The pallet felt unsteady as I picked it up. The cardboards were so long and heavy that their sides sagged toward the ground, and the weight of the pallet was so precariously distributed that it could make the forklift tip if not carried correctly.

Sleepy Bear walked beside me as I edged the forklift closer and closer to our workstation, finally stopping when we reached a narrow walkway that was bordered by a wall on one side and a line of coils on the other.

"Okay," Sleepy Bear said, motioning for me to stop. "Now lift up the pallet as high as it'll go so you can clear these coils. You'll have to drive like that until we get to our shanty. Then you're gonna have to turn hard, but you've gotta watch out. See that pipe there?"

He pointed toward a silvery pipe that snaked along the wall of the building.

"Yeah," I said. "I see it."

"That's a gas line. You're going to have to cut really close to it, but you don't want to hit it. Just be careful. Keep an eye on your pallet."

Sleepy Bear walked out in front of me and beckoned me forward with his hands. The forklift bounced under the weight of the huge pallet, and my heart raced as I worked the brake pedal. I didn't want to tip the forklift, as I had done before, and the gas line made me nervous. I kept glancing toward Sleepy Bear to give myself courage. He guided me gently with his hands, keeping me on course.

The speech Trump had given at the RNC had been directed toward industrial workers like me and Sleepy Bear. Trump had caught us in his sights, trying to sow discord in our midst, and there were certainly many steelworkers who supported him. *He shoots straight*, these steelworkers said. *He's not a politician. He doesn't dress shit up with flowery language.* They believed Trump was just like them, even though the billionaire had inherited a fortune, and I couldn't understand why so many people refused to see reality for what it was.

Sleepy Bear beckoned me forward, and I held my breath as I made the turn beside the gas line. The forklift crawled along, turning by slow degrees, but I followed Sleepy Bear's advice, keeping a watchful eye on the pallet. When I cleared the turn, he put both of his arms up in the air, as if I'd made a touchdown, and then he nodded me toward our workstation, where I dropped the pallet on the ground.

"You did great," Sleepy Bear said before I parked the forklift. His words made me puff out my chest a little with pride.

In that moment, I resented the fact that Trump was trying to build his platform on the backs of steelworkers. All of his animosity and vitriol didn't belong in the mill. This place was about history, about family, about the fight for fairness and equality. It was about a seasoned steelworker showing an Orange Hat the ropes. It was about building camaraderie in the midst of machines that could kill you. It was about bolstering your union sisters and brothers when they were down on their luck. It was about making sure everyone—regardless of race, creed, gender, or orientation—went home safely at the end of every shift.

I thought back to the two lawyers who had talked to me about

Chinese steel. I had dismissed them with the same nonchalance that they had used to dismiss me. Those lawyers didn't know what it was like to stand beside steel coils day after day, praying that you wouldn't be caught beneath the weight. They didn't know what it was like to achieve a small victory with a forklift, and they didn't know the confidence that a Yellow Hat could build with his advice. Those lawyers didn't know steel—not really, anyway—but I didn't know much about their worlds, either. I didn't know their battles, their goals, their demons. I assumed that they reduced me to a stereotype, so I did the same to them. Tit for tat. An eye for an eye. It never occurred to me that my animosity was the rift that divided the country. This rift was more than political parties and economics. It went beyond Congress, beyond the White House, beyond our weekly paychecks and our job titles. The rift had been born from a particularly human failing. We had forgotten how to see each other. We had let down our guard. We had closed our eyes. Now the weavers of shrouds and fantasies had come along, recognizing our self-imposed darkness. They believed that we were too blind to know better, so they covered our eyes carefully, hoping that none of us—both steelworkers and lawyers alike— would ever see clearly again.

9

A feverish chill ran through my body as I trudged slowly toward the shanty I shared with Sleepy Bear. A wad of tissues packed my pockets, and a fleece blanket was stuffed into the backpack I carried to the job every day. I wasn't the type to bring a blanket to the mill, but fall had descended on Cleveland, bringing with it billowy white clouds and a bout of the flu.

Sleepy Bear was already sitting in the shanty by the time I arrived. He pitched forward in his seat and studied a packet of dirty wrinkled papers that were covered in codes, numbers, and decimal points. Most of the information contained on the pages was completely indecipherable, but the few parts we did understand gave us an idea of how many coils we would need to band over the next twelve hours.

"How's it going?" I asked.

Sleepy Bear looked up from the papers for a moment. He was wearing the signature headpiece of the cold-weather mill, which was a blue-and-red aviator hat with dangly earflaps. The hats were provided by the company for free, which meant that steelworkers across the valley could be seen sporting the look. Like most people, Sleepy Bear wore his hat with the earflaps turned upward, which prevented him from overheating.

"Oh, I'm all right," he said, "but you look tired."

"Yeah, I'm not feeling well."

I slung my book bag to the floor and plopped down in my chair.

Someone had recently changed the cup of vinegar that was used to catch fruit flies, and the smell was making me nauseous.

"Do you want to go home?" Sleepy Bear said, a look of concern on his face. "The shift manager might let you take the night off."

I pointed to my orange hard hat, which I was too tired to take off my head. Sleepy Bear nodded knowingly. Until I earned my yellow hard hat, the company still considered me an at-will employee, and the rules regarding absence were strict.

"You're probably right," he agreed. "You don't want to risk it, but I've got some bad news for you."

"Don't tell me that we've got splits," I said.

"Worse." Sleepy Bear sighed, handing me the dirty packet of papers. "We have heavy-gauge GM splits."

"What the fuck?" I said, examining the schedule. "How is that even possible?"

In the life of a Bander, a night filled with heavy-gauge GM splits was like winning the bad-luck lottery. Heavy-gauge coils were produced much faster than light-gauge coils, which meant that they needed to be banded more quickly, and a GM coil was packaged with four bands instead of the usual two. To make matters worse, a split coil was basically a regular coil that had been cut in half, which meant that every split could be produced in half the time.

"It sucks," Sleepy Bear said, "but we'll just do the best that we can."

I put the papers aside and pulled the blanket from my backpack, wadding it up and propping it against my shoulder like a pillow. The splits weren't set to arrive for at least another hour, so I thumbed through articles about the upcoming election on my phone, scanning the headlines that predicted Clinton's chances of winning against Trump. Most articles repeated the same sentiment. Trump didn't have a shot against the likes of a career politician. We were all safe. There was no way he could disrupt the system, and I wanted to believe the articles, even though I had my doubts. The longer I read the cramped words on the screen, the foggier my mind felt. After a while, I put the phone aside and tried to get a few minutes of rest.

My eyes were closed when the splits finally arrived, but I wasn't sleeping. My head rested against my blanket, heavy with snot and exhaustion, and I sighed when I heard the rumble of the crane overhead. I prayed that Crazy Joe would bring us the coils more slowly than usual. I wanted a few more minutes of downtime.

"Eliese," Sleepy Bear said loudly, our roles suddenly reversed. "The splits are here."

I opened my eyes to a line of glistening coils, all of which were much shorter than the ones we usually banded. The splits stood only three or four feet high. We called them *baby coils* inside the mill, even though they still weighed more than a handful of fully loaded sedans.

Sleepy Bear and I grabbed our hard hats and Kevlar sleeves, venturing out into the cold. A dull pain radiated through my back every time I bent over to put the protective rings in the eyes of the tiny coils, and my arms felt like rubber as I flipped the long strips of cardboard from the pallet. I kept banding despite my pains. It didn't matter that my body was failing me. My sore arms and throbbing back belonged to the mill, which stopped for nothing.

I worked as quickly as possible, but my tape kept wrinkling onto itself whenever I tried to fasten each piece of cardboard around the steel. The tape gun I was using for the purpose had seen better days. Its teeth were bent and dull, and the little wheel that held the tape in place was always threatening to come loose. All of the other Banders—even Sleepy Bear—had hidden the good tape guns in their lockers, which wasn't an uncommon practice in the mill. Steelworkers were like anxious squirrels. They gathered up the best tools and stowed them in safe places, always fearful that the tools would be taken by someone else. I had yet to get my hands on a good tape gun of my own, and I had been struggling with the shabby one for months.

Sleepy Bear and I moved down the line of coils, placing cardboard around their bare edges. When I got to the fourth coil, I placed my tape gun on top of the steel, like always, and flipped a piece of cardboard from the pallet. After wrapping the cardboard around the coil, I held it in place with my left hand and reached for the tape gun with my right. As I went to secure the cardboard with the tape, the entire roll popped out of my gun and tumbled to the ground. I looked down and sighed. It felt like someone had poured melted plastic into my bones. They throbbed with every movement, and the oil that seeped out of the coils, which smelled vaguely of mold and car exhaust, was making me queasy.

The fallen tape landed a few feet away—too far to reach without letting go of the cardboard—so I stuck out my foot and hooked the edge of the roll with my toe. Somehow I managed to inch it closer while keeping the cardboard in place with my fingertips. When the tape was close enough to grab with my free hand, I carefully put it back into the gun and tried again.

As I reached to secure the cardboard for a second time, the tape did the same thing. It bounced on the floor and rolled even farther away. I tried to reach it with my foot, but I lost my balance. My fingertips slipped from the cardboard, which popped off the coil and landed in oil, and I nearly toppled to the ground with it.

"Fucking piece of shit," I said, throwing the tape gun at the ground. Banding coils hadn't been this challenging since I'd learned the job with Gunner, and my body was making everything more difficult. I was tired and achy, and I craved my bed like a thirsty man craves water.

Sleepy Bear walked over to me, and I struggled to hold back my tears.

"Here," he said, holding out a clean, glistening tape gun. "Use mine. You can keep it. I have another one in my locker."

The tape gun felt to me like freshly folded laundry or a newly vacuumed carpet. It was a sigh of relief, and it made the splits far less daunting. Even so, the coils kept coming. No matter how quickly we banded, there was always another round of splits waiting to be brought over by Crazy Joe.

It was nearly two o'clock in the morning when Sleepy Bear and I finally got a break. I curled up for a nap in the shanty, but Sleepy Bear didn't do the same.

"I'm going to hang out somewhere else," he said. "I don't want to get whatever you've got."

"Okay," I told him, wrapping my blanket around my shoulders.

Once alone, I cranked the heaters on high to ward away the goose bumps that had risen on my arms. The shanty felt like a sauna after a few minutes, but the heat didn't have much of an effect. My body ached and shivered, and my nose started to run.

For the next few hours, I tried to trick myself into sleep. I meditated. I did breathing exercises. I counted sheep. Nothing worked. I couldn't turn off my mind, which had started to race.

Around me, the mill felt strangely quiet, which only amplified my sleep-deprived delirium. Sleepy Bear wasn't snoring next to me, and there weren't any buggies whizzing past. Even the cranes had taken a break for the night, leaving a heavy silence over everything. I pulled the blanket over my head, as if the warm fleece could somehow dampen my thoughts, but my mind was just as loud as ever.

I obsessed over the cold sweat that was seeping through my undershirt, wondering if my weakened immune system was evidence of something worse. Maybe I had urachal cancer after all. Maybe there was a larger sickness growing. I pined over the minutes that ticked away. Each second was one less moment of rest, making my recovery from the flu that much more difficult. I dreaded the next few nights, when I would have to come back to the mill and do it all over again, and I feared the upcoming election. What if everyone was wrong? What if Trump surprised us all?

I took a deep breath and started counting sheep again, conjuring their woolly images in my head—*one sheep, two sheep*—but every fuzzy body was saddled with worries that wouldn't go away. They jumped over a wall only to return again with more of their partners—*thirty sheep, forty sheep*—until I started thinking back to 2004, when I was a bright-eyed freshman at the Franciscan University of Steubenville. Bush won against Kerry that year, and everyone at my college rejoiced. Ten days after the election, I woke up to a perfect morning. The cool air and fluffy clouds were too beautiful to be spoiled by textbooks, so I skipped my Friday classes to watch Bob Ross's *The Joy of Painting* with one of the pot-smoking men I had befriended on campus. When we weren't mesmerized by Ross's happy little trees, we were chain-smoking cigarettes beneath the autumn sky or gorging ourselves on spice cake in the cafeteria.

After a while, the pot-smoking friend and I parted ways. He wanted an early night, and I was itching for something to do. I wasn't quite ready to let this perfect day slide into the next, so I sat outside my dorm until two men, both of whom were freshmen who I barely knew, asked me to have a few drinks with them. My gut told me to stay home, but I ignored it. I was desperate to keep the day alive, and I didn't have many friends to help me pass the time. Most of the other women on campus had alienated me completely, so I accepted the men's invitation. It was the only offer I had.

Long after the sun set, I followed the men to a small patch of woods just outside campus. We stumbled slowly through the dark and sat down beneath trees that had already lost their leaves. The ground was cold but dry, and a strong breeze whistled between the bare branches overhead. The first man, Ben, pulled a few bottles from his backpack, and it wasn't long before I felt lighter and looser. I drank quickly, and my body warmed against the chill air.

"I'll tell you guys a secret," Ben said, looking sly as he lifted a bottle to his lips. He was one of the most handsome men I'd ever met—he had brawny biceps and dirty-blond hair—but he also struck me as an unreliable type of person.

The second man, Aaron, leaned against the trunk of a tree and crossed one arm over his bent knees. Aaron was a pale, lanky boy who always seemed to be brooding. In the dim light, it was hard to tell what he was thinking as he stared at me, and I started to wish that he hadn't come with us. His sullen mood put a damper on everything.

"What secret?" I asked Ben, trying to ignore Aaron's gaze.

Ben wiped the corner of his mouth to build tension. "My girlfriend came to visit me a few weeks ago, and we had sex in front of the Fieldhouse."

I shook my head in disbelief. "On campus? Out in the open?" I said. Even if I had a boyfriend, I would never have thought to do something so risky in the middle of a Catholic university.

Ben nodded in satisfaction and took another swig from his bottle.

"Someone told me your girlfriend is a stripper," I blurted out. The alcohol had loosened my tongue just enough to give voice to the rumor.

Ben gave me a quick wink, and I couldn't tell if he was bluffing. Aaron just smiled and tossed his bottle into a bush. He didn't say much while we drank another round, but Ben was the life of the party. He talked about his high school antics, which had been punctuated by liquor and drugs and adventurous sex. I, on the other hand, had been an overly serious student, always intent on good grades and perfection. My stories about physics tests and book reports couldn't quite contend with Ben's tales of ecstasy and sexy cheerleaders, so I drank and listened. Even though my lips had grown numb, the alcohol wasn't strong enough to put me in a stupor. I laughed a bit more easily, but I was still very much myself.

"Wait a second," Ben said halfway through one of his stories. "Do you guys hear that?"

A few voices echoed in the distance, and we all perked our ears to listen. Even Aaron came to life.

"Let's get out of here," Ben whispered. "I don't want to get caught."

We packed up what was left of the alcohol and walked through the little swath of woods. I followed behind Ben, who led the way. I couldn't help but notice that we were heading straight toward the voices, but I didn't say anything. After all, Ben had more experience in these kinds of matters, so we kept walking until the woods opened into a field. The voices were so close that I could almost hear what they were saying. Through the darkness, I could see a few men driving golf balls into the night. They seemed harmless enough—they certainly weren't cops—and Ben went right up to them. He held his head high, as if he belonged, but he left the backpack of alcohol with Aaron and me. We were both helpless introverts, and the small amount of alcohol we'd consumed hadn't been enough to make us bold.

Ben returned with an offer a few minutes later. "It's just a bunch of drunk guys over there. They said we can come to their apartment if we want. It'll be warmer, and they have more booze."

Aaron shrugged and grunted in agreement, but I wasn't quite

so eager. I had never liked big groups of people, and the thought of attending a party full of strangers made me feel exhausted.

"I don't know," I said. "I might just head back."

"Oh, come on," Ben crooned. "It's not even midnight."

"I know," I told him, kicking at the grass with my foot. "I'm just getting tired."

"All right," he said. "Do you know how to find your way back?"

I thought for a moment. Ben was right. I had never been to this place. I knew we weren't far from campus, but I also wasn't sure how to get home.

"No," I admitted. "How do I get back?"

"Just come with us," Ben said. "We won't stay long. I promise."

Somewhere in the quiet of the mill, Crazy Joe started moving his crane aimlessly through the dark. The gentle whine of his motor broke my attention, tearing my thoughts away from Aaron and Ben. The memory evaporated just as quickly as it had been called to the surface, but I knew it couldn't be held back for long. Eventually the men would reappear in my mind. They always did. As the crane rumbled slowly overhead, I pulled my blanket more snugly around my shoulders. Maybe if I tugged the corners tight enough the stretched fleece could guard against the things I didn't want to recall.

My fever lingered, stubbornly worsening during the cold hours at the mill. I suffered through a few more shifts with Sleepy Bear, hugging my blanket and popping decongestants, but the illness didn't relent. I had barely recovered when Sleepy Bear and I were scheduled to work another round of nights together. It was the same old thing. A cup of coffee from the gas station—the largest you can find—chased with an energy drink for good measure. Then the sound of Crazy Joe hurrying overhead. The gloves. The Kevlar sleeves. *Cardboard, plastic, bands. Ratchet. Crimp. Repeat.* A little gossip. Did you hear about the man who had a heart attack in Steel Producing? Who was he? How old? You know a lot about the mill by now. The size of Sleepy Bear's Tupperware suggests that his wife made him a spectacular dinner. Crazy

Joe is moving coils for no reason, which means that he's had more caffeine than usual, and the woman who operates a crane called Warehouse 4 is having a bad day. She's already flipped a coil, and the night has barely started. It might be boyfriend troubles again. You glance at a few articles about the election. Try to find some more coffee in the Social Shanty. *Cardboard, plastic, bands.* Check your eyes in the bathroom mirror. The bags just won't go away. Then off to the vending machine for a candy bar. Pick one. Reconsider. Not long ago, someone found a dead mouse in one of these machines. Reconsider again. You need the sugar. You need something to keep you going. You've climbed mountains before, but scrambling up bluffs felt less difficult than moving your body through a night at the mill. One candy bar won't hurt. Don't think about the mice. Then it's back to the coils. *Ratchet. Crimp. Repeat.* Count the hours you have left. Count sheep. Try to rest. Fight your reeling mind. Before you know it, Crazy Joe is moving overhead. Then it's more cardboard. And repeat.

After finishing one of these twelve-hour shifts, Sleepy Bear and I waved our goodbyes and headed for our cars. My body desperately needed a few hours of sleep before we would have to do it all over again.

I threw my book bag beside the door when I arrived home that morning. The sun had just begun to rise, casting a dusky gloom over the apartment. I slipped off my shoes and headed straight for bed, but I stopped short in the living room. A shadow flashed in the corner of my eye, darting over the burgundy carpet before disappearing. I looked around for its source, peeking under the couch and behind a bookshelf, but I barely had enough energy to walk. Exhausted, I shrugged and fell into bed.

I had seen shadows before. They sometimes came when I was in the throes of an episode. They fluttered on the edge of my vision, flashing so quickly that I often thought they were ghosts. I knew that my mental state was growing worse by the day. Some mornings, when I got off work from the mill, I would cry in my bed for no reason. Other times, I flew off the handle at Tony. My obsession with belly buttons was just as strong as ever, but I told myself to keep it together. I had to muscle through. I had to be stronger than my ailing mind. I still had my orange hard hat, and I didn't want to risk failing at the first full-time job I'd ever worked.

Once in bed, I fell asleep quickly, burying myself in a down comforter that was thick enough to dull any chill, and I stayed asleep until my alarm went off in the afternoon. I didn't want to be late for my shift with Sleepy Bear, so I trudged toward the bathroom for a hot shower. I lingered in the steam, breathing in the floral body wash, and I felt renewed as I wrapped a towel around my chest. I could make it through one more night. I could hold it together long enough to band a few coils. I could keep myself afloat until I earned the yellow hard hat.

Then I walked back into my bedroom. A squirrel sat on the floor, near the foot of the bed, looking mangy and thin. Some of the fur on its tail had fallen out, like an eyebrow that had been plucked too often, and the rest of its coat was dull and unkempt. The squirrel just stared at me, as if I were the intruder, and I felt every cell in my body suddenly come alive with a fury that could have wrenched the earth in two. All of the damage I'd been holding together cracked beneath the tiny weight of that squirrel. He was the last straw, the final stroke, the ultimate indignity, and I was like a shudder that swallowed cities whole. Who did this squirrel think he was, dancing around my apartment while I slept, infecting me with whatever sickness he carried? Didn't he know that I had enough sickness as it was? My throat still ached with the remnants of the flu, and I barely had enough strength to carry myself through one more night at the mill.

I grabbed a book from a nearby desk and hurled it at the little animal. I wanted to knock its skull into a pulp, but I missed. The squirrel ran out of the bedroom, and I jumped back as it dove into the kitchen, where it weaseled its way into a cupboard that wouldn't latch. I threw anything I could grab at the cabinet. Pots. Shoes. Plastic cups.

"Fuck you!" I screamed, a few tears rolling down my cheeks.

I opened the silverware drawer and started hurling forks and knives at the cabinet door. They clattered on the ground in a pile, but I kept throwing them, denting the cabinets in my rage. The squirrel had unleashed something inside me. I wasn't just trying to scare it into submission. Everything in my life was crumbling more quickly than I could manage. I felt exhausted, no matter how hard I tried to trick myself with a warm shower. I felt depressed and unhinged, no matter how hard I tried to level my moods. My relationship with Tony was struggling. I barely saw my family or my friends. The mill was sucking me dry. It was dredging up old nightmares. And now I had to ignore the squirrel in my apartment so that I could band coils through the night.

"Fuck you," I said, lobbing another knife at the door. "Fuck you. Fuck you."

When I opened the cabinet, the squirrel was gone. It had probably exited the apartment when it first crawled inside, weaseling its way through a hole that extended into the wall. I had been flinging silverware at nothing.

I went back to the bedroom and grabbed my phone to call Tony.

"There was a squirrel, and now it's gone, and I don't know what to do," I blurted out when he answered the phone.

"Slow down," he said. "What happened?"

I explained the situation through my tears. "I need to sleep at your house. I can't stay here."

"Okay," Tony said. "That's fine. Come here after work. But call your landlord too."

I followed his advice and left a rambling message on my landlord's cell, but there was nothing else I could do. I had to be at the mill for my shift, so I packed a bag with some clothes and ran out of the apartment.

Later that night I told Sleepy Bear about the squirrel.

"What?" he asked, his brown eyes even bigger than usual. "A squirrel?"

"Yeah," I told him. "A fucking squirrel."

Sleepy Bear lifted his arms and shuddered with disgust, as if he had seen the squirrel himself.

"Oh, Eliese, you're a mess," he said.

"I know," I agreed.

The squirrel had split me open, and I knew a total unraveling wasn't long behind. The swing shifts, the delusions, the fever—it was all too much. I tried to steady myself by looking at my phone, where an article about urachal cancer was waiting to be read, but the words blended together. It felt as if a shroud had been drawn over my eyes, and my mind started slipping down paths I couldn't control. The memory of that perfect afternoon in Steubenville kept creeping back into my thoughts. I could still taste the clear autumn air. I could see the bare branches of the trees. I could hear the men who had beckoned me into the woods. Their voices flooded back to me with sudden force, pulling me away from the mill. I tried my best to shake off the memory, but my fever made me powerless to stop it.

As I followed Ben and Aaron into the strange men's apartment, I was struck by the smell of body odor and cheese curls. The walls were sparsely decorated, and a retro-looking table with red-vinyl seats had been nestled into the corner of the living room. There were empty bottles on the coffee table and an empty bag of chips on the floor. I sat down on a worn plaid couch, which I quickly recognized as the source of the smell.

As I sat there, I noticed that I was the only woman. There was a whole apartment full of men—ten or twelve, at least—and I was the lone female. Some of the men introduced themselves, and one of them handed me a beer. They all acted as if they'd known me for years. For a moment it felt like I belonged in this man's world. I was more at home here, among this boisterous, freewheeling masculinity, than I was with the girls who protested abortion rights with me.

All of a sudden Aaron tapped my shoulder and nodded toward the kitchen. I followed him, leaving Ben in the living room with the rest of the men. The kitchen was small and cramped. There were dirty dishes in the sink and an empty pot on the stove. Aaron handed me a red cup. I hadn't watched him pour the contents. I would later come to believe that he had slipped something inside, but I didn't think of that then. I wanted to show that I belonged in this man's world, so I drank quickly. It wasn't long before everything started to blur.

The rest of the night happened in fragments.

I woke up in the bathroom. Aaron was standing in the doorway. I tried to walk out, but he pushed me backward. I fell into a bathtub and hit my head on the faucet. Aaron unbuckled his pants.

I woke up outside and on my knees. Ben stood over me, exposed. He grabbed my hair and forced himself inside my mouth. Vomit ran down my chin and my chest, but he didn't care.

I woke up, and I was on my back. I stared up at the bare branches of a tree. The roots dug into my naked thighs. Aaron was on top of me.

"Come on," Ben said, "we gotta go. Someone's gonna see."

I woke up, and the two men were dragging me somewhere. They each had me by the arm, but I was too unsteady. My body lurched forward, and I fell to my hands and knees.

"Get up," the men said.

I couldn't move. My body didn't feel like it belonged to me.

"Get up."

I remained motionless on all fours, like a dog. The men grabbed my arms and pulled.

"You can't tell anyone about this," they said again and again as they led me slowly through the night.

I came to beside the entrance of my dorm, unable to stand. The world felt pixelated, like a television with bad reception, and I was spliced between frames. The men were gone, but I heard voices. Women's voices. There were arms lifting me, pulling me, guiding me up a flight of stairs. There was the door of my room, then more hands, then words flying too fast to hear. There were footsteps and whispers. A click. A thud. Then darkness.

The morning after the rape, I woke up in my own bed, wearing my pajamas. I had no recollection of dressing myself or crawling beneath the comforter, but I knew that my head throbbed and my legs hurt. I wanted nothing more than a shower, so I shuffled to the bathroom and let the water run until a thick steam obscured the tile walls. When I slipped inside, I didn't adjust the temperature. I let the hot water scald my skin while I picked pieces of gravel from my hands and knees. The tiny stones, which were too heavy to be swallowed by the drain, sat stubbornly in the basin, and I tried to piece together my memories of the night before. I wasn't quite sure what had happened. I had gone out drinking. We had met up with strangers who were driving golf balls into the night. I had swallowed whatever was in the red cup. Then—what?—I had sex with two men? I lost my virginity?

The stones in the shower kept getting caught beneath my feet, and I could smell Aaron and Ben on my body. Their sweat lingered in the back of my throat. It clung to the steam around me, growing sharper with each whiff. I poured body wash on a loofa and ran it over every inch of skin, but the smell of sweet pea didn't mask whatever stench still lingered from the men. No matter how hard I scrubbed, their smell just wouldn't go away.

As I reached for more soap, everything inside me suddenly shifted. My mind broke away from the rest of me. I was looking at myself from above. I noticed, quite calmly, that my body was crying, but the tears belonged to someone else. I was no longer connected to this vulnerable, pink skin. I had been removed from its pains and its problems, and now I was floating outside time, plucked from the carcass that had carried me for so long. I felt like a tiny diamond loosened from the earth. Safe. Precious. Unencumbered. For a moment I wondered if I was dying. Maybe I had gotten caught in the limbo between living and dead, but the feeling didn't last.

Just as quickly as I had been whisked away from my body, I was thrown back into it. I didn't understand why I had felt so fractured, so unreal. It would be many months until I learned that dissociation—this severing of the self—is often a symptom of trauma.

When I finished in the shower, I dressed in the baggiest outfit I could find. I wanted to hide beneath thick layers of fabric, but I also didn't want to be alone. I needed someone to tell me what to do next, so I went outside and implored the help of a woman who lived in my dorm. Her name was Emma, and she was the closest thing I had to a female friend on campus. She had been present when the men had brought me back, and she had been one of the women who had helped me back to my room.

We sat in a courtyard outside our dorm and smoked cigarettes in silence. The afternoon was just as beautiful as the one before it. Big fall clouds floated across the blue sky, and the air was crisp and clean. I tried not to cry, but I was helpless to stop the tears.

"What happened with Aaron and Ben last night?" Emma asked, snuffing out her cigarette on the pavement.

I wiped the snot from my nose, gasping for air. "I don't know. I think I got drunk and lost my virginity or something, but now I feel really weird. I just want to curl up in bed and cry."

Emma rolled her eyes, obviously annoyed at my reaction.

"Did you bleed?" she said suddenly.

I looked up at her big brown eyes, which sat beneath a perfectly smooth pair of bangs.

The smoke from my cigarette curled into the air, but the odor wasn't pungent enough to mask the smell of the men's sweat, which followed me everywhere.

"What did you say?" I asked Emma. I wasn't sure I had heard her correctly.

"Did you bleed after it happened?"

"I have a few cuts and scrapes," I told her.

Emma huffed and crossed her legs. "That's not what I mean. Did you bleed after you had sex?"

"Oh. No. I don't think so."

"I thought you said that you were a virgin."

"I am a virgin," I told her, but then I stopped myself.

I didn't know if I *was* a virgin anymore. No one had ever explained rape to me, at least not in a real and practical way. I had never learned the meaning of *consent*. I didn't even know how to tell if I had been raped in the first place.

"I don't know," I said. "I guess I *was* a virgin."

"Listen," Emma said, "if those guys really did what you said they did, then you would have bled."

I didn't know what to tell her, and I was too distraught to fully comprehend the accusation that was being made against me.

"I don't know why I didn't bleed," I said. "I rode horses as a kid. I fell a lot. Maybe I tore my hymen then."

Emma scoffed and lit another cigarette. An uncomfortable silence settled between us.

"What should I do?" I asked.

"Listen, Eliese," Emma said with conviction. "If you really had sex with two guys in one night, then I think you need to go to confession."

I had gone to her for guidance, and she had given it to me. For all I knew, she was right. Maybe I couldn't stop crying because I had tarnished my soul. I didn't know what else to do, so I went to the rectory and asked for a priest.

The man who answered my request was Father Scanlan. He was chancellor of the university at the time, and before becoming chancellor, he had served as the university's president for twenty-six years. It was his leadership that had turned the Franciscan University of Steubenville into a well-known institution of Catholic learning, and many considered him the holiest of men. We sat across from one another in a pair of wingback chairs, and I found comfort in Father Scanlan's presence. He was already an old man at the time, and he had a thick wave of white hair. His eyes were sober and thoughtful, but they weren't morose. Had he not been a priest, he would have been some child's favorite grandfather.

I bowed my head as Father Scanlan made the sign of the cross over me.

"Forgive me, Father," I said in the customary way, "for I have sinned."

I recounted the normal litany of everyday sins—using the Lord's name in vain, forgetting my daily prayers, smoking pot in the cemetery. When I ran out of things to say, I panicked. My stomach dropped in the way it does after a sudden fall, and it felt like every breath contained less oxygen than the one before it. I started inventing sins that I had never committed. Stealing. Fighting. Things that weren't in my nature. I didn't want to tell this old man, whose eyes were bright and patient, that I had unwillingly lost my virginity to two men I barely knew.

"Last night," I finally said, tears already in my eyes, "I got drunk with these two guys."

Every gritty detail came pouring out. The woods, the red cup, the men. I told him of the bathtub and the vomit. I told him of the smell of their bodies, which wouldn't go away. I spoke of a violence that I didn't yet recognize.

As the story tumbled out of me, my mind kept jumping out of my body, just as it had in the shower. It didn't feel like I was confessing to a priest—it felt like I was watching myself in slow motion on a screen.

"For these and all my sins," I said when I was finished, "I am truly sorry."

I tried to speak the apology with meaning and conviction, but I didn't quite believe it. I wasn't sorry. I was too raw for remorse.

Father Scanlan gathered his thoughts with a sigh.

"When we don't love ourselves," he told me, "we end up in situations that are contrary to God's law. We use alcohol and marijuana to fill the void that's left by a lack of self-love. Sexual immorality, in particular, occurs when we don't honor our bodies. It shows that we haven't accepted God's love into our lives."

I sobbed bitterly as he spoke. My whole body shook, and tiny gasps escaped from my throat. No matter how hard I tried to keep silent, the sadness couldn't be contained.

"For your penance," Father Scanlan said, folding his hands in his lap, "I want you to pray to the Virgin Mary. Ask her to help you learn how to love yourself as a woman."

The words made me cry even harder. Snot dripped from my nose, and my mouth twisted with grief. It felt like everything had been my fault. My poor judgment had made me drink the red cup, and my lack of self-love had landed me in the dirt. *You can't tell anyone about this*, the men had warned as they dragged me home. Maybe they were looking out for my own good. They didn't want everyone to know that I was a broken, immodest woman who had done something so horrific that she could barely breathe through her tears.

Looking back, I don't know exactly what Father Scanlan should have said to me during my confession, but the words he spoke weren't the ones I needed to hear. In many ways, he was right. I was an insecure girl who was trying to find herself, and sometimes I tried to find myself in all the wrong places. But when I sat before him, I didn't need to be reminded that I'd brought this sorrow upon myself. I felt enough shame already. In that moment, I needed to be directed to mental health services. I needed to be told that you can't give consent when you're gravely impaired. I needed someone to tell me that I had, in fact, been raped.

I recited the Act of Contrition—a Catholic prayer of repentance—in front of Father Scanlan, and he absolved me of my sins. Up until that point, I had often felt renewed by the sacrament of confession. There was a catharsis that came when I unburdened my shortcomings to a priest. This confession was different. I didn't feel restored or forgiven. I could still smell the bodies of those men, and my tears came just as quickly as ever.

Nearly thirteen years later, Father Scanlan passed away. Upon his death, Catholics sang his praises. There are many who still believe that Father Scanlan should be canonized and named a saint. For all I know, he should be. One lapse in judgment doesn't negate the good we do, and even the saints among us have sinned. I do, however, know that women have carried the burdens of men for far too long. For generations, we have been painted as temptresses with flawed natures. We're the intemperate ones who beckon men into sin. Adam only ate the apple because Eve ate it first. Aaron and Ben took advantage of me because I didn't love myself enough, and the priest who absolved me of my rape might one day be revered as a saint. Eve did eat that apple first. It held within it the knowledge of good and evil. Maybe she already knew that Adam couldn't be trusted to tell her the difference between the two.

I recovered from the fever in between my shifts at the mill, but my life was swept into a continuing state of upheaval. The squirrel prompted me to finally find another apartment and buy new furniture, which wasn't the exciting endeavor I had expected it to be. My free hours were now spent touring different floor plans and mulling over new mattresses, and I had trouble finding an open apartment that suited my needs. Every hour spent talking to leasing agents was one less hour I had to sleep, and the mill was demanding even more of my time than ever. The old-timers were using up their last vacation days of the year, and I was stuck filling in for their shifts on my off days. When I wasn't at the mill, I was searching for a new couch or packing boxes or crossing my fingers for a vacancy in my price range.

Tony let me stay with him for the duration of the apartment search, but he made it clear that the arrangement wasn't permanent.

"We've been together for a while," I said one evening while we cleared the dishes from dinner. "Maybe it's silly for me to sign a lease. Maybe we should just move in together."

Tony scraped some leftover spaghetti into a bowl, focusing all of his attention on the limp noodles.

"Maybe," he said. "Can you see if there are any more paper towels in the pantry?"

The conversation ended there, and I knew better than to push it. The apartment search wasn't going as quickly as either of us had hoped, and it took me several weeks to find something that I liked well enough to rent. During that time, the tension continued to build in our relationship. The fights grew more frequent now that we were in such close proximity. Tony tried his best to tour apartments with me, but his heart wasn't in it. He didn't have the same enthusiasm he had shown in my hunt for a new car, and he left most of the research to me.

One afternoon, while I was working a shift at the mill, Sleepy Bear and I picked up our pay stubs in the Social Shanty. He tore into his and nodded in approval before turning to me.

"Aren't you getting close to earning your yellow hat?" he asked.

"I'm not sure," I told him with a shrug. "I've been too busy to think about it."

"Well, check your hours. I bet you're close."

I opened my own pay stub, which was chock-full of overtime, and searched for the total hours I'd worked over the past several months. It turned out that Sleepy Bear was right. I was well over the 1,040 hours required to complete my probation. Somewhere in the chaos of my life, I had become a full-fledged member of the union.

Over the next few days, I expected some kind of fanfare—or at least an email—but no one from the company noticed. There wasn't the slightest mention of my yellow hard hat, so I went to the man who served as the secretary of the Finishing Department.

"Talk to Jeremy," he told me.

I talked to Jeremy.

"Talk to the shift manager," he said.

I talked to the shift manager, who served as a low-level supervisor inside the mill. He was a few years younger than me, and he had a mop of shaggy brown hair.

"Sure, I'll get you a yellow hat," he promised.

It took him a few days, but he finally brought the hard hat to my shanty while I was working the night shift with Sleepy Bear.

"There it is," the shift manager said, tossing the yellow hat into my lap.

He walked out of the shanty before I had time to remove the hard hat from its plastic wrapping, but Sleepy Bear sat up to witness the momentous occasion.

"Try it on," he said with a smile.

The new hard hat looked dazzlingly clean compared to the orange one I had been wearing, which was scratched and dirty from six months in the mill. During that time, I had learned the language of the cranes and the lingo of the steelworkers. I had spent slow mornings drinking burnt coffee to the sound of Sleepy Bear's snores. I had spent long nights praying for dawn, and I had gained a few pounds from eating too many Danishes in the Social Shanty. But when I put on the hard hat for first time, I didn't feel the sense of triumph I had expected. I was relieved that my job was secure. I was proud of myself for making it through the swing shifts, and I was grateful that I was now a member of one of the biggest unions in the country. But something was missing. I couldn't quite put my finger on it at the time—and I didn't want to dwell—so I smiled and turned to Sleepy Bear for approval.

"That's the right color," he said with a wink. "You're a union woman now."

The confession with Father Scanlan did little to ease my anxiety, and I continued to decline in the days that followed. I didn't eat, and I didn't go to class. I barely even got out of bed. By the time I finally called my parents for help, I was in shambles. They didn't know what to do—they could barely understand me through my tears—so they drove down to Steubenville and took me back home to Cleveland. They also scheduled an appointment with a therapist. The woman had a gentle demeanor, but she wasn't afraid to be direct.

"It sounds like you were raped," she said when I told her what had happened.

The word *rape* came like a revelation. The minute I heard it, I knew in my gut that it described that night in the woods. My tears stopped, and my body relaxed. I had been inconsolable for nearly a week, but I suddenly felt the catharsis that I had been unable to find with Father Scanlan.

After speaking with the therapist, I spent several days with my parents in Cleveland. They both wanted me to gather my things from the university and come home for good, but I wasn't convinced. I didn't want to crawl back to the safety of my childhood home while Aaron and Ben finished the semester without any repercussions. I didn't want to wallow in victimhood, and I didn't want to succumb quietly to what had been done to me. More than anything, I wanted to protect other women on campus. Aaron and Ben were both freshmen. They had three and a half years of college ahead of them, and I didn't want them to do the same thing to anyone else. It was too late to go to the police about my own rape, but I could seek justice at the institutional level. I could bring the matter to the college's attention, but I hadn't yet resolved to do so. I already sensed that my complaint might bring the condemnation and animosity of my peers, and I didn't know if I had the nerve to fight the battle that might ensue.

While I was weighing my options in the living room one afternoon, my father sat down in a chair across from me.

"I have something for you," he said.

He held out a little box that had come from the pawnshop where he worked. When I opened the lid, I found a gold necklace and two tiny charms. One charm was a golden heart with a keyhole in it, and the other charm was a delicate golden key.

"This is the key to your heart," my father said when he gave it to me. "No one can take it from you."

The gesture gave me just enough courage to make a decision. I fastened the charms around my neck and silently resolved to speak out about my experience. I would finish the semester at Franciscan University, and I would lodge a formal complaint with college administrators.

When I got back to campus, I was required to provide a written account of the rape. Aaron and Ben were both given a chance to read my testimony, and then they were faced with a choice: If they agreed that my account was accurate, they could voluntarily withdraw from the university without an expulsion on their records; if they thought that I was lying, they could ask for a trial that would be judged by a panel of professors and peers. The trial posed the greater risk. If the men won the trial, they wouldn't be subject to any disciplinary action whatsoever. If they lost, however, they would be formally expelled from the school.

Each man decided his fate separately, and each one made a different choice. Aaron said that my record of events was accurate. He agreed that he was guilty, so he took his punishment and left the school. Ben, on the other hand, claimed that I was mistaking him for someone else. He wanted a trial.

Over the course of a few days, the university assembled a panel that was composed of students and professionals. The students on the panel were barely older than I was at the time. One woman had a pair of doe eyes behind her thick lashes, and the others were men in pressed pants and button-down shirts.

Both Ben and I were allowed to have two support people in the room with us. Ben chose to have his parents with him, but I didn't. My mother had taken off work to help me through the trial, but I had asked her to wait outside. I didn't want to be seen as a little girl who still needed her mommy. In retrospect, I'd made the wrong decision. My mother would have gone to battle for me, but I was too distraught to realize it. I chose instead to be accompanied by Emma—the same woman who had told me to go to confession—and a school psychologist who was on the university's payroll. At the time, I thought that both people would corroborate my story. The psychologist could define date rape to the tribunal, and Emma could tell them about the night it happened. She had seen me when the men brought me back to the dorm, and she could testify that I had been too incapacitated to consent.

Everyone gathered in a large conference room attached to the library. The room smelled of wood paneling and old books, and Ben was already there when I walked inside. He sat at the head of a long oak table beside his parents. They were all perfectly dressed in business attire. Ties and sport coats. A pencil skirt for the mother. I had tried to look equally professional in a blouse and black pants, but my makeup had already gotten smeared from crying.

A thin man in a sweater vest directed me to the middle of the table, where I sat down between Emma and the psychologist.

"I think we're ready to begin the proceedings," the man said, explaining that Ben and I would both provide a statement before the panel asked us a series of questions. "Eliese, you can begin by reading the written testimony that you filed with your complaint."

It was the same account that Ben had already seen, but I obeyed the man with the sweater vest, reciting the words in front of the panel. I spoke quickly, stifling the tears that were threatening to betray how badly I'd been hurt. I didn't want to show any weakness. I didn't want to collapse in front of the people who held my fate in their hands, so I showed no emotion whatsoever. I read the account like a robot, with little affect and great efficiency.

When it was Ben's turn to give his account, he insisted that he hadn't been in the woods with me that night.

"She's mistaking me for someone else," he kept saying. He denied his involvement so many times that I found myself growing frustrated.

"You're lying," I interrupted. "I know it was you."

"Do you know what she does?" Ben said to the panel. "She smokes pot in the cemetery with these guys from my dorm. They're always out there, getting high."

"Why does that matter?" I said.

The panel ignored me. I could feel them grasping at the implications of my questionable character. At first I considered attacking Ben in a similar manner. He was no saint. He had bragged about having sex with his girlfriend in front of the university's Fieldhouse, and he was certainly no stranger to pot and booze. But I didn't want to sink to Ben's level, and I figured that everyone would see his attacks for what they were: distractions. The panel wasn't there to judge anyone's character. They were supposed to judge the accuracy of my account, which Aaron had already deemed to be true.

"Okay, okay," the man in the sweater vest said, holding up his hands. "I think things are getting a little out of hand. Ben, if you're done with your testimony, then I think we'll proceed with the questioning."

Ben and his parents nodded, satisfied that they had given a full account. The panel asked Ben a few questions about his involvement, pressing him to admit that he was there. He didn't budge in his denial. "She's mistaking me for someone else."

Eventually the man in the sweater vest turned to me, folding his hands on the table. "Eliese," he said, "we have to ask you an important question. Did you say no?"

I stared at the oak table, noticing the grain that ran through the wood. I wasn't sure if I had said no. Pieces of the night blurred together, making it impossible to give a definitive answer. I thought back to the old adage from the Gospel of John. "The truth will set you free." I gave the man in the sweater vest the most honest answer possible.

"I don't know," I said. "I don't remember."

I tried to explain that I was too incapacitated to consent, but my words fell on deaf ears. The psychologist didn't offer much in the way of validation, and Emma wasn't helpful either. When it was her turn to testify, she sat squarely in her seat.

"Emma," the man in the sweater vest said, "you're here as Eliese's witness. What are your thoughts about the matter?"

Emma perked up and brushed her bangs away from her forehead.

"I think they're both to blame," she said with unshakable conviction.

The panel finished their questioning a short time later and went into deliberations. I was sitting in a restaurant with my mother, eating a salad, when her cell phone rang in her purse. It was the man in the sweater vest calling with the verdict. The panel agreed that Ben had been in the woods with me, but they decided that whatever took place had been consensual.

"I can't believe this," my mother said. She threw the cell phone back into her purse and shook her head, and I knew from her wrinkled brow and quivering lip that she was beyond angry. "I want to talk to the president of the college and give him a piece of my mind. Or maybe we'll talk to Father Scanlan. Someone has to listen to us."

I sat there and picked through the lettuce on my plate. I was no longer hungry, but I didn't have the same reaction as my mother. I was numb. I thought that I had done the right thing in coming forward—I thought I was helping other women by taking a stand—but nothing had been accomplished. Ben would escape without punishment, and I had to bear the weight of the panel's decision. *It was consensual. You just don't love yourself as a woman.*

Many years after hearing that verdict, I went on a backpacking trip in Kentucky's Red River Gorge. At night I sat at a makeshift campsite with a group of strangers I had met on the trail. A bottle of rye passed between us as a campfire sputtered embers into the darkness. We were sharing our best stories with one another. I told a short, funny quip about dildos and cocaine. Someone else told a long tale about losing his front teeth in a bar fight. Then a middle-aged woman took the rye and began to speak.

"When my son was little," she said, wringing the bottle in her hands, "I took him to a beach, and we spent all day building sandcastles. He loved astronomy, so he made a castle that looked like a space station. It took him hours to build, and he was so proud when he finished. But then the tide started to come in, and I explained to him that the water would wash his castle away. I said that the water didn't have anything against him. It was just the way things were."

The woman took a sip of rye, and all of the other hikers leaned forward around the heat of the fire. The flames danced in the pit, casting shadows on the surrounding trees.

"Well," the woman continued, "my son and I left the beach for the night and went to bed. Before falling asleep, he prayed and prayed. He asked God to spare his sandcastle, and I was a little worried. I figured that he would be pretty mad at God the next morning when he found out the sandcastle was gone. But then the strangest thing happened. We got to the beach early in the morning, and the sandcastle was still there. The tide had washed everything else away. I mean, the beach was completely smooth. There wasn't so much as a footprint on it, but my son's sandcastle was standing right in the middle, totally untouched. I couldn't figure out how it survived. There wasn't a logical explanation for it, so I started to wonder if God had intervened somehow. Maybe that sandcastle was my son's sign from God."

There was a brief moment of silence before everyone complimented the story and passed the rye. Someone threw a log onto the fire, and a new storyteller began telling a tale. I didn't listen, though. I was crying softly to myself.

As I sat beside the fire, I thought about the sign I had received from God when I was a little girl. It was just a cage full of doves, but it had meant everything to me. It meant that I had a purpose and a place in this world. It meant that I was supposed to become a nun, so I followed that sign to the doors of Franciscan University. Then the rape took my faith away.

As a child, I had been told that God was a great, protective force. He was our savior, who loved us all equally. He was the true source of freedom and opportunity, and I was raised to believe in his providence. Beside that campfire, however, God seemed to me like a great boulder rolling down a hillside. He was an angry, unpredictable weight tumbling at random, and I felt like the small, hapless thing that had gotten in his way. This loving God had granted the trivial wish of a little boy who probably didn't even appreciate the gesture, and yet he had taken the world away from me. He saved the sandcastle, but he didn't spare my body. He changed the tides for the sake of a child, but he let my dream of the religious life fall at the feet of two men who didn't blink twice at my pain.

After donning my yellow hat for the first time, I took my buggy outside for a drive. It was a little past midnight, and the stars were hidden behind a thick layer of cloud. The fall air felt cold on my face as I rode to the west end of the Finishing Department, where I drove alongside a sharp precipice that dropped off into the Cuyahoga River. It was too dark to see the water, but I could sense it as I sped past. There was a certain calm about the riverbank, as if a little slice of nature could dampen the fury of the mill.

The road quickly curved away from the Cuyahoga, leading me past the white circular tanks of the Water Treatment Plant. I never knew what was contained in those tanks, but there were a few of them standing in a cluster behind a concrete barrier. They were several feet high and thirty feet across, and they always looked to me like crop circles that had been turned inside out.

From the tanks, I turned left and drove past the brick locker rooms and the Hot Dip Galvanizing Line until I came to the northern border of the Finishing Department. The Blast Furnace, which made the iron that would one day be turned into steel, was located a few hundred yards away, and I paused to stare at the two blue flames that rose out of its smokestacks.

The flames of the Blast Furnace weren't as aggressive as the orange one that came from the Basic Oxygen Furnace, and they looked nearly holy in the midnight quiet of the mill. Each flame lapped in the breeze like a piece of blue lace caught on a tree branch, and I imagined that the goddess of steel had snagged her dress while running past. The goddess was far away by now, over in China somewhere, and this lace was the only thing left of her. The men and women in yellow hats cared for it like priests at an altar. They had been tasked with keeping the memory of the goddess alive, and I was now one of them.

As I sat in my buggy, looking up at the flames, a niggling unease stirred inside me. It wasn't quite sadness—not exactly—but it wasn't far off, either. I felt like a cracked jug of water or a puckered balloon losing air. Something was slipping out of me, and I couldn't seem to put a stopper on it.

You can be anything you want to be, adults had said to me when I was young. *If you dream it, you can do it!* Others in my generation had heard some version of the same in their childhoods, and many of us dreamed of changing the world. We wanted to leave an indelible mark on humanity, which was the reason I had once been so attracted to both the convent and the classroom, but reality hadn't lived up to the grandiose expectations we'd set for ourselves as children.

After the trial at Franciscan University, my parents urged me to drop out of school. They wanted me to stay home for a semester and reenroll at another college, but I didn't want to admit defeat. I wasn't about to withdraw from the school while Ben went unpunished, so I finished the fall semester and went back the following spring.

Life at the university quickly became untenable. My fellow students gave me sidelong glances as they walked past, and my pot-smoking friends distanced themselves from me. *She's the slut who lied*, people whispered behind my back. Everyone knew who I was, and they did their best to steer clear.

To cope, I filled every moment of my time with some activity or another. I started training with the swim team, and I stage-managed the spring play, and I tutored kids in the afternoons, and I did an internship at a local elementary school. I was taking a full load of senior-level classes, and I was reading extra books on the side. I told myself that I was handling the situation well, even though I had stopped eating and sleeping. My nights were spent in one of two ways: I would either cry in my bed for hours or roam the streets around the university. Sometimes I played chicken with oncoming traffic. There was a part of me that wanted to die, but there was also a part of me that felt invincible. Whenever I stood in front of a pair of approaching headlights, I didn't really think that they could kill me.

As the weeks passed, my mind became a treacherous thing that raced wildly. A paper about Dante's *Vita Nuova* would turn into flashbacks of that night, and the flashbacks would induce an immense sadness, and the immense sadness made me think that I had been possessed by the Devil, and the Devil made me think of the impending apocalypse, and the impending apocalypse made it very difficult to finish a paper about Dante's *Vita Nuova*.

Every so often, I cut the skin on my upper thighs with a razor. It wasn't a cry for help, or else I would have done it in an area that wasn't so easily hidden. I wanted the adrenaline, which was the only substance that seemed to quiet my mind for a moment. I didn't know it then, but I was experiencing my first mixed episode. I had the frenetic, grandiose energy that is so common in mania, but I also had the destructive apathy of depression.

I continued to decline for several months. Then, on a cold night in early spring, I found myself wandering around campus in the rain. I didn't know where I was walking—or *why* I was walking—but I wasn't wearing a coat. The rain created a hazy aura around the streetlamps in the dark, and I crept around a soccer field at the edge of campus until I stumbled on a herd of deer.

The deer let me inch toward them, lifting their necks from the grass with apprehension. There was a tiny doe on the edge of the herd whose wet fur glistened in the lamplight. I paused to look into her bright, kind eyes, and then I was overcome by a sudden urge to kill her. I didn't want to take her life with a bow or a rifle. I didn't want to do it from a distance. I wanted to tackle the doe with my bare hands. I wanted to pounce, like something hungry and wild, and I wanted to rip into her rigid body as she struggled beneath me.

The doe flicked her ears, as if she had read my thoughts. We both stared at each other, locked in the stillness that comes before the chase. My mind raced violently. I thought of Aaron and Ben, and I thought of the cold night that I had spent with them in the woods. I thought of the doe's slender neck, her soft spots, her vulnerable points. I thought of her twitching ears and her glassy eyes. Then it was Aaron and Ben again, grabbing hold of my mind. Their bodies. Their smells. I thought of my bare thighs on the ground and my scabbed knees the morning after. Then it was the doe again. Her soft spots, her soaked fur. The confession. The Virgin Mary. The question, *Did you bleed?* Then Aaron and Ben, the cold night in the woods, the men golfing, the men laughing, the belt unbuckling, the red cup, the bare thighs, the doe, her slender neck, her soft spots, her broken bones, her blood.

I ran toward the doe at full tilt, and I actually believed that I could catch her. She turned effortlessly on slender legs that floated over the new spring grass. In an instant she had disappeared with the herd into the darkness. I sank down onto my knees and cried. It was the first time that I had ever been afraid of myself.

When I finally walked back to my dorm room, I had enough sense to call my parents. It was the middle of the night, but they answered. Without hesitation, they made the two-hour trek from Cleveland to Steubenville to take me home.

The following day, my mother made an appointment with a psychiatrist. The doctor listened to my symptoms and explained that I was experiencing an episode of mania, which meant that I had bipolar disorder. She prescribed a mood stabilizer and recommended a partial-hospitalization program that involved daily therapy sessions at a Cleveland-based mental health center. I consented to the treatment and moved back in with my parents. After some balking, I finally agreed to leave Franciscan University. I made arrangements to finish my remaining coursework from Cleveland, and I enrolled at a local college the following fall.

Even though the psychiatrist never said that there was a causal relationship between the rape and the mania, the proximity of the two has always stood out to me. Doctors still don't know exactly what causes bipolar disorder, but they believe that three main factors contribute to its onset: a genetic predisposition, a biological predisposition, and environmental circumstances. People who eventually develop the disease may have relatives with mental illness, or they may have biological differences in the structure or function of their brains. Additionally, they may have a past history of trauma, such as childhood sexual abuse, or they may have an acute trauma, known as an environmental trigger, that prompts the onset of the disease. Any combination of these factors can cause bipolar disorder to manifest. The more factors you have, the more likely you are to become sick.

At the time of the rape, I already had two strikes against me. I had a genetic predisposition for mental illness. My grandmother was bipolar, and my uncle was schizophrenic, and my father had suffered from anxiety for most of his life. It's also likely that I had a biological predisposition. I tended toward emotional extremes as a child, and I was prone to melancholy as a teen. I may have developed bipolar disorder as a result of biology and genetics alone, but there is another possibility. Aaron and Ben may have provided the trigger that set my mind spinning. There is a chance, however slight, that the rape was the third strike that sealed my fate.

Granted, I'll never know if those men caused the disease to manifest, and there's no sense in wondering for too long about maybes and what-ifs. The cause doesn't change the reality of what happened. I went to college wanting to save the world, but I left with a disease that would ravage me for years. I was struck hard by the realization that the possibilities weren't as endless as I had come to believe. Men could crush you without suffering any repercussions. Tribunals could damn you with their verdict. Justice wasn't merely blind—she was also indifferent and weak—and even God couldn't save the dreams that he had once instilled in me. Maybe he could preserve something as simple as a sandcastle, but changing the tide was a far cry from fixing the bigger inequities that existed around every corner.

More than a decade after the rape, I learned that Franciscan University continued to mishandle cases of sexual violence. There were other women, like me, who were told that they were responsible for injustices done to them. One woman went to college administrators after a man forcibly restrained her. The man bit her, kneed her in the groin, and then stuck his hand down her pants. The college told the woman that the event didn't qualify as sexual assault. Another woman contacted the same administrators after a male student continued to make aggressive, unwanted advances. Sometimes the man grabbed the woman's hand and placed it over his pants, forcing her to feel his erection. The administrators dissuaded the woman from contacting police. They also required that she see a counselor to make sure she "wasn't bipolar." They insinuated that she wouldn't be taken seriously if she was.

When I came forward about my own sexual assault, I did so to protect those women. I believed it was my duty to take a stand. I thought that my voice would actually have an effect, and yet so many women had been victimized since then. Over the course of those years, I often listened to older Americans describe the shortcomings of young people like me. They said we were entitled and self-absorbed. We didn't have a good work ethic. We wanted instant gratification, and we lacked the discipline and follow-through of those who came before us. Such criticisms always miss the point. My generation was raised to believe that we had the power to make a difference—*if you dream it, you can do it*—but our idealism got swallowed up in a country ravaged by abuse and inertia. The ambitions of our childhoods no longer seemed feasible. All of our best intentions had nowhere to go, so they burrowed inward and turned sour, giving birth to a deeply rooted egotism that was as delicate as glass. In the end, the very same children who wanted to save the world awoke to find that they had gotten lost in a world where they didn't know how to save themselves.

As I sat beside the blue flames of the Blast Furnace, I took off the yellow hard hat and turned it over in my hands. My thirtieth birthday was only a few days away, and I wasn't sure what I had to show for it. I hadn't joined a convent. I hadn't saved souls or cured poverty. I hadn't made a positive impact on anything, and I feared that the yellow hard hat would lull me into apathy. Maybe I would stop trying to make a difference. Maybe I would accept the inertia and shrug, content with the niceties that my paycheck could buy. That was the reason I balked when I first donned the hard hat in front of Sleepy Bear. I valued what the hat represented—I felt a deep affection for the mill and its people, and I knew that I was lucky to be a member of a union—but I was also afraid of what the hard hat meant in my own life. Not only had I fallen short of what my younger self had set out to do, I had also lost the will to keep striving after the ideals that had been so important to me as a child. My hopes of changing the world had morphed into hopes of a bigger salary. My faith in my own potential had withered. Even the hatchback I had purchased at a killer price from the sleazy salesman suggested that I'd lost myself. The girl I used to be would have paid a higher price out of principle, but that girl was hiding somewhere. She had disappeared from view, and I was worried that the long hours in the mill would keep me too distracted to find her again.

10

I didn't have any desire to celebrate my birthday, but Tony insisted on a night out. He took me to a local wine bar for a few drinks before dinner, but he seemed jumpy and nervous when we walked through the door. He practically bowled me over before grabbing my arm and ushering me into a private room on the side of the building.

My stomach sank when I saw that both of our families were gathered together for a party. Our parents sat on couches near a fireplace, and Tony's younger sister sat with her husband in a set of matching wingback chairs. Laurel hadn't been able to make it—she lived in Michigan with her husband—so the party was small and intimate. Even so, I wasn't looking forward to a gathering held in honor of my first thirty years. I felt that all I had to show for them was poverty, underemployment, and the constant upheaval of my bipolar moods.

I walked into the room, trying my best to act chipper. Tony had orchestrated the whole event. He'd bought pizza and Thai food for dinner because it was our tradition to eat both at the same time, and he ordered a cassata cake, my favorite, for dessert. The room he rented for the occasion was stately and old-fashioned. The maroon wallpaper was decorated with tiny flowers, and the antique couches had a Victorian flair. A warm glow emanated from the fireplace, and the feet on the coffee table looked like tiny claws.

Someone poured me a glass of wine, and I sat down on a couch next to Tony.

"How do you feel now that your twenties are gone?" my mother asked playfully.

"Okay, I guess," I said, forcing a smile.

"Are you proud of what you've accomplished in thirty years?" Tony's sister asked.

She was six years older than me, which meant that she had been born right at the tail end of Generation X. Her job suited her well, and she owned a house. She had two daughters in middle school, and I had to fight back tears when I answered her question.

"No," I said. "I didn't accomplish everything I thought I would."

I grew quiet and sipped my wine. It was the first time Tony's family had met mine, and everyone talked excitedly as they got to know one another. Our parents laughed. Tony chattered about *Star Trek*. Everyone around me filled the silence, and I felt more and more invisible with each passing moment.

When it came time to open gifts, Tony gave me a large present shaped like a flat rectangle. I removed the paper to reveal an original black-and-white photograph of a horse. It was absolutely stunning. Most of the portrait was dominated by shadow, creating a landscape of black broken only by the horse's head. The animal stared forward with fearless eyes, and the right side of his face gently faded into the darkness that engulfed the rest of him.

I had loved horses since I was a child, so the picture was perfectly suited for me. I would come to cherish it over the following weeks, but I was filled with sadness when I looked at it for the first time. The image of the horse was slipping away into the picture's black background. His power and potential had been overtaken by something cold and indifferent, and it seemed like the same thing was happening to me.

Tears kept welling in my eyes as the party went on, so Tony took me outside to get some air. A cold November wind swept through the street, and the trees on the sidewalk were dressed in little white lights.

Tony looked at me with concern. His hands were tucked into his pockets to ward off the chill, and he pitched forward slightly, as if the breeze had pushed him off-balance.

"Did I do something wrong?" he asked.

I stared down at the pavement, kicking at a piece of concrete that had come loose. Around me, the night felt magical. The crisp air. The stars in a clear sky. The twinkle of the lights on the trees.

"You didn't do anything wrong," I said without lifting my eyes.

"Are you sure?"

I felt guilty as I wiped a tear that was rolling down my cheek, and my selfishness wasn't lost on me. The party was the most thoughtful thing that anyone had ever done for me, but I couldn't let myself enjoy it. The narcissism that was so notorious in my generation wouldn't be held at bay, and I had spent most of the party wallowing in self-pity.

"I promise," I said. "You didn't do anything wrong. Really, I mean it. The party is wonderful, and I'm so grateful that you put it all together."

"Then why are you so sad?" Tony asked, pulling his hands from his pockets and putting them on my shoulders.

I didn't know how to explain it to him in a way that didn't sound petty or melodramatic. I hadn't done anything important with my life and it was barreling ahead nonetheless. I didn't become a nun, and I wasn't saving the world, and I technically hadn't even received my master's degree. I wasn't a professor or a teacher, which would have at least given me a sense of purpose, and one of my parents' friends recently congratulated me for abandoning my unrealistic childhood ambitions in favor of something more practical.

"Please, tell me what's wrong," Tony said.

"I don't know," I told him. "I'm just disappointed in myself, I guess. I feel like I should have done more by now, and I'm worried that I'll get stuck in the mill."

After six months as a steelworker, I already felt reliant on the mill's income. I found myself wanting more and more money, even though I had plenty, and I quickly developed a taste for spending. The new car I'd bought after totaling mine in the accident came with a hefty monthly payment and a higher insurance bill. I had cleared up some outstanding debts, and I was finally making payments on my student loans. I no longer shopped the clearance rack at clothing stores. I was still in the process of moving out of my squirrel-infested apartment and into one with a vaulted ceiling, and I was also spending thousands of dollars to replace all of my secondhand furniture. I didn't hesitate to buy expensive French cheeses at the grocery store. I paid for a lawn service for my parents' yard. I no longer felt a need to keep track of every penny. Through it all, a little voice in my head kept repeating the advice I had been given before I started in the mill: *People get used to the money. They buy new cars and new houses. Before you know it, they're trapped.*

"Don't worry," Tony said, ever gracious despite my sullenness. "I think the mill will be a springboard for you. It's been a blessing for the short term, but you're not going to get stuck there."

He drew me in for a long hug, and I relished the reassurance of his embrace. Tony was always calm and confident in the face of my fears, which helped to ease my mind for a moment. I looked up at him and summoned a smile. There was still a cake that needed to be cut, and there was more wine that needed to be passed around. The party wasn't yet over, and I wanted to enjoy what was left of it.

"It's cold out here," I said. "Let's go back inside."

Two days after my birthday I went back to the squirrel-infested apartment to pack up some boxes. The landlord had patched the hole that the squirrel had breached, promising me that it was just a fluke, so I went over everything with bleach and decided to stay the night. When I woke up early the next morning, I stared at the clock. It was Election Day and I wanted to vote before the polls got too crowded, but I couldn't bring myself to get out of bed.

A deep depression had overtaken me, and my mind raced. My thoughts were barely coherent, and they flew through my head so quickly that I couldn't grab ahold of them. I thought about the mill, my hard hat, my unrealized goals. I thought about the laundry that needed to be done, the bills that needed to be paid, the groceries that needed to be bought. I thought about taking a shower, which seemed a herculean task, and I thought about the minutes that were ticking slowly away.

I was supposed to meet Tony after voting—he had the day off for the election—and I was already running behind. Like always, Tony wanted to maximize his time away from work. I didn't feel like maximizing anything at the moment, and I didn't know if I had the energy to put on a smile to hide my worsening mood.

I stared at the clock in a state of paralysis, and I did what I often do when a bipolar episode begins raging in full force. I berated myself for being lazy and dumb.

You're a piece of shit, I thought to myself. *You're a failure. You don't deserve to be alive.*

I said the types of things that I wouldn't say to my worst enemies, and I worked myself into a fit of hysterical tears. My back stiffened and my chest shook, and I knew that the tears needed to be stopped in a pinch if I had any hope of making it to the polls.

In that agitated state, it was impossible to calm myself with the coping mechanisms I had been taught over the years, which meant that there was only one way to put a quick end to the sadness. It wasn't ideal, but I didn't have any other options. I needed to get up out of bed and maximize the day with Tony, so I raised my hand and hit myself on the side of the head.

The light in the room grew momentarily brighter, and a dull ache spread across my scalp. I took a few more blows at my temples and cheeks, and the sadness began to ease. My tears stopped. My thoughts no longer raced. In an instant, my mood settled back down to baseline.

It was a trick I had learned after years with bipolar disorder. Whatever neurotransmitters my body released in response to pain had the ability to calm my mind long enough for me to function, and the physical aftermath of a blow to the head was far easier to hide than other forms of self-harm. Any bruises would be covered by my hair, and a slap on the cheek or temple rarely left anything more than a red mark that could be blamed on facial scrubs and chemical peels.

After the tears stopped, I quickly got out of bed and showered. I went to my polling center and cast my vote before heading over to Tony's house for the day.

Shortly after I arrived, we hopped in his car and went out for coffee together. As usual, Tony played electronic dance music in the car. The miraculous effects of hitting my head were already wearing off, and I was finding it difficult to keep my sadness and irritability at bay.

"Can't we listen to something other than techno?" I snapped.

"It's not techno," Tony said. "It's house music."

"Well, can't we change it? We always listen to this electronic stuff. I just can't handle it today."

With a huff, Tony turned the volume down on the radio and we drove the rest of the way in silence.

Later we tried playing a game of dominoes. I was losing miserably, and my competitive nature got the best of me.

"Why do you have to annihilate me every time?" I pouted.

Tony rolled his eyes and started to put the dominoes back in the box.

"What are you doing?" I asked. "We're not done."

"Let's just stop playing," he said.

"Why are you so angry at me?"

Tony looked up and shrugged.

"You're the one who's always angry with me," he said.

After dominoes we went for a hike in a nearby park. As we walked, Tony started talking about finances.

"If you just put aside a little bit from each paycheck," he said, "you can build up a pretty good savings account."

Tony had been talking in a general way about a theoretical *you*, but I took the words personally. There was something in his voice that struck me as condescending, and I thought his haughtiness was directed at me. I didn't need a lecture about saving money. Even though I was spending more than I ever had before, I was also putting huge chunks of cash into a savings account. In six months' time, I had accumulated more than enough money to cover my rent for a year, which seemed pretty respectable for someone who had started with nothing.

"Listen," I said to Tony, "I know how to handle my money."

"I wasn't saying that you didn't know how to handle it," he said.

"Really? That's kind of what it sounded like to me."

Tony clenched his jaw and let out a sigh.

"I just can't do anything right, can I?" he said.

I didn't respond, and we finished the hike without saying a word.

My bipolar disorder was warping the world, and I was seeing hostility and aggression where none existed. The most innocent comments became biting insults, and I reacted like an open wound without a scab. Even the slightest pressure sent me reeling, and it was difficult to stem the pain once it began. While it's impossible to know if my ennui at the birthday party and my irritability with Tony were symptomatic of a mixed episode, it's clear my overblown reactions certainly were. The two halves of my disease were clashing with disastrous effect, and Tony was taking the brunt of the punishment.

Our day together was peppered with small spats, but we reconciled long enough to get through a peaceful dinner. Since Tony cooked the meal, I did the dishes afterward. I was in the midst of scrubbing silverware when the preliminary results of the election started scrolling across the television screen.

Tony sat down in the living room with a cup of tea. His house was small and open enough that the entire downstairs felt like one giant room, which meant that I could still see him from my position in front of the sink.

"Who's winning?" I asked with a soapy plate in my hand.

"Well, it's still early, but it looks like Hillary has a good lead."

"Thank God," I said, rinsing the plate and setting it aside to dry.

As I strained to hear the newscasters over the sound of the running tap, Tony turned to me from the living room.

"Do you love me?" he said with a smile.

"A little," I told him. "Do you love me?"

"I guess."

When I finally finished the dishes, I curled up with Tony on the couch. We watched the election coverage for a while, and Scout sidled up next to me. The little black pit bull wanted a piece of the fuzzy blanket I had laid across my lap and insisted that I sacrifice a corner for her. When she got comfortable, she quickly fell into a deep sleep. Her paws twitched, as if running, and tiny yips escape from her closed mouth.

The dog's dreams were contagious, and my eyes began to grow

heavy. While I didn't need to be back at work in the morning, there were night shifts on the horizon. I would have to pull a twenty-four-hour turnaround soon, and I was still trying to recover from the shifts I had just completed.

Even though most of the electoral votes hadn't yet been reported, it seemed like Hillary would win, just as all the pundits had expected. There was no sense in waiting up any longer, so I slowly climbed off the couch without rousing the dog.

"I think I'm going to go to bed," I whispered to Tony.

His brow twisted with concern.

"Are you mad at me?" he asked.

That sentence had become the refrain of our relationship. We were always asking it of each other throughout the day, and it didn't really matter if the answer was yes or no. The question itself was exhausting for both of us.

"No," I said. "I'm not mad. I'm just tired."

I kissed Tony good night and went to bed under the belief that the first female president would be elected while I slept.

The following morning, Tony woke me before he left for work. I opened my eyes for a moment, but I was too groggy to raise my head from the pillow.

"Have a good day," he said, kissing me on the forehead.

As he backed away, I closed my eyes and started to drift back into sleep. I listened to the familiar sound of Tony's footsteps, and then I suddenly remembered that it was the day after the election.

"Wait," I said without opening my eyes. "Who won?"

"Trump did."

I pulled the edge of the comforter close to my cheek. "Really?"

"Yeah," Tony said, "I was surprised too."

"What about Ohio?" I asked. "Did Ohio vote for him?"

"Yep, it sure did."

Tony gave me another kiss on the forehead before he left for the day, and I fell back asleep for a few hours. When I finally got up, I showered quickly and headed back to my apartment. I did a few loads of laundry and packed my books into boxes. I didn't give much thought to Clinton or Trump. Life chugged along with its usual burdens, distracting me from thoughts about the presidency. It wasn't until much later, when I went to buy groceries for the week, that the results of the election finally hit me.

As I walked through the automatic doors of the grocery store, I thought about my early-morning conversation with Tony. Donald Trump was the president-elect. Millions of Americans had voted for him, and my own state had leaned in Trump's direction.

I quickly grabbed a cart and headed for the peaches. As I tested each one for ripeness, I glanced around at the other people who were also picking through the produce. A plump woman in a floral blouse was bagging tomatoes. A gray-haired man in plaid was looking at the celery. A young man with gauged ears was feigning interest in the apples so that he could size up a young woman who was holding a cantaloupe in each hand.

For the first time in my life, I looked at my fellow Americans with suspicion and disdain. I eyed up the people in the produce section. I wanted to know which ones were my enemies. Did the woman bagging tomatoes secretly hate me? Was the man near the celery a bigot?

Of course, I didn't need to go to the grocery store to find Trump supporters. There were already two people in my life who had certainly voted for him in the election. My parents were still die-hard Republicans, and even a reality-star billionaire couldn't shake them from their views. At one point during the campaign, I went over to their house for dinner. We gathered around their kitchen table, passing a bottle of red wine that had started going to my head.

"I don't understand how Christian people can support a guy like Trump," I said, picking at the salad my mother had made.

I looked across the table at my father, who squared his shoulders. A smug look spread across his face as he took a sip of wine. My mother, on the other hand, looked down at her dinner plate. Her political views had always been more tempered than those of my father, and she could sense a fight coming.

"I just don't think Trump is very Christlike," I said. "Did you hear what he said about grabbing women by the pussy? I don't think Jesus would be on board with that."

I put down my fork and ran my fingers over the smooth black granite of my parents' kitchen table. It was flecked with tiny specks of silver that reminded me of the graphite that was peppered throughout the mill.

"Oh, you're talking about that stupid *Access Hollywood* thing," my father huffed, leaning back and crossing his arms. "You can't judge a person for a comment he made a long time ago. Besides, it's just locker room talk. He didn't mean anything by it."

I pitched forward in my seat, letting the chicken cutlets on my plate grow cold. My father and I were both itching for a fight, and it didn't matter that my mother had spent all day preparing one of our favorite meals.

"But Trump did mean something by it," I said. "He meant that women are objects to be used at his discretion. He was saying that wealthy, privileged men have the right to treat women with disrespect. It's that attitude of male entitlement that leads to a culture of rape and harassment, and I'm surprised it's something that a self-proclaimed Christian would defend."

"What about Bill Clinton?" my father asked, nearly spitting the words at me. "I think he was pretty disrespectful toward women, don't you?"

My fist tightened around the stem of my wineglass, and I finished the last swig that was left inside. It went down easy, tasting rich and peppery. My father had brought it out just for dinner. He knew wine like he knew guns—with precision and certainty—and he liked to bring the best bottles to the table when I came over.

"We're not talking about Bill Clinton," I said. "We're talking about Trump, and it's not just his view of women that's the problem. It's the whole package. He's hostile to minorities. He's not interested in protecting the environment. Aren't Christians supposed to treat everyone with compassion? Aren't they supposed to be stewards of the Earth?"

I poured another glass of wine and sat back in my seat. My mother listened quietly with her hands folded on the table, and my father seemed to grow taller in his chair.

"Oh," he said, "all of that environmental stuff is just a big conspiracy meant to line someone's pockets."

"Whose pockets are being lined, though?" I asked.

"The elites," my father told me. He picked up his fork and shoved a big piece of chicken into his mouth.

I could feel myself growing angrier with each exchange. "Who are these elites?"

"They're the ones with all of the money and power," my father said, still chewing. "People like George Soros. They're the ones who benefit from the conspiracy."

"But it's not a conspiracy," I told him, throwing my hands in the air in exasperation. "It's science. At the end of the day, it shouldn't even matter if you don't believe in climate change. You're supposed to be a Christian person. If God really gave people dominion over the Earth, then we should do everything in our power to protect it. Even the pope says that we should try to minimize our environmental impact."

My father bit into another piece of chicken, which rendered him speechless for a moment, so my mother chimed in from her corner of the table.

"Oh," she said softly, "we don't really like this pope."

"Yeah," my father agreed after gulping down his food, "this pope is just another Marxist who's pushing a leftist agenda."

"But he's the pope," I said, my voice trembling. My parents had always been the most devout people I knew, and I couldn't quite fathom their sudden lack of loyalty. "You believe that the pope was chosen by the Holy Spirit to lead the Church."

"Yes," my mother told me, skewering a tomato with her fork, "but the will of the Holy Spirit has to be translated through men, and men are fallible. They can misinterpret the message."

I buried my face in my wineglass, trying to soothe my growing unease. Trump was shaking everything, even my parents' faith, and I wanted to get through to them. After a few more sips of wine, I put the glass aside and glanced around the table.

"Did you ever think that you're misinterpreting Trump?" I said with every ounce of calm I could muster. "Did you ever think that you see him as something good when he's actually the opposite?"

Neither of my parents flinched. My father ate a few green beans from his plate, and my mother shrugged.

"Well," she said, "Trump isn't a perfect person, but he can help with the abortion issue. That's really what we need to focus on right now."

I took another sip of wine and cut my chicken into tiny pieces. Both of my parents were waiting for me to retort, but I didn't have the energy to make any more appeals to reason or religion. There was something else nagging at me, and it had very little to do with politics or Christianity. When I first heard Trump say that he could grab women by the pussy if he wanted, I thought back to the aftermath of my own rape. The locker-room banter that my father defended felt reminiscent of the judgment I had received at Franciscan University. The tribunal said that the men and I were both to blame, which meant that my ability to consent didn't really matter much.

After leaving the Franciscan University of Steubenville, I enrolled at a much more liberal college on the east side of Cleveland. During my time there, I befriended a lot of Democrats. As it turned out, they weren't as scary as I had been led to believe. In fact, they were generally reasonable and well-informed. They believed in social justice, and they acted the part. They put together renditions of *The Vagina Monologues* every winter, and they were involved in an ALLIES club that advocated for the LGBTQIA community. They marched for AIDS awareness. They did volunteer work. They recognized the needs of the marginalized and oppressed, and they tried their best to use their talents to make positive changes.

All my life, I had dreamed of helping the poor and feeding the sick. That was partly the reason I'd decided to become a nun. I wanted to do something big and important with my life, and I was led to believe that prayer, contemplation, and antiabortion rallies were the best way to do so. People said that God would take care of the rest, except he didn't. These liberals, on the other hand, actually seemed to be making a difference, or at least trying to. So I decided to get involved in the women's rights groups and the ALLIES group and the AIDS walk. For the first time in my life, it actually felt like I was doing something that mattered.

Through this, I found a group of people who talked openly about the type of violence that I had experienced. They acknowledged what had been done to me, and they tried to raise awareness to prevent it from happening to others. In the conservative world at the Franciscan University of Steubenville, I'd found only judgment, abandonment, and injustice. In this new world, I found acceptance, validation, and support. It didn't sound like an evil leftist plot meant to indoctrinate me.

As I sat with my parents around the dinner table, I asked the real question that was on my mind.

"How can you support a man like Trump when your own daughter has been raped?"

A heavy silence fell over the kitchen after I asked the question. We all picked at our plates and sipped at our wine for what felt like hours. Eventually someone changed the subject. For the rest of our meal we talked about trivial things. We discussed our plans for Thanksgiving, and we raved about the chocolate pie my mother had bought for dessert. There was a lingering tension below the surface, though. Both of my parents had witnessed the damage caused when men felt entitled to grab someone by the pussy. My mother had wiped away my tears after the rape, and my father had given me a golden necklace. Now, twelve years later, Trump was a poster boy for male privilege, and my parents weren't just willing to support him. They were ready to forsake the pope for him, and yet they ignored the daughter who had been hurt by the misogynistic views that Trump condoned.

When I got in my car after dinner, I couldn't shake the feeling that I had been abandoned by the very people who were supposed to love me most.

In the weeks following the election, my mental health took a rapid turn for the worse. I could barely get out of bed on most mornings, and I often found myself growing teary-eyed for no reason. My fights with Tony intensified. My memories of Aaron and Ben kept bubbling to the surface, reminding me of the damage that had set me on a path toward the mill. My mind felt like gunpowder mixed with broken glass, and my obsession with belly buttons turned into an obsession with Trump. I read news about him with the same vigor that had once been reserved for articles about urachal cancer, and I fixated on his tweets. The world itself began to feel hostile and unforgiving. Every-thing had been turned on its head. A reality star was going to be pres-ident, and the people I loved had voted for him.

As the days wore on, even my visual perception of reality began to change. Tree branches became monstrous arms waving in the breeze, and the dead leaves that clung to their fingertips looked like razor-blades or stained glass, depending on the light. The yellow lines on the highway jumped off the road like ribbons, and the serrated clouds all had bloated stomachs. The world felt sharp and jagged in my chaotic mind, and I was a soft, malleable thing getting snagged around the edges.

Through it all, I continued to work my shifts at the mill, but climb-ing out of bed had become a constant challenge. I started hitting my-self more and more often, and the quick jolt of adrenaline would give me enough motivation to brush my teeth and get to work on time. Otherwise, my days were spent in misery.

One morning, I woke up at Tony's house before a shift in the mill. I tiptoed through the dark, so as not to wake him, and put on a pair of jeans and a bra. I went downstairs half dressed with the rest of my clothes in hand. When I got to the living room, I slipped into my shirt and collapsed on the couch.

As I sat there and stared at the wall, my mind raged like one of the huge machines that roared inside the mill. Those machines groaned and squealed and spit steam into the air, and they operated with an intensity too powerful to be steadied by sheer force of will. If you got too close to their moving parts, they would suck you up and hold you helpless in their jaws. That was exactly how I felt as I stared at the dark living room. I wondered if the Devil had gotten inside me again, filling my head with pranks and whispers. I got the feeling that the furniture was taunting me. The television had a sinister look in its eye. The blinking red light on the fire detector was keeping track of my movements, and the stereo hissed crude insults that I could just barely hear. It felt like I was caught inside the spinning gears of something too powerful to be tamed, so I bent forward and hit myself on the head over and over.

I was giving myself a violent blow to the temple when Tony's dog came bounding down the stairs. She jumped up on the couch beside me and began licking my face, trembling slightly at the sight of my distress. I gently pushed her away and hit myself with a strength I didn't know I had. Every strike cracked against my skull, echoing through the quiet house.

The dog watched, anxious and confused.

"It's okay," I said, gasping through my tears. My words only made the dog tremble more, so I ran my hand over her head to calm her.

"What's going on down here?" Tony asked, walking into the living room. He wasn't wearing his glasses, so he squinted with tired eyes.

I sat up, startled. I hadn't heard him approach, and I felt like a child who had been caught setting fire to the curtains.

"Nothing's going on," I said with exaggerated nonchalance.

Tony stood over me and looked down at the tears that were still on my cheeks. I grabbed my socks and started fiddling with them.

"What's wrong?" Tony said. "Are you okay?"

"Yeah, I'm okay," I told him, my voice quaking.

Tony looked over at the dog, who had jumped off the couch and moved to the corner of the room. She was lying with her head between her paws, and her whole body was shaking uncontrollably.

"What was that noise?" Tony asked. "It was really loud. I could hear it upstairs."

"I don't know," I said. I twisted the socks in my hands, running my fingertips over the soft fabric. "I didn't hear anything."

Tony crossed his arms and wrinkled his brow. "I don't think you're telling me the truth. What were you doing down here?"

He glanced over at the dog. She got up and ran to him before pressing her chest into his knee.

"Did you do something to Scout?" Tony asked.

I sighed loudly, offended by what he was suggesting.

"No," I said. "I would never hurt the dog."

"Then what was that noise? Be honest with me."

I slowly put my socks over my feet, wondering what lie I could possibly tell. When I couldn't delay my response any longer, I looked up and stiffened my shoulders.

"I was hitting myself, okay?" I said defensively. "Are you happy?"

Tony shook his head, as if trying to remove a bug from his ear. "What did you say?"

"I was hitting myself. That's the noise you heard."

"Why would you do that?"

I crossed my legs and shrugged. "It calms me down."

Tony paused for a moment and ran his hand over the dog's back. Then he stared at me with dismay.

"We have to talk about this," he said. "I'm worried about you."

I stood up suddenly and headed to the front door, where I slipped on a pair of boots.

"Well, I can't talk now," I said, tying my laces slowly to avoid meeting Tony's eyes. "I'm running late. I have to get to work."

"Well, we'll talk about it later then."

"Yeah, okay," I told him, although I had no desire to talk about anything.

I quickly walked out the door and got in my car. The blows I'd given myself hadn't done the trick, so I drove to work in tears. I could barely hold myself together for the duration of my shift, and I went to the bathroom several times just to sit on the toilet and cry. With each coil I banded, I became more and more convinced that the Devil had possessed me.

After my workday ended, I went back to Tony's house for the night. We had an awkward dinner filled with long silences, and the world hit me like a freight train as I scrubbed the dishes. Everything around me seemed to be moving amazingly fast, as if someone had pressed the pause button on my body while the rest of time accelerated at double the speed. When every dish was finally washed, I sat down with Tony on the couch.

"We have to talk," he said.

"Can't we just forget it?" I asked. I actually believed it was the type of thing we could sweep under the rug. "I won't do it again. I promise."

"No," Tony answered. His voice sounded measured and stern. "We have to talk."

I sat on my hands and sank into the couch, preparing for a lecture.

"I don't know what's been going on with you lately," Tony began, "but I don't think this relationship is healthy for either one of us. I don't think that I can be what you need me to be."

"Wait, what?" I said. His words were moving too fast for me to process, and they all turned into a garbled mess when they reached my ears. "I don't understand."

"I know that you don't want to be in a relationship that isn't moving forward," Tony told me, "and I don't think I can see us moving forward after all the trouble we've been having."

"Hold on," I said, shaking my head. "Are you breaking up with me?"

"Yeah, I guess I am."

I exhaled sharply and looked up at the ceiling. "Holy shit. I don't need this right now."

I hadn't expected our conversation to take such a sudden turn, and my mind wasn't working well enough to deal with what was happening. The blank screen of the television across the room glared at me. Everything felt sinister and unreal.

"Holy shit," I said again. "You're dumping me?"

"I still want to be friends," Tony crooned, as if friendship could lessen the blow.

With that, every ounce of willpower slipped out of me. A delicate barrier had been holding my emotions at bay for weeks, and it finally shattered. My world was falling apart, and I no longer had the ability to stop myself from adding to the disaster. I went upstairs and closed myself into the bathroom, where I sank to the floor and cried. I hit myself on the head, but it no longer had any effect. I needed to release the pressure that had built up inside my mind, so I grabbed a porcelain toothbrush holder and chucked it at the wall.

"What are you doing in there?" Tony yelled, trying to open the door.

"Nothing."

The toothbrush holder had shattered into tiny shards, which I tried to gather in my hands. Tony forced his way into the bathroom and looked down at me, running his hands over his head in shock.

"Leave it," he said. "Just leave it."

I dropped the broken pieces to the ground and pushed past him, storming into the bedroom. I curled up on the bed and sobbed while Tony kneeled down next to me. He tried to take my hands, but I pulled them away.

"You're scaring me," he said. "You're not acting like yourself."

When I looked into his eyes, I was suddenly struck by the urge to laugh. I had tried so hard to keep everything together, and it was crumbling despite my best efforts. My failure struck me as insanely funny just then, so I looked Tony in the eye and started to chuckle softly.

"None of it matters," I said, as if the words were a punch line. "None of it fucking matters."

Tony's eyes widened with fear. He might as well have been looking at a wild bull that was ready to charge. "Are you laughing right now?"

His question only made me laugh harder.

"Stop it," he said, touching my shoulder. "You're scaring me."

"Oh, I'm scaring you?" I asked, nearly out of breath from tears and laughter. "This is scary?"

"Yes," Tony pleaded. "I don't even recognize you. You're not yourself. You're not you."

"Of course I'm not myself," I said. I was now entirely convinced that the Devil had gotten into my chest. He was the one laughing, not me. "I'm not myself," I said again. "I'm not me."

"What are you talking about?" Tony asked. Scout had sidled up to his shoulder, as if trying to diffuse the situation. "Why do you keep laughing?"

I didn't have enough sense to explain that my disease was taking hold of me and turning me into a different person, and I didn't know how to tell him that I was losing control of everything so quickly that I needed someone to take me to a hospital.

All of a sudden I stopped laughing and grew sullen.

"I don't know what I'm talking about," I told him. "I'm just going to leave."

Tony stood up and took a few steps backward, giving me space. "Why don't you spend the night?" he said. "I'm worried about you."

I swung my legs over the side of the bed and looked him in the eye.

"Are we going to forget everything that happened and start over tomorrow?" I asked.

Tony's brow twisted above his glasses. He seemed confused. "No, of course we can't forget this."

"Then I'm leaving," I told him sharply.

I rose from the bed and bolted out of the room, heading back downstairs. Tony followed behind, begging me to stay, but I refused. I didn't want to spend the night in a house that would remind me of everything I had lost, so I put on my coat and darted toward the door.

Tony stood on the other side of the living room with his arms crossed. The rims of his eyes had turned red, although he hadn't yet started to cry. Scout crept over to Tony's leg and pushed herself into him, her black fur glistening under the lights.

"What about the clothes you have upstairs?" Tony asked.

I put on my boots as fast as I could, nearly toppling over in my rush to get out. "Just throw them away."

"Won't you please stay tonight?"

"No," I told him, opening the door on the cold December night.

As I turned to walk outside, Tony called to me one last time.

"Wait, please, hold on," he said, his voice on the edge of tears. "Can you just wait a second so I can ask you one thing?"

I couldn't tell what kind of question was lingering in his head, but I steadied myself and closed the door. We stood in silence for a moment, and I desperately hoped that he would ask me to forget the whole thing. I wanted him to say it was all a big mistake. Everything could be forgiven and forgotten. The breakup was just a huge joke.

"What is it?" I asked.

Tony took a few steps forward with Scout close on his heels. "If you're really leaving, then can I get my key back?"

My stomach dropped, and I had to bite my lip to keep from crying. It felt like someone had split me open and thrown an anchor into my chest, and I wondered if my body would sink down into the floor. I searched for his key, which was mixed in with my own, but my hands were shaking too much to get a good grasp on anything.

"You know what?" I said, still fighting with the keys. "Fuck you."

"What?" Tony asked.

I brought my eyes to his.

"Fuck you. Fuck you."

He was abandoning me when I needed him most, and I felt more alone than I ever had before. My friendships had taken a back burner to my job, and my sister lived five hours away, and my parents had cast a vote against me. Tony felt like the one beacon of support in my life, and now he was leaving too.

I handed Tony my keys, and he took his from the ring before giving them back.

"Please," he said, "just stay tonight."

I opened the door and stepped over the threshold, shaking my head. "I'm not staying."

I turned toward Tony one last time, and we looked at each other for a beat. A cold winter wind blew into the house, and I could see that he was crying.

"I love you," he said.

There was desperation in his voice, and I felt it too. Neither of us had expected things to end so quickly and violently, and it seemed as if we were both being swept toward a conclusion, like leaves on a flooding river. We wanted to cling to something—we wanted to slow ourselves down—but we couldn't. The water was moving too fast for us to get our bearings, and the only thing we could have held on to was each other.

"I love you," Tony said again.

"Yeah, okay," I told him. Then I slammed the door.

When I got into my car, I drove aimlessly through Tony's neighborhood with the music blaring. I didn't know where to go. I didn't want to spend the night alone in my apartment, and I felt too disconnected from my parents to show up on their doorstep. It was well past midnight, which meant that I needed to be at the mill in a few hours, and I knew I wouldn't be able to sleep after what had just happened.

My mind raced as I sped along the sleepy residential streets, and a light snow fell onto the wet pavement. I was sick of feeling alone, and I was tired of building myself up only to have everything torn down again by my disease. I had yet to find a medication that controlled my symptoms without causing disastrous side effects, and I didn't know if I had the strength or the willpower to recover again. It felt like I had gotten lost somewhere inside my mind, and I was still convinced that a demon had wheedled his way into my head in the hopes of setting off an Armageddon. I needed to push the Devil out, so I drove to a nearby park that overlooked Lake Erie.

I could hear the waves crashing against a break wall as I got out of the car and headed toward the shore. Every wave sent a spray of water into the air, covering the surrounding area in a thick layer of ice. The moonlight reflected on the frozen ground, and the trees and bushes that lined the lake looked as if they had been formed in glass.

I walked up to the break wall and let the huge bursts of water wash over me. They quickly drenched my hair and soaked my jacket, and I laid myself down on the snow-covered shore, pressing my cheek against the ice. Someone had once told me that hypothermia was an easy death. You were supposed to slip into a delirious sleep, but sleep seemed very far away. My fingers and toes were being pricked by needles, and my entire body shivered in protest against the cold. I gave off steam like something broken, and the rest of the world felt eerily quiet beside the rhythmic swell of the lake. The thin air wasn't heavy enough to stir the glazed trees. The stars stood motionless in a clear black sky. A few intermittent lampposts cast a yellow haze on the ground, and the water kept raining down on me with each new wave.

I stayed beside the lake until tiny icicles formed in my hair, and I didn't move from the ground when the breeze stung my bare neck. I wanted my body to relent and go numb. I craved the deep void that sleep would bring, but something shifted as I waited to fade away. I slowly began to feel like a seamless extension of everything around me. The skin on my forearms was knitted to the trees, the bushes, the sky, the earth. When one piece moved, I could sense its burden. I could feel the pull of the breeze through the branches, the tug of the lake over the break wall, the draw of the horizon under the heavy sky. There was something strangely transcendent about the feeling, even if it was only the result of mania. It seemed as if I could reach out and touch the spirit that held the world together, and I was suddenly struck by a brief moment of clarity. In an instant I realized that I wasn't trying to kill myself because I wanted to die. I was trying to kill myself because I didn't know how to live.

I didn't know how to find contentment in a job that offered me money without meaning, and I didn't know how to manage a disease that divided me into Jekyll and Hyde, and I didn't know how to reconcile the dreams of my childhood with the reality of a steel mill. Despite it all, the deepest part of me still wanted to believe that there was a solution other than self-destruction.

The same impulsiveness that had brought me to the lake made me pick myself up off the ground. Without a second thought, I began walking back to my car. My body moved slowly, and my legs were too cold to coordinate anything faster than a sloppy stagger. When I finally coaxed my fingers to open the car door, I had enough sense to drive myself to an emergency room.

Once inside, the nurse checked me into the computer system and put my belongings in a clear plastic bag. She wheeled me to a hospital room intended for psychiatric patients like me. It consisted of only white walls and a hospital bed. There wasn't a privacy screen, and one wall of the room was made of Plexiglas to allow for easy monitoring.

Another nurse came in to measure my vital signs. She was middle-aged with long dark hair, which was frizzy from being dyed one too many times, and she seemed to have a chip on her shoulder.

"Do you want to call your family?" she asked after recording my blood pressure.

"No," I said, pulling a white blanket over my arms. The election still felt like a wedge between me and my parents, and there was no one else to call.

"Are you sure you don't want to use the phone?" the nurse asked again.

"Well," I told her, "I guess there's one call I have to make."

The nurse checked my pulse and temperature before bringing a portable telephone into the room. She waited with arms crossed while I dialed the number for the mill, leaving a garbled message to let them know that I wouldn't be at work for a few days. When I was finished, the nurse took the phone away and started asking me a few more questions.

"So, what brings you here today?"

"I don't know," I said. "I'm just not doing well. My mind isn't right."

I tried to tell her about my symptoms, but my brain was too jumbled to explain anything accurately. I couldn't find the right words to describe the mixed mania I seemed to be experiencing, and I didn't have the sense to tell her about the months of slowly declining mental health. I didn't tell her about my obsessiveness, my sadness, or the episode by the lake. I didn't mention the swing shifts, which had triggered my symptoms, and I didn't tell her that my mind felt like a wounded animal. During our brief conversation, I only thought to tell her about Tony.

"So your boyfriend broke up with you and you thought that you'd come to the emergency room?" she said, her voice heavy with sarcasm.

Up until that point, I thought there was nothing left inside me to break. Everything awful had already ruptured, but I couldn't have been more wrong. The nurse's dismissive tone cracked open a flood of anger. I was angry at Tony for leaving me. I was angry at my mind for betraying me. I was angry at my parents for their vote, but mostly I was angry at myself. I had failed at the one thing I set out to prove with the mill. My bipolar disorder had gotten in the way of my job, as I feared it would. As I seethed in the hospital bed, staring at the crow's feet that patterned the nurse's smug eyes, I was filled with such rage that I lurched forward and pushed her shoulder as hard as I could.

"Fuck you, lady," I howled. "You don't fucking know shit."

The nurse recoiled and ran out of the room, yelling. "Security! I need a security guard, please."

A burly man dressed in blue came into the room in a matter of seconds, followed by a few other nurses. They tethered my arms to the handles of the hospital bed, and the security guard stood in the corner of the room after everyone else left.

"I don't really need to be guarded," I said to him, trying my best to sound calm. "It was just that nurse. She was kind of a bitch."

"I have to stay," the guard said, picking absently at his fingernails.

I sighed and stared through the Plexiglas wall, noticing a wooden crucifix that was hanging outside my room. The hospital was owned by the Cleveland Clinic, but it had a Catholic heritage. It used to be managed by nuns, and there were still a few sisters who lived on the premises. The crucifix looked like one I used to have as a child. Christ's body was a little too pink, and the streaks of blood that stained his sides were a little too neat. His head hung down gently, as if he'd just nodded off to sleep, and his crown of thorns wouldn't have struck fear into a toddler. As I studied the crucifix, I thought for a moment about what Tony had said before I left. *You're not yourself.* He was right. All of my polish had been stripped away, revealing the raw mess I held inside. I was no longer the sweet little girl who believed that she had an important place in the world, and I wasn't quite sure how to find her again.

It took a few hours before the hospital was able to prepare a place for me in the psych ward, but an orderly finally wheeled me to a room just before dawn. I sat down on the thin mattress of a long low-lying bed and curled up beneath the scratchy white sheets. The open doorway let in a stream of fluorescent light, and a few nurses chattered in the halls. I stared for a while at a tall bureau that loomed in the corner of the room. Its pressboard doors were marred by two tiny holes, which were all that remained of the door handles. There was no doubt that the handles had been unscrewed and hidden away for safety reasons. To the suicidal and depressed, a door handle could look very much like a weapon.

As I lay awake in the childproof room, a man in a hospital gown shuffled past my door. His feet dragged on the linoleum floor, and he stared squarely at the empty air in front of him, singing a song I had never heard before. It sounded like a dirge of sorts.

"Into the darkness we walk, we walk, we walk, we walk," the man sang.

He trudged up and down the hallway, repeating that same line over and over again. His hospital gown was stained with what looked to be gravy, and his curly black hair stood on end. A few streaks of gray could be seen at his temples, giving him a world-weary appearance, and he walked with exceptionally good posture despite the way he lugged his feet behind him.

"Into the darkness we walk, we walk, we walk, we walk."

There was something otherworldly in his eyes as he sang, as if he'd gotten stuck in a trance. Had the halls of the psych ward suddenly become a desert, he could have easily been mistaken for a new messiah.

I listened to the man's song for a while, but the exhaustion of the mill eventually overcame me. I fell asleep to the sound of his voice, and I stayed that way for hours. It was a heavy, dreamless sleep, the likes of which I hadn't had in months. When I awoke, the man had stopped singing. Different voices filled the hallways, and a television played somewhere in the distance.

A young nurse popped her head into my room as I rolled over in bed.

"The doctor is ready to see you now," she said.

I slowly stood up and shuffled over to the door, wrapping my arms around my waist to keep the thin hospital gown securely fastened. The nurse ushered me into a small room where a psychiatrist waited with a file of papers stacked on his desk. He was a middle-aged man and his face was twisted into a perpetual scowl.

"Have a seat," he said without a hint of warmth. There was a vague accent in his voice that sounded Eastern European, as if he'd emigrated to the United States as a child. "What brings you here today?"

I did my best to explain my symptoms while the psychiatrist took notes. I told him about the sadness, the racing thoughts, the self-harm, and the Devil. I told him about Tony and the lake, and I told him about my history with bipolar disorder. When I finished recounting everything that seemed pertinent, the psychiatrist put down his pen and looked me in the eye.

"So what is it about your life that's so horrible?" he said.

I hesitated. I didn't know what else to tell him.

"Come on," he said, looking annoyed. "Tell me. What's so horrible?"

I sat across from him, feeling cold and exposed in my thin hospital gown, and tried to think of the best way to summarize my malaise.

"Well?" the psychiatrist said.

The answer to his question began to feel like a word that I'd forgotten. It was right on the tip of my tongue, just barely out of reach.

"Come on," he goaded, "tell me. What's so horrible?"

"I don't know," I said. "I'm not sure."

"Come on. Tell me."

The man's persistence made my shoulders tense. I pitched forward in my seat while the answer simmered in my chest.

"I just," I said, faltering.

"Yes? Spit it out."

"I just hate living in this fucking country, all right?"

The response surprised me. It slipped out of my mouth with astonishing force, even though I hadn't been thinking about America or my place within it. I sank down into my chair as a brief silence settled over the room.

"How dare you say such a thing?" the psychiatrist boomed. "You live in the best country in the world. You have all of the opportunity you could ask for. How dare you say that you hate living here? Why would you say a thing like that?"

"I don't know," I said. "I just feel trapped."

The psychiatrist rolled his eyes and wrote something in his notes.

There was no doubt in my mind that he was calling me obstinate and resistant, even though I had given him the only response that made sense to me. My sadness couldn't be understood outside the context of the country. From the ever-increasing demands of making a decent living and the ever-increasing divisions that separated the country on party lines to the madness of a reality-star president and my stymied dreams of making a difference—every aspect of my current situation had been born in a very particular American experience. To view the resulting sadness as somehow separate from my place within the country would have been woefully incomplete.

After a few more hurried questions, the psychiatrist prescribed a low dose of lithium and dismissed me for the day, which left me feeling both misunderstood and dejected. I wandered into the psych ward's common room and sat down at a table that was covered in magazines. While I leafed through a copy of *The New Yorker*, I noticed that the same man who had sung the dirge in front of my door was now busying himself with a notebook and a pencil. He sat beside a television that played a constant stream of music and recorded the names of songs and artists as they appeared on the screen. Occasionally the man sang along with the lyrics. As I watched him out of the corner of my eye, an older nurse came over to me with the pills that the doctor had ordered. She smiled and handed me a plastic cup of water.

"You don't seem like someone who should be in this place," she said.

I shrugged.

"Well," I told her before popping the pill into my mouth, "I *am* in this place."

I took a sip of water and swallowed the medication.

"Just try to stay positive," the nurse said. "You'll be out of here in no time."

I sighed and handed her the disposable cup of water. Before walking away, she leaned over and lowered her voice.

"I mean, at least you're not like that guy," she whispered, nodding toward the man with the notebook.

I gave her a vacant stare. Perhaps her words were meant to encourage me, but they seemed entirely devoid of compassion. With that one sentence, she laid down a dividing line. *We* were better than *him*.

"Sure," I said, but I didn't mean it. I was very much like the man with the notebook. We had both found ourselves in a place of loneliness and despair.

The nurse went back to her work, and I brought the copy of *The New Yorker* to my room to read. I curled up beneath a thin blanket and opened the crisp pages. It had been a while since I'd read anything other than articles about urachal cancer or Donald Trump, and the words in the magazine sated a desire for substance that I didn't even know I had.

I was growing drowsy from a poem when I heard a light knock at my door. I looked up, thinking it was a nurse, only to find my parents standing in the hall.

My mother rushed into the room with tears in her eyes. Her hair was rumpled and undone, and she wasn't wearing any makeup.

"I've been looking everywhere for you," she said, sitting down on the bed and wrapping her arms around me. Her body trembled next to mine. "Tony called and told me that you weren't doing well, and then you weren't answering your phone, and I got so worried. I called the mill a bunch of times to see if you were there, and they said you didn't come into work. I was calling the police and the hospitals. I thought something had happened to you. I would've died if something had happened to you."

My father stood over us, slowly adjusting his glasses, and I let myself sink into my mother's arms. I could smell the sweet floral aroma of the soap she had used that morning, and I could feel her soft, smooth shoulders pressing into my cheek. My father put his hand on my head, and I began to cry.

"Your mother would have gone to the chief of police if I hadn't been there to stop her," he said.

My mother slowly drew away from me.

"He's not joking," she told me. There were still tears in her eyes, but she started to laugh. "The chief of police is a patient where I work, and I was going to find his address and go to his house."

My father smiled. "She probably would have gotten arrested."

We all laughed a little if only to lighten the mood. When I was a little kid growing up in the Catholic Church, the teachers told me that there were three different kinds of love: *philía*, *éros*, and *agápe*. *Philía* was the brotherly kind of love, and *éros* was the romantic kind. *Agápe*, on the other hand, was unconditional and sacrificial love. It was the kind of love that made you lay down your life for someone else, and it was supposedly the love that God had for his creation.

As I sat there with my parents, I couldn't tell if there was an all-loving god in the sky, even if I wanted it to be true. In that moment, I only knew what was right in front of me. I had put my parents through hell, and yet their love for me didn't falter. Our politics didn't matter just then, and our votes were trumped by something larger.

"Thanks for coming," I said to them. "I mean, thanks for finding me. You didn't have to."

"What are you talking about?" my mother asked with a look of confusion on her face. "You're our daughter. We will always find you when you're lost."

I stayed in the hospital for nearly a week, which gave me ample time to befriend the man who had sung the dirge in front of my door. We colored pictures of gingerbread houses during art therapy, and we sat next to each other during our group sessions. He showed me the songs and artists he had recorded in his notebook, and we had a long discussion about the Red Hot Chili Peppers. The man was probably in his mid-fifties, but I far preferred his company over that of the younger patients. Many of the people my own age had been brought in for drug abuse and opioid addition, and they had been slotted into the psych ward because there was no room for them in local addiction recovery units. These patients were all so lost in their own hells that it was difficult for me to connect with them, so I found friendship with the older man, who always greeted me with a warm smile.

One evening we sat down together for dinner.

"How are you doing?" I asked, pulling my napkin from its plastic sheath.

"I-I-I-I'm f-f-f-ine," he said. "Y-y-y-you?"

"I'm okay." I prodded the sallow piece of turkey on my tray and frowned. "What did they give you for dinner?"

"R-r-r-roast b-b-b-b," the man said, looking at me with desperation in his eyes. It sounded like a great stone had gotten stuck in his throat, and his eyes were begging me to break it loose.

"Roast beef?" I whispered.

The man nodded with a smile, and we both delved into our sickly-looking meals. Our plastic knives buckled from the tough meat. The mashed potatoes were runny, and the green beans had been cooked into a mash. After a few bites, the man held up the best of the dinner, which was dessert.

"P-p-p-pudding?" he asked, offering me the cup from his tray.

"No, I can't take your pudding," I told him, grateful for the gesture. My own dinner had come with cookies that were hard enough to break your teeth. "You keep it."

The man shrugged and set the pudding aside. We ate in silence for a while, buttering our rolls and picking through our potatoes. When we were scraping up the last remnants of gravy, the man suddenly looked up from his tray and began talking about his childhood.

"M-m-m-my f-f-f-father," the man said, shaking his head in disgust.

Up until that point, our conversations had mostly consisted of polite banter. We talked about the weather and the mediocre hospital food. We talked about Christmas, which was quickly approaching, and we talked about our favorite music. During all of our conversations, neither of us asked why the other one was there. Strangely, that question doesn't arise much in a psych ward. There is an unspoken understanding between patients. Everyone already knows the kind of pain that brings you to such a place, so there's no sense in rehashing it without need. At the same time, there also exists a strange intimacy in the hospital, which allows for the most heartfelt confessions at the most unexpected times. People will tell you their deepest secrets and their darkest memories. They'll utter the words that no other soul has ever heard.

I put down my fork and listened to the man tell his story. It took a great deal of attention to piece together his words, but I gathered that his father had been a nasty man and a habitual drunk. The father was always angry and unforgiving, and his belt had a heavy buckle, which was often used for beatings. One day, when the man from the psych ward was just a little boy, he hid the belt from his father to stop the bruises. Later that night his father came home in a belligerent stupor and tore through the house in search of the belt. He knocked over dressers and turned up the mattresses, but he came up empty-handed. Enraged and weaponless, the father grabbed his young son by the arms and threw him down a flight of stairs.

"Th-th-that's w-w-w-why I-I-I," the man said, pointing to his mouth. There were tears streaming down his cheeks, and I sensed that he was trying to utter words that were too painful to speak.

"That's why you stutter?" I said quietly.

He nodded.

"I'm so sorry," I told him. "That's awful."

We finished the rest of the dinner without speaking another word, and the man seemed relieved by the silence. At the end of the meal, he offered me his pudding a second time. I could tell that he needed me to accept this kindness—he wanted me to take what he offered—so I held out my hand.

"Thanks," I said, and he smiled when I sank my spoon inside.

The next morning, we ate breakfast together. As we sipped our coffees and picked through our imitation eggs, I tried to make some light conversation.

"You really like to sing," I said.

He put down his fork and wiped his hands with a crumpled napkin.

"I d-d-don't talk so g-g-good," he said, pointing again to his mouth, "s-s-so I sing."

I thought back to the dirge he had repeated in front of my door, and I realized that his song hadn't been affected by the stutter. In fact, his words came out easily whenever there was music involved. He didn't stumble over lyrics when he sang along with the television set, and his voice didn't waver when he chanted a line from the Red Hot Chili Peppers.

I gave the man a quick smile, but I could already feel the emotions welling in the back of my throat. I fussed with my coffee to keep from crying. I added a little more cream, a little more sugar. As I watched the black coffee slowly lighten, I thought about what the nurse had said to me a few days earlier. *At least you're not like that guy.* Maybe she had been right all along. Maybe I was nothing like this man. For months I had been so caught up in everything that was wrong with my life that I had lost the will to make it right again. When I told the psychiatrist that I hated my country—that I felt trapped within it—I was giving voice to a thought that had been rising within me for years. I did feel lost and ineffective. My dreams of change appeared vain and fruitless. America was a gear that crushed the vulnerable with its force, but the psychiatrist was right to scold me. From his seat, he saw the country with different eyes. In his America, an immigrant could rise to the rank of physician. This was a place of refuge and opportunity. A grand experiment. The best country on Earth. It had its flaws, many of them severe, but despair solved nothing. The stuttering man was proof of that. He could have nursed his own feelings of desolation, but he wasn't so defeated and self-absorbed. He held within him a deep and incurable sadness, and yet he sang. He sang in the face of a father he should have been able to trust. He sang in the face of a violence that had stolen his words. His pain wasn't an excuse to grow cynical. He didn't wear his anger like a shield, and he didn't collapse under its pressure. Life had burdened him with a voice that most would overlook, so he did the most difficult thing in the world. He found a new way to be heard.

11

When I returned to the mill, the company didn't put me back in the Shipping Department with Sleepy Bear. The psychiatrist demanded that I avoid swing shifts at all costs, so I was moved to a place called the Temper Mill, which was one of the few areas of Finishing that worked a straight daylight schedule.

On my first morning with the new assignment, I crossed paths with Sleepy Bear in the parking lot. A light snow fell on the surrounding cars as he walked toward me, dressed in sweatpants and a thin jacket. He was just getting off the night shift, and he had already showered in the locker room. I barely recognized him without his uniform and hard hat. His eyes looked bigger than ever, and the well-tailored jacket had a slimming effect.

"Hey, baby girl," he said with a wave. "When did you come back? I didn't see you on the schedule."

"Oh," I told him, my teeth chattering in the cold, "I'm working in the Temper Mill now."

"What?" he huffed. "The Temper Mill? Why on earth did the company put you there?"

I didn't want to admit that the swing shifts had driven me into a bipolar episode, so I shrugged and feigned ignorance. "You know how the company is. They do crazy stuff sometimes."

"They sure do." He laughed. "Well, I'm glad you're feeling better. And don't worry about the Temper Mill. I'm sure it'll be fine."

We talked for a few more minutes until the brisk air forced us apart. He caught me up on the gossip like old times. Jeremy was writing more memos. Charlie was training as a Shipper, and Gunner was the same old Gunner.

"Stay safe," Sleepy Bear said as we started walking our separate ways.

"You too," I told him.

We wouldn't see much of each other after that. The Temper Mill was a long walk from the Shipping Department, and we rarely had reason to interact. I visited him once in the little shanty we used to share, but it wasn't the same. He had a new partner to replace me, and the shanty felt cramped when I tried to weasel my way inside. I didn't stay long. I didn't want to spoil the memory of what we'd once shared. Sleepy Bear had gotten me over my fear of forklifts. He was there when I got my yellow hat. He guided me through the mill and made a steelworker out of me. Sometimes I even missed the way he snored.

The Temper Mill was a far cry from my old home in Shipping. The paint wasn't as crisp. The floors weren't as clean. The machinery looked tired and the roof leaked, but the Temper Mill was real steelmaking. The motors whined at a deafening pitch as the steel wound onto a tension reel at three thousand feet per minute. The cranes picked up coils while you were standing a few feet away. The finished steel plopped onto a wobbly conveyor belt that could mangle your leg like a sausage grinder, but I found that I was eager to get a firsthand view of the action.

A tall blue-eyed manager had given me a brief tour of the department before bringing me to my post, where I started banding coils with a mousy woman named Evelyn. The mill roared a few feet away, screeching and sputtering as it rolled the steel through its jaws.

Evelyn had grayish-blond hair that fell softly on her shoulders, and her wide eyes looked kind and forbearing behind a pair of thick-rimmed safety glasses. She could have been reading picture books to feisty children in a library, not banding coils in a steel mill. Despite her meek appearance, Evelyn banded by hopping directly onto the conveyor belt, something I was never allowed to do while working with Sleepy Bear. In Shipping we always waited for the crane to put the coils safely on the ground, but the Temper Mill was more rough-and-tumble than anything I'd experienced in the mill so far. The coils came faster. The cranes swooped closer. The employees joked with one another over the radio, and Evelyn and I did our job beside a steel table where we placed our gloves every day.

We always stood directly between the coils and the table when we banded, which made me think of the story I'd heard during orientation about the woman who had been crushed. I still remembered the details—a coil had slipped from a rickety conveyor belt, pinning the woman against a steel table just as she reached for her gloves—and the similarities weren't lost on me. The woman's words lingered in the back of my mind. *Get it off me*, she'd said. *Get it off me.*

Shortly after I started in the new department, Evelyn and I were banding together with plugs crammed in our ears to dull the never-ending noise. It felt like I was working inside a crack of thunder, and I didn't think the sound could get much louder until the ground beneath me began to shake. The mill shrieked and shuddered, as if it were grinding a dying animal in its teeth, and the sound cut right through my earplugs.

"Wreck!" Evelyn yelled when I looked over at her. A wreck on the mill was a dangerous thing. It could send shrapnel flying through the air. It could launch sheets of steel far above the conveyor belt, creating razor-sharp guillotines that fell at random, but the surge of adrenaline that ran through my fingertips didn't paralyze me.

Evelyn dropped the piece of cardboard that she had been holding, and we both rushed to a safe spot at the edge of the mill until the machines had been powered down. When everything grew eerily quiet, Evelyn smiled and turned to me.

"Do you want to go look at the pit and see what a piece of wrecked steel looks like?" she asked.

"Absolutely," I said, slipping my earplugs into my pocket.

Evelyn led me to the south side of the Conveyor Booth, which was located a few feet away from the pit. There was a heavy yellow handrail surrounding the hole to prevent people from falling inside, and we both leaned against it as we looked down.

Most of the steel had been coiled perfectly on the tension reel, but the last few feet that had come through the mill sat in tangled heaps far below. The steel bent and folded like a used ribbon carelessly ripped from a present, except the ribbon inside the mill was smoking from the friction.

"See how it tore?" Evelyn said, gesturing toward the pit.

The coil had been moving with such speed and pressure that a tiny wobble had caused its momentum to go haywire, and the enormous power of the mill had ripped the steel like paper, rendering it worthless. Through the steam, I could see several cuts and gashes in the metal. Parts of the ribbon had torn nearly in half, and other parts were marred by jagged oblong holes. Even the portion of steel that was still coiled on the reel had received a vicious blow, creating a long ellipse-shaped wound that curled in on the edges and revealed a few layers of mangled steel beneath. I couldn't help but think that the gouge looked unnervingly similar to a deep cut in human skin.

"Just think of how much force it takes to tear the steel like that," Evelyn said.

I nodded in silence, struck by a feeling of awe. Back when I was first starting as an Orange Hat, the wreck would have scared me senseless. I would have cowered from the force of the mill, feeling small and timid, just as I had done in countless ways since I started on the job. I could still remember the panic I felt in the Hot Dip, when I leaned over the zinc to clean Robbie the Robot. I could recall the anxiety that had overtaken me when the forklift tipped under the weight of the ingots, and I could taste the dread I had experienced around the cranes. Now I was the type of person who put her body between the coils and the steel table. I could keep my wits about me during a wreck, and I knew how to band coils in my sleep. I had spent so many months sinking into the throes of my disease that I hadn't noticed myself changing in other ways. My fear had dissolved, leaving a steelworker in its wake.

As Evelyn and I studied the twisted jumble of steel in the pit, a woman popped her head out of the Conveyor Booth, opening the door with such force that it cracked against the side of the building. She flipped a hard hat over her hair, which was shaved on one side and blue on the other, and she stomped toward us with a furrowed brow.

"Are you guys going to let the crane take this steel out of the pit, or are you just going to stand there like dumbasses for an hour?" It was Tackle Box, the same woman I'd seen hurling obscenities at the lazy-eyed crane operator in the Shipping Department. I felt myself shrink in her presence. Her gauged ears and pierced septum gave her a hardened edge, and the baggy uniform that hung from her shoulders did little to hide her beauty. She had the wide eyes and high cheekbones of the genetically gifted, and I saw that her real name, Lea, had been printed on the front of her hard hat.

"Oh, look," Lea said, gesturing toward a tall man with hunched shoulders. "Here comes Frenchie. I told him that this shit wasn't running right, but did he listen?"

Frenchie ambled over to me and Evelyn. His long hair was still fairly thick despite his age, and I imagined that it had once been a shock of red in his younger years.

"Are we having fun yet?" he said to no one in particular. He spoke a half a decibel too loud for polite conversation, and his words grated on my ears.

Evelyn mumbled in response, and Lea stormed off, so Frenchie turned to me.

"Hey," he said. "You must be the new Utility Worker down here."

"Yeah," I answered softly. "That's me."

"What's your name, again?"

"Eliese."

"Elsie?" Frenchie shouted, leaning forward and cocking his head.

"No," I said. "It's Eliese."

"Alyssa?"

"No. Eliese."

"Oh, well, I'm Frenchie," he said with the vacant smile of someone who doesn't want to admit that he has no idea what you're saying. "I'm the Maintenance Manager. I fix stuff when it breaks."

"Well," I said, "it looks like today's your day."

Frenchie let out a long, tired sigh. His shoulders curved forward, as if his spine had decided to grow in the wrong direction or a great load had been saddled around his neck.

"Around here," he said, "today is always my day. Speaking of which, I better see what my mechanics are doing."

With that, Frenchie walked over to the pit. Some of the mechanics were kneeling beside the damage, shining their flashlights this way and that, while a few others were still shaking their heads in dismay. The entire group looked up when Frenchie came over.

"Why are you all standing there?" Frenchie said. "This isn't a party. Lock out the conveyor. Call the crane. Get this mess out of here."

He barked other orders and gestured passionately with his arms, leaning down over the wrecked steel and examining it with expert eyes that had been trained by decades in the mill. Meanwhile, the rest of the crew buzzed around the Temper Mill. Evelyn walked away to get a bottle of water, smiling like a gentle grandmother who was in the middle of baking chocolate chip cookies. Lea had disappeared into the Conveyor Booth, muttering a string of obscenities.

Somewhere in the nearby shanties, there were others in hiding. There was the Feeder, who had been nicknamed Black Widow after someone she'd dated had turned up dead. The Stocker, who always had a nervous glint in his eyes. The Roller, who called everyone *kid*. There was the Inspector, who was the only sane one of the bunch, and then there was the Catcher, who knew how to handle a fifth of whiskey. Three years ago, his doctor had given him two years to live. A more motley crew couldn't have been imagined, and Frenchie was right there in the middle of it all, waving his hands above the pit like a mad conductor in the performance of a lifetime.

I scampered past Frenchie and into the safety of the Conveyor Booth, where another worker named Morales was cooking his lunch in the microwave. Before scolding me and Evelyn, Lea had been telling him a story about doing psychedelics at some sort of music festival, and now she resumed her tale while a crane lifted the ruined steel from the pit.

I had seen Lea several times since we'd first crossed paths in Shipping, and I hadn't been looking forward to working with her. She drove a decommissioned police car to the mill every morning, and her face was usually shrouded in anger. I always averted my eyes when she walked past, because I was afraid to meet her gaze.

For a moment I thought about nestling into a lonely nook next to the refrigerator, but I didn't want to fade into the background of the Temper Mill. I didn't want to be the person who could be pushed around, tucked away and forgotten, so I sat down in a seat close to Lea and Morales.

"Up," Lea said immediately, scowling at me.

I was in no mood to obey her commands, so I leaned back and crossed my arms.

"Fuck you," I told her. "Find your own damn seat."

A look of shock flooded Lea's face. Her eyes went blank as we stared at each other, our shoulders squared. Then, without warning, Lea smiled.

"Holy shit." She laughed. Morales smiled too. "I've seen you around the mill a lot, and I figured you were too pious to tell anyone to fuck off. I thought you were just this quiet judgmental bitch."

"Yeah?" I told her, relieved by her sudden change in mood. "Well, I thought you were a raging bitch."

Lea slouched into the chair next to mine. "I *am* a raging bitch."

"Tell me about it."

"Fuck you," Lea said, feigning outrage.

I shrugged. "Only if you insist."

Later that afternoon, when the coils had all been tempered for the day, Lea and I emptied the garbage cans that were scattered throughout the mill. I grabbed a blue can that was filled with plastic bottles and newspapers, and I started tipping it into a dumpster.

"Hey," Lea said, putting her hand on the edge of the can. "What are you doing? That's recycling."

I immediately put the blue can back on the ground, thinking of all the bottles I had once tried to save in the Shipping Department. I had long assumed that all of the plastic in the mill ended up in a landfill somewhere.

"This is really recycling?" I asked, my voice full of wonder.

"Yeah, you crazy fuck," Lea told me. "It's really recycling."

I put my hand on my hip. "Well, show me where to dump it, asshole."

Lea shook her head and smiled. We each grabbed one side of the blue can and headed outside, where the winter wind whipped against our bare cheeks. The blue flames of the Blast Furnace burned in the distance, and the rest of the mill stretched out in front of us. This place never failed to remind me that power is double-pronged. The very forces that could rip everything apart were the same ones that tempered something strong and resilient, but you couldn't stand by passively, hoping that everything would work out all right. You had to plant your feet and take control, or else a little wobble might turn dangerous.

Together, Lea and I hoisted the contents of the blue can into an empty recycling bin. I had once feared her—and I had certainly disliked her—but now, as the plastic bottles thudded softly at the bottom of the bin, I sensed that we would be just fine, maybe friends even. Life had handed me wrecked steel and a slippery conveyor belt, but I had managed far worse. As I gathered up the blue bin and headed back inside, I knew that I was home.

Every day, when the machinery was running, I stood on the conveyor belt and put my body between the coils and the steel table. That's just what people did in the valley. They stirred zinc and tapped iron and stood beside molten steel that could cook you alive. In the furnaces, people did their jobs under the constant threat of being gassed with carbon monoxide. In the Pickle Line, they worked under tanks of hydrochloric acid that could leak into the air. Steelworkers sucked it up and moved forward. They did what needed to be done, and sometimes they earned respect with a few well-timed *fuck yous*.

Make no mistake, people in the Rust Belt weren't simple, and they didn't respond to the blunt and relatable merely because they were unsophisticated or naive. If anything, they were guarded. For years they had been wounded by well-spoken politicians who fed them flowery speeches instead of results, and those wounds had scabbed over and grown scars, hardening into a deep, contemptuous distrust. They didn't want your promises until they were sufficiently convinced that you wouldn't take anyone's shit. You had to speak their language, which was brusque and no-nonsense, if you were ever going to gain their trust. Once you did, their shells would crack open, revealing a depth that you assumed couldn't exist.

They might even lay themselves bare for you, as Lea came to do with me. They might thumb their blue hair and tell stories through pierced lips about a daughter called Pumpkin, or an aloof boyfriend who always criticized the unwashed dishes in the sink, or a grandmother who had been a rock in harrowing times. At the bar, they might mention the battles they had fought as a young single mother in a steel mill. At the hibachi restaurant, they might share their excitement about the old Victorian house that they could finally afford to buy. After one too many cocktails, they might even tell you things you promise to keep secret—*cross-your-heart-and-hope-to-die secret*— and in these deep intimacies, which were born from a bit of bravado, you might discover that the anger and the posturing were just masks worn to cover the fragile identity beating underneath.

When I found my way into the Temper Mill, there was still part of my own identity that was just as raw as it was when I was eighteen years old. I had dealt with the rape as best I could with therapy and time, but I never stopped being the broken girl who was resentful of a God that hadn't saved her. I wasn't looking for spiritual renewal inside the mill, not even when a fellow steelworker asked if I wanted to go to the first-ever Women's March in Washington, D.C.

"It's going to be huge," the woman said in a soft voice that reminded me of organic tomatoes and cage-free eggs. "The union's paying for the trip. All you have to do is show up."

I smiled and said I would think about it, but I was lying. The thought of driving through the night with a busload of strangers made me shudder, and I far preferred to stay home and read about the event on my phone. As the days wore on, however, there was something inside my head that kept urging me to go. The feeling grew like a deep and familiar ache, waking parts of me that had long gone numb, and I was helpless to ignore it. I recognized the twinge of conscience that wouldn't let me sink into apathy, and I slowly began to feel the same hunger that I had once experienced as a child. Back then, I believed that every life, however small, had a point, an objective, a marvelous end goal, even if we couldn't see it at the time, and the feeling made me long to be part of something larger than myself.

On the night before the march, I boarded a bus full of female steelworkers. We drove through the night, winding along the precipitous curves of the Pennsylvania Turnpike, but the gentle hum of the engine wasn't enough to lull anyone to sleep. We watched a few movies about activists and suffragettes while thumbing the signs that the union had provided for us. Mine had a crisp blue sheen on it. In the middle, the word *SOLIDARITY* had been printed in gold.

We arrived in the city a few hours after sunrise, and the bus dropped us on a busy street that was already thick with protesters. There were people in pink hats, people in brightly colored shirts, people with Mardi Gras beads that flopped from their necks. Women held signs that said, *Nasty Woman*, and men held signs that said, *I'm with Her*. The older children carried pom-poms and noisemakers. The younger ones rode in strollers or sat atop the shoulders of their parents. Cheeks were covered in glitter and hands were encased in gloves, and everyone seemed charged with the same energy.

I stayed close to my union sisters as we slowly descended the long stairs to the Metro, bumping shoulders with strangers in the tight space, before squeezing into a train car that was already packed with people. You could spot the locals on the train by their briefcases and business suits. They all looked a little put out by yet another protest, but it didn't stop the excited chatter that echoed throughout the train. Nearly everyone exited onto the National Mall and headed toward Independence Avenue, where several speakers were scheduled to address the crowd from a stage that was already obscured by thousands of eager bodies.

I wove my way through throngs of people, slipping between tiny gaps in a sea of arms and shoulders, turning sideways to shimmy through momentary openings that could close without warning, trying hard to get as close to the stage as possible. As I did so, I passed a group of counterprotesters who carried antiabortion signs and stood behind a barricade that was guarded by police.

"You're doing the Devil's work!" they yelled through megaphones. "You'll pay for your sins."

Most of the counterprotesters were white men, although a few women were standing alongside them, and they all had the wide, frenzied eyes of the religiously blind. They pitched forward at the waist, as if fire and brimstone had scarred their bodies into bent rods, and their fingers wagged with a fury that couldn't be tamed.

"Hell awaits the handmaids of the Devil!" one of them shouted.

A fellow union sister looked over at me, shaking her head.

"Don't pay any attention to them," she told me, but I couldn't keep myself from staring. There was a time in my life when I would have been the one standing behind that barricade, and it felt strange that the same conscience that had once inspired me to pray rosaries at a John Kerry rally now prompted me to protest for the other side.

All of a sudden, as I stared at the barricade, one of the counterprotesters caught my eye. His gray beard ended in scraggly curls that barely brushed his chest, and the dusty-brown coat that hung limply from his shoulders made it look like he was little more than a skeleton underneath.

"God's wrath will reign down on you!" he cried.

"There will be wailing and gnashing of teeth," said another.

For a moment the thick crowd of protesters that I had been trying to navigate closed in front of me, leaving no gaps or holes through which to squeeze, and I had no choice but to stand there, trapped in front of the counterprotesters and their insults. As I waited for an opening that would allow me to move forward, my childhood fear of the Devil started creeping back into my mind. The fear slipped on easily, like a perfectly sized jacket, and I was surprised how naturally I wore it.

I thought back to something my parents had always told me as a child. *The Devil's greatest trick is to make you feel good about sinning*, they said. I did, indeed, feel good about marching on Washington, which gave me pause. Maybe my thoughts had been co-opted by something evil. Maybe my conscience, which had prompted me to march, couldn't be trusted. Maybe the counterprotesters were right: I was just an unwitting handmaid of the Devil who would suffer God's wrath.

"You're all murderers!" one of those counterprotesters shouted, and the absurdity of the accusation rattled me awake.

I stared out at a sea of pink hats, sensing the pulse that had brought us all there. People carried signs covered in pink fallopian tubes and upraised fists. Some held the words *Love Trumps Hate* up over their heads, and it seemed to me that there was something holy moving through the crowd. It wasn't a righteous or overwhelming force that demanded judgment, and it wasn't bound by political ideologies or manmade institutions. It was like a whisper, the faraway promise of something better, and I was reminded of the voice I had once heard in a church when I was nine years old. *Okay, goodbye*, the voice said to me after I asked the Virgin Mary if I was supposed to become a nun. It didn't matter if the words were nonsense or if the prediction was wrong or if the voice itself was all in my head. What mattered was that I had felt a deep faith stirring within, which had given me hope for the future. Now I felt something similar as I stood with the thousands of protesters who had converged on the capital.

It had been a long time since I'd felt that kind of faith, although I could still remember when it left me. I had been kneeling inside a small chapel that was made to look older than it was. The walls were a jigsaw of stone and mortar, each rock fitting perfectly alongside the next, and the doors were great arches made of solid wood. A handful of simple pews perched on the stone floor, and the altar, which had been constructed from plain blocks of dark wood, was adorned with nothing more than a gold monstrance.

It was the day after the rape, and I had just come from my confession with Father Scanlan. He had given a very specific penance to perform—*pray to the Virgin Mary and ask her to help you learn how to love yourself as a woman*—and I was too distraught to do otherwise.

A few other students were scattered inside the chapel. They had bowed heads and folded hands, and they wore pressed khakis and tasteful skirts. I wore a hooded sweatshirt and baggy sweatpants. My hair was tangled and my eyes were swollen from crying, but I began to pray my penance anyway.

"Let me learn to love myself as a woman," I said under my breath.

I dug my nails into the pew to keep myself from crying, but it did little to stop the tears.

A student in a flowing skirt walked past and asked if I was all right, but I brushed her off.

"I'm fine," I said.

I wasn't.

"Let me learn to love myself as a woman," I prayed again.

My thoughts turned toward Aaron and Ben. As far as I could tell, they hadn't used condoms. I wasn't on any type of birth control at the time. Plan B had not yet been approved for over-the-counter sale in the United States, and I was too scared to ask anyone on campus about Planned Parenthood. I began to worry. *What if I get pregnant?* I was barely eighteen years old, and I certainly couldn't support a child on my own. As I kneeled in that chapel, I wondered what I would do with an unwanted pregnancy. My stomach dropped, and I started to cry for a different reason.

"Please," I begged, "don't let me get pregnant."

I spent several hours in that chapel, praying for my period. It would come a few days later, but I didn't know it at the time.

"Please, Mary," I said, "don't let me get pregnant."

There was no answer, no acknowledgment, no relief. The wooden pews creaked under the weight of praying bodies, echoing in the vaulted ceiling overhead, and I was struck by a loneliness I had never felt before. It seemed as if a great ocean had swallowed me up in waters so deep that no sunlight could shine through, and I was swimming blindly toward a barbed, ugly thing that waited for me in the dark.

No matter how hard I prayed, the Virgin didn't reach down to pull me from the depths and God became a light I could no longer see.

I spent years inside that darkness, trying in vain to rekindle something akin to faith, but I only ever got a glimmer of the thing I'd lost. I didn't feel the holy spark whenever I tried to go to Mass, and no amount of prayer could shake my feelings of loss.

"Murderers," the counterprotester said again, but the crowd had opened up, allowing me to move toward the stage.

I slipped away from the man's damning accusations, carrying my SOLIDARITY sign in my hand, and my fear began to snap like the brittle thing it was. I was walking within a great crowd of people, inspired not by reproductive rights or political agendas, as I had initially thought, but rather by a faith that had never really left me. This faith brought me to both sides of the barricade—once as a self-righteous teenager who fawned over her own holiness, and again as a woman who had prayed her penance in the dark—and I was no longer beholden to the fear I had learned as a child. The cries of the counterprotesters grew fainter with distance, swallowed in a wave of pink hats, and I knew that something deeper than my politics had changed. Maybe, after many years of darkness, the prayer I'd said in that chapel—*let me learn to love myself as a woman*—had been answered all along.

The Temper Mill turned out to be a godsend for me. My moods continued to improve from the consistency of a daylight schedule. The nausea that was a side effect from a new medication I was taking slowly subsided, and the sadness and obsessions that had plagued me months earlier evaporated completely.

In the past, the nausea would have been enough to scare me away from medication. I had a low tolerance for side effects, which meant that I rarely stayed on drugs for long, but I was determined to do things differently this time around. I was tired of letting my brain get the best of me, and I didn't want to end up in the hospital yet again. If the stuttering man could sing, then I could muscle through an upset stomach.

Everything was coming back into focus. While Tony's absence left me with a feeling of loss, I was learning to adapt and keep myself occupied. I went camping in the dead of winter with a group of strangers I'd met on the Internet. I visited my best friend in Washington, D.C. I reveled in weekends spent drinking tea and reading novels.

One morning, as I was trudging toward the Conveyor Booth, a middle-aged man I'd become friendly with in my new post stuck his head out of his shanty and waved to me. His name was Nelson and he worked as the Stocker on the line, which meant that he sorted through the coils before they went through the Temper Mill. Every coil that he handled had been baked in a series of large furnaces that cooked the steel to temperatures well over one thousand degrees, and the resulting smell clung to his skin and his clothes. He'd been working in the mill for more than twenty years, but he still had an anxious demeanor and nervous eyes.

The sun outside hadn't yet risen, and a chill breeze blew in through a nearby truck dock. I wanted nothing more than to spend the next few minutes in the warmth of the Conveyor Booth with the big cup of coffee I held in my hand, but Nelson insisted.

"Come here," he called, and I turned to meet him with a sigh. It couldn't be helped. Once Nelson caught you in his sights, he wouldn't let you leave.

"What's up?" I said as I stepped into his shanty, which was sweltering inside.

"Did you hear the news?"

"What news?"

"The company's gonna close the Temper Mill," he whispered.

"What?" I asked, suspicious of anything dubbed "news" in the Rumor Mill. "Where did you hear that?"

Nelson narrowed his eyes, looking sly. "I have my sources."

"What sources?" I said before taking a sip of coffee.

"Just sources," he told me. He had tighter lips than a journalist protecting a high-level government asset.

"Did you ask Cheryl about it?" I asked, referring to one of the managers who oversaw the Temper Mill. I wasn't going to trust any news about a shutdown unless it came directly from someone with authority. Steelworkers would go to absurd lengths to churn up a little gossip, and it seemed unlikely that the rumors were true. The Temper Mill could pump out a coil every three minutes, and Cleveland was known for being one of the most productive steel mills in the country. It seemed silly for the company to shut down a small piece of a highly functional whole, but even if Nelson was right, the other parts of the mill wouldn't be in danger. The Blast Furnace would keep making iron, and the Basic Oxygen Furnace would keep making steel, and the rest of the Finishing Department would keep chugging along. The union would find jobs for us in other locations throughout the mill, but Nelson couldn't face the prospect of a shutdown with such nonchalance. He was a worrier. Change made him nervous, and his stomach turned at the thought of the unknown.

"I asked Cheryl about it," he said, rubbing his oil-stained boots on the floor, "but she said it's just a rumor."

"How about the committeeman?" I said. "Did you talk to him?"

"He told me not to worry about it."

"Well, there you go," I said, trying my best to soothe Nelson's nerves. "They're not gonna shut this place down."

The rumors kept circling for months. No one from the union or company gave them any credence, but those of us in the Temper Mill started to see bad omens. Things kept malfunctioning after my first day on the line. The huge motor that ran the mill broke. The conveyor belt broke. The scale went out, and the oiler failed again and again. It seemed that every week brought some new disaster, but Frenchie was always there to clean it up and we worked like dogs when everything was going well. We met our quotas and tempered the steel furiously, and we hoped that the company would have mercy.

Due to all the mechanical problems, I occasionally found myself in the cab of a crane, acting as a second set of eyes for the operator when repairmen were working in the area. One afternoon, when crews were fixing a leaky pipe with a boom lift, I sat on a folding chair in the doorway of a crane's cab with a tattooed operator who navigated a coil field with expert precision. His hands darted around like those of a

piano virtuoso, manipulating the various levers and buttons that controlled the crane's movements, making a thousand small adjustments
to account for the swing in the huge pendulum that carried the coils
through the air.

The whole crane bounced and jerked as we coasted up and down
the building. Every time the operator lifted a coil from the ground, it
felt like the whole crane was going to bend in half and give way. When
he went rumbling along at high speeds, it felt like I was sitting inside
the Zipper or the Scrambler at a two-bit carnival run by hacks who
didn't care if the rides were missing a few screws.

The operator and I spent a good portion of the morning moving
coils before we finally got a break. He parked the crane in the middle
of the building and reclined in the black throne that sat in front of the
controls.

"So, I hear that you're a liberal," he said, completely unprompted.
He stretched out his legs, resting his feet on the window of the cab,
and I let out a long sigh. Sometimes I felt like a curiosity in the mill.
People often asked if I was a liberal, and quite a few were eager to get
into political discussions with me. When I tried to enjoy my lunch,
they launched into monologues about health care or affirmative action. When I picked bottles out of the garbage and put them in the
recycling bin, they called me Greenpeace.

"Yeah," I told the crane operator, "I'm a liberal."

The man stared absently out of the window, nodding slowly. He
had a buzzed head and a row of exceptionally white teeth, and if we
had known each other in high school, he would have been the cool kid
and I would have been the nerd.

"I guess that means you're a feminist or whatever," he said.

"Yes. I'm a feminist."

The operator suddenly turned to look me in the eye. "You're not one
of those crazy feminists, right?"

He was staring at me intently, but there didn't seem to be any mal-
ice in his expression. He could have been asking me if I preferred
ketchup over mayo. It felt as if the question was a standard one in his
mind, so I took a deep breath and bit my lip. Productive conversations

rarely started out with the words *crazy feminist*, and I couldn't just walk away if things got heated. I was stuck in the cab of this crane for the foreseeable future, so I prepared myself for a conversation that would probably end in disaster.

"I'm a feminist," I said more sternly, hoping to avoid any more mention of the word *crazy*.

"I just don't understand some of these feminists," he told me. "They don't want men to hold doors for them anymore. They don't want men to pick up the check. They don't want chivalry, but I was raised to treat women with respect."

I had heard the same kind of argument from my father, and I always stumbled through my response, which inevitably left me feeling dumb and inarticulate. Discussions about feminism in my family usually ended in anger, and I was already afraid that the same thing would happen here.

"There are a lot of women—feminists even—who won't care if you hold the door or pick up the check," I told the crane operator, my voice quaking slightly. "There's nothing wrong with being respectful toward women, but you also have to be sensitive to women's boundaries."

"But I want to be a provider for my wife and kids," he pushed, taking his feet off the window of the cab and leaning forward in his seat. "It gives men a sense of purpose. It's like feminists don't want to let men be men."

I looked down at my lap and picked at the cuffs of my blue uniform, trying to think of the best way to keep the conversation from devolving into bitterness.

"Feminism isn't about taking things away from men," I said after a long pause. "That's the wrong way to look at it. It's about redefining gender roles. It's about making sure that everyone's treated equally."

The crane operator crossed his arms, causing the well-defined muscles beneath his tattoos to ripple. We went back and forth about gender for a while, each of us speaking a different language. Finally, when we were both exhausted, the man shook his head with a glazed look in his eyes. He was like a student who had just been forced to diagram sentences or solve complex geometry proofs, so we sat in silence for a moment while the mill bustled around us. A few Yellow Hats were painting the floors near the Temper Mill, and the men on the boom lift were tackling the leaky pipe with an arsenal of wrenches. A few buggies whizzed on the walkways far below, and a crane on the other side of the building was quickly lowering coils onto truck beds. I stared absently at my hands until the crane operator rustled in his seat.

"There's one thing I don't understand," he said with renewed enthusiasm. "Why do women have to make such a big deal out of this sexism stuff? I mean, I don't agree with sexual harassment or whatever, but I don't understand why women want to dwell on it. Why can't they just deal with it and move on?"

I could feel my calm quickly slipping away. The crane operator's statement struck a nerve, but I figured his views were just par for the course. I knew from earlier conversations that the man was a staunch conservative. He was white. He owned guns. He didn't understand feminism, and now he was saying that women should just deal with sexual assault in silence.

"Listen," I said just as sternly as I'd rebutted his "crazy feminist" comment. "Women face a lot of criticism and blame when they come forward about sexual assault. It's not something to be taken lightly, and it's not fair that many women are humiliated for speaking up. I was raped when I was in college. I spoke out about it, and no one believed me. People said it was my own fault. Their reaction was almost as bad as the rape itself."

A heavy silence filled the crane, and I sat back in my folding chair, feeling triumphant.

"I'm sorry that happened to you," the operator said. "I really am. I know what it's like."

"Do you?" I asked, my voice heavy with an accusation that barely needed to be named. "Do you really know what it's like?"

"I don't know," he said. My tone had made him sink down into his seat with a look of resignation on his face. "Maybe it's different, but I was molested as a kid. Someone who I trusted abused me, and I felt like I couldn't tell anyone about it. Men aren't supposed to cry about that kind of shit. They're supposed to suck it up and deal with it, so that's what I did. I figured it out on my own."

By the time the crane operator finished speaking, I was the one sinking into my seat in embarrassment. Up until that point, I would have pointed to the man and said he was *the problem*. He was the reason for the wage gap. He was the reason that the Equal Rights Amendment hadn't been passed, and he was the reason that rape culture still existed.

"I'm so sorry," I said to him. "I'm sorry that happened during your childhood. I'm sorry that you didn't have anyone to help you through it."

The man shrugged. "Thanks. I'm sorry about what happened to you too."

With that, the crane operator grasped his controls and flipped the crane into gear.

"Looks like we have some coils to move," he told me, and we both stared out in silence, watching the crane's cables slowly coast through the sky.

A knot was growing in my stomach, as if the man's confession had unearthed a stone deep inside me, and my thoughts turned to my father, who once let my imagination run wild in a pawnshop filled with old coins. Back then, he entrusted me with magical relics that had once lined the pocketbooks of nineteenth-century Americans. He gave me buckets of old nickels and the promise of hidden treasure. He was the same man who read the scriptures at church every Sunday. He was the same man who shared my love of lobster bisque and baked Brie, and when I was lost in the maze of my own despair, he was the man who came to the psych ward to find me.

This man, whom I so loved and admired, had never forgiven the universe for dealing him a shitty hand, and yet he hadn't done much to turn his hand around. He never forgave his mother for abusing him as a child. He didn't manage the type 2 diabetes that he had been struggling with for more than a decade. He still had a few years before retirement, but he was jumping from one job to the next, leaving himself unsuccessful in all of them. He took two-hour naps at work. He disappeared at lunch. He insisted on taking too much time off, and he always blamed his managers whenever he got fired. He latched onto right-wing politics, which told him that he was entitled to a good hand. He deserved the right cards. He shouldn't have to work for the jackpot, which meant that it was someone else's responsibility to turn his jokers into aces.

Bubbling beneath the surface of my father's sense of entitlement was the very human delusion that we are each the center of the universe. *My perspective matters most. My problems deserve to be solved. I am the spotless protagonist in the epic poem of my life, and I want a distraction from my pain.* If you can step away from that delusion, even if only for a moment, you start to see the mess that connects us, even in places we're reluctant to look. The conservative crane operator, who initially struck me as a misogynist, actually understood the pain I had carried for so long. My father, who seemed to have abandoned me with his politics, was the same person who sacrificed everything to give me miracles, and I was the liberal daughter who owed him the world.

When I left the mill that afternoon, I got into my car and drove to the university where I had once been a graduate student. I was still dressed in my blue uniform and my work boots, but I walked into the administrative offices and found the woman who was in charge of posting degrees.

"What do I need to do to get my diploma?" I asked.

The woman stared at me, her shoulders swimming in a blazer that was one size too big. In truth, I already knew the answer to my own question. It had been more than four years since I'd completed the coursework and finished the thesis, and I had tried to sort out the problem several times before. I had been to this office, and I had been told what to do by the woman behind the desk.

"It should be pretty simple," she told me once again. "You just need to reformat the approval page on your thesis, and then your thesis committee needs to sign it."

That was all. One piece of paper and three signatures. For four years, the problem had seemed an insurmountable challenge. Every time I went through the ritual of visiting the woman in her office, I stopped short of getting the signatures. I always shrugged and fell into apathy, and I told myself that the degree didn't matter. Of course, the degree mattered greatly. I was just afraid to get it. I was afraid of success, afraid of failure, afraid of my disease, afraid of my potential, afraid to give myself a chance. When my father was in his prime, he had likewise failed to get a degree that he had worked so hard to earn. He had talent and skill, and he was only a few credits away from his bachelor's in music when he quit. I never forgot what my mother had said to me about it: *I think he was afraid to get that degree.* My father had formed me and shaped me. He guided me into the world. For so long, we were sidekicks and comrades—two souls cut from the same mold—but I wasn't my father. I didn't have to go down his path.

As I walked out of the administrative offices in my oily boots, I knew that something had shifted. The air outside was quite crisp, but the sun shone in a cloudless sky. A few flowers were trying to poke through the soil, and robins flitted through the bare branches of a nearby tree. Cleveland was thawing into spring, which meant that I had been at the mill for nearly a year. I had spent much of that time being frightened by the gruesome stories, the molten zinc, and the forklifts, but now I was the type of person who knew how to handle herself in the mill. In a year's time, I had learned that you couldn't dwell too long on your fear.

I cleared up the administrative snafu in a matter of weeks. The diploma came in the mail a few months later, encased in a brown envelope, and I looked at it for only a moment before storing it in a closet. The diploma itself had never been the point. Its absence was always about my inability to move forward, and while I once feared that my yellow hat would be the thing that kept me stuck, it turned out that the mill—this place where I thought I didn't belong—gave me what I needed to forge ahead.

I tossed my hard hat onto the ground in the Conveyor Booth and plunked down in a chair next to Lea, who was already absorbed in the pages of a fantasy novel. Frenchie stood outside the door, yelling at a few union mechanics who were dressed in white jumpsuits.

"Why hasn't somebody locked out the oiler?" he screamed. "This isn't a picnic! Do I have to do everything myself?"

Some of the mechanics shook their heads, and others gave their fellow union workers knowing glances behind Frenchie's back. I didn't begrudge them their frustrations. When it came to the mill, Frenchie could be as fierce as a dictator, as defensive as a soccer mom, and as condescending as a scholar peering down from an ivory tower. If you disagreed with his assessment of a mechanical problem, he would tell you that your brain was a slush pile and your father's father was an idiot. If, however, you agreed with him, you would still be met with biting arrogance. His style was all bark and all bite. It was mostly vinegar and no honey.

Just as I was about to pull out my phone and read the news, the door flew open, letting in a waft of cool air, and a man waltzed into the booth with the morning paper in his hand.

"Crossword, anyone?" he said, waving the paper in front of me and Lea like a baker tempting a line of hungry customers with a tray of muffins.

Lea perked up immediately and placed her book on a little metal table that was sitting between us.

"Gimme," she said with her hand outstretched, but the man waved the paper above her head, just out of reach. "Come on, Ethan. Let me have it."

Ethan smiled behind his well-groomed goatee, which was specked with a few sprouts of gray. He was a conservative navy veteran who bid into the Temper Mill a few weeks after I arrived, and he was also something of a trickster. If you were lost in thought on the job, Ethan would startle you from behind. If you put your lunch in the microwave, he might slip it back into the fridge while your back was turned. He often regaled us with stories about his three daughters, who sometimes found cream cheese in their deodorant or fake insects on the kitchen floor, and he was always looking for an innocent prank to play in good spirits.

Lea stared at Ethan with pleading eyes, and he finally handed her the paper with a flourish. She opened to the crossword, grabbing a pencil that was lying on the metal table near her book, and Ethan sat across from us on a tall chair that was positioned beside a control panel.

"Okay," Lea said, "what's a four-letter word for a photo mishap?"

Ethan and I both squinted at the air in front of us. We were trying to visualize the puzzle in our heads when Lea sat up with a sudden revelation.

"How about *bomb*?" she said, pausing to get our input. There were rules to our daily crosswords. If the mill was down and we had time to work on the puzzle together, then we would wait for everyone to agree before writing down an answer. If, however, the mill was plugging away, then we were allowed to pencil in our answers whenever we had a free minute.

Ethan and I nodded in agreement, and Lea put the dulled tip of her pencil to the page.

"A five-letter word for finger or toe?" she asked.

"*Digit*," Ethan said.

As Lea carefully transcribed the answer, Ethan turned his attention to a window on the side of the booth.

"Hey, look," he said, a mischievous smile spreading across his face. "The Orange Hats are getting a tour of the mill."

Lea and I both stood up to get a look at them. There were only four or five newbies, and they stuck out like sore thumbs. Stiff creases ran down the legs of their blue pants, and the cuffs of their blue shirts hadn't yet softened from countless washings in the industrial machines that the mill used to launder our uniforms. Eventually the rich color, which was a cross between indigo and navy, would fade into a dirty cobalt, and their sparkly orange hard hats would grow duller by the day.

"Aw," Lea crooned, "don't they look so innocent and cute?"

"Oh, they'll learn," I said, which made everyone smile.

Ethan turned to us with raised eyebrows. "I think that we're getting one. At least, that's the rumor I've been hearing."

Lea sat back down and readied her pencil.

"Yeah," she said with a nod, "Morales was saying something about that. I wonder which one we'll get."

From the window, I watched as the Orange Hats walked down the green path that led to other parts of the mill, heading toward their new lives in the valley.

"I don't know," I said as they disappeared from view. "I just hope we get a good one."

12

The entire crew of the Temper Mill gathered in a conference room located in the heart of the Finishing Department. Like most things in the mill, the room felt dingy and tired. The bottom halves of the walls were paneled in dark wood, and you could smack a cloud of dust from an old projector screen that hung in front of a whiteboard that someone had marred with permanent marker. The linoleum floors, which had once been cream, were now gray. The ceiling tiles sagged from water damage, and the door frames had splintered with age.

A row of chairs had been laid out on three sides of the room, forming a crescent of union workers who fit right into the space. We were dressed in blackened boots and oily pants, and soiled gloves dangled from our pockets.

Nelson and I plopped down next to each other, and Ethan removed his hard hat a few chairs away. Morales and Lea hunkered down on the opposite side of the room, both laughing about something under their breath. Evelyn had been out sick for some time, but there wasn't an empty chair in the room. Anyone who had anything to do with the Temper Mill had been beckoned to the meeting. The Roller was there, along with the Catcher and the Feeder. There were mechanics, inspectors, crane operators, and managers. Our boss, Cheryl, stood in the back of the room with her hands on her hips, and Frenchie sulked beside her.

Nearly everyone in the room was carrying on a different conversation at once, creating a din in the small space. People talked about the weather, the gossip, the mill, the weekly production report. We were all in denial about the long table at the front of the room, which had only two seats behind it. One was occupied by a bald man with a long gray beard, and the other was taken by a portly Italian with wide eyes and black hair. Both men were union officials, and their presence boded poorly for whatever was on the horizon. Union officials were busy people, always flitting around the mill on some errand or another, always attending to other people's problems and grievances. Sometimes bad news was the only thing that could pin them down for more than a few seconds.

When everyone had settled into their seats, the black-haired union official cleared his throat and raised his hand. The conversations quieted in an instant, but you could still hear the rumble of a crane moving somewhere in the distance.

"I'm sure you've all been hearing rumors about the Temper Mill," the union official said. "Up until this point, they've just been rumors. The union has been trying to work with the company to keep the line running, and nobody knew how those negotiations would go. Well, we finally have some answers for you guys. Despite our best efforts, the company has decided to shutter operations at the Cleveland Temper Mill."

A hush fell over the room. Even the crane in the distance stopped moving, as if it, too, had heard the news, and together we went through the stages of grief.

"What about those tariffs Trump has been talking about?" a mechanic said from the back of the room. "Those tariffs will change things. Business will pick up."

The bald-headed union official looked at his partner before shaking his head.

"We don't know what's going to happen with those tariffs," he told us, "and the company seems to think that they won't matter much anyway."

"But what's going to happen to our customers?" a brusque old-timer said next. He served as the SOT on the line, and he had been working in the Temper Mill for decades. "What will they do with our customers?"

"Management will slowly transfer our orders to the plant in Indiana," the black-haired union official said, referring to a facility owned by the same company that controlled the Cleveland mill. "You guys will keep rolling for a while, but you'll get fewer orders every week."

Morales threw his hands up in the air. "This is bullshit."

He had a deep fondness for the Temper Mill, taking pride in its cleanliness and productivity. The news was almost too much for him, and I could see a thick blue vein throbbing on his forehead.

"I knew this would happen," Morales continued. "Frenchie has been fixing the mill with chewing gum and duct tape for years. Nothing works right anymore. It's no wonder the company wants to close us down."

Frenchie sprang into action, jumping forward with sudden ferocity.

"I've done the best damned job I could with the money the company gave me," he said, pointing a long finger at Morales. The two men weren't so different from each other. They both saw the mill as their baby, and the news of its closing was a blow to their pride. "Maybe if the workers on this crew weren't so fucking lazy, we wouldn't be shutting down."

"Who the fuck are you calling lazy, old man?" someone said from the front of the room, which prompted the union officials to raise their hands in tandem.

"Whoa, whoa, whoa," the bald-headed union official said. "Let's not go at each other's throats. It's nobody's fault that this happened. Orders are down. It's beyond anyone's control."

The seething tempers settled back into a simmer, but the mood was still tense. The crane started moving again. This time, it rumbled right past the conference room, which caused the walls to shake for a moment.

"What if we start rolling better?" Morales asked. "Won't that change things?"

"I don't think so," the union official said. "This is already in the works, but it's not all bad news. We were able to negotiate a hot idle, which means the company can't come in and start tearing apart our equipment. They've agreed to maintain the Temper Mill. If orders start to pick up again, then we can restart the mill at a moment's notice."

"Oh, come on," the SOT said on the far side of the room. "You've said it a million times. Once the company takes something away, there's no getting it back."

The union official started playing with a pen that had been resting on the table.

"When it comes to pay and benefits, you're right," he said, "but closures are different. As long as we maintain our equipment, there's always a possibility that the business could come back. Now, you guys shouldn't bank on it. Don't assume the Temper Mill's gonna be saved by tariffs, and don't assume that it's gonna reopen once it shuts down. The company seems pretty adamant about this closure, and I'd take them seriously."

Nelson raised his hand timidly, and I could tell that his old insecurities had come hurtling back with the news. One of the union officials nodded in his direction, but it took Nelson a few seconds to speak.

"What's going to happen to us?" he said when he gathered his nerve. "Where will we go?"

"Well," the black-haired union official said, "I can definitely assure you that no one's getting laid off. No one's losing their job or anything. I'd advise you all to sign bids when they come out. Try to find yourselves a new home. If you don't get a bid between now and the official closing date, then we'll slot you in where you're needed."

"When's the official closing date?" Morales asked.

"We're not sure yet, but we'll keep you updated. It'll probably be sometime in the summer."

It was the middle of January 2018 when we shuffled out of the conference room with our heads held low, and we would keep working in the Temper Mill until July.

During those last few months on the line, I devoured crossword puzzles with Lea and Ethan. Our downtime increased with each passing week, so we bought books full of crosswords to supplement the morning paper. One afternoon, when we had done enough puzzles to make our heads spin, we sat together in the Conveyor Booth. We were all a bit restless, and our shift was slowly drawing to a close. To help pass the last hour, I started reading the news on my phone. I was completely absorbed in an article about tariffs when Cheryl barged into the booth. It didn't matter if the Temper Mill was shutting down. She was still our boss, and she wouldn't let us forget it.

I quickly put my phone down on my thigh and glanced up at Cheryl, trying to look innocent. She turned toward Ethan, who had hidden a Sudoku puzzle when he saw her approaching.

"I really hope you're all staying on top of your duties, even though we're closing," Cheryl said. Like Frenchie, she had been a manager on the Temper Mill for years. She, too, seemed to take the closure personally, although she didn't convert her disappointment into anger or outrage. If Cheryl blamed anyone, she blamed herself. Now she was trying to rally her troops to show that she still could. She was putting her managerial foot forward to prove that she still had a place in this world.

"Don't worry, Cheryl," Ethan said. The smile on his face was too wide to be sincere. "We're not shirking our duties."

Cheryl took a deep breath and prepared to say something inspiring. "It's easy to get complacent around here," she told us. "It's easy to cut corners or dodge work, but you can get a real sense of accomplishment when you take ownership of the mill. Just look at Morales. He takes pride in his work. He keeps his area clean, and he's always willing to do extra projects when we have downtime. That kind of spirit really makes a difference."

Cheryl paused and looked around at us. We all smiled and nodded in agreement, but Ethan and Lea were more effusive in their praise. "I totally know what you mean, Cheryl. You're right, Cheryl. Don't worry, Cheryl. We got it."

An air of victory spread across Cheryl's face.

"Around here," she said, "you can either take initiative and get stuff done, or you can play games on your phone like Joe Schmo."

Cheryl glared at me as she said the words, and I looked down at the phone on my thigh. She wanted me to know that I'd been caught red-handed. She wanted me to know that I was Joe Schmo. For a moment I thought of clarifying her worst assumptions. I had been reading the news, not playing games, but I knew the distinction wouldn't matter.

I glanced over at Lea, who raised an eyebrow. Ethan was sitting on the opposite side of the booth, but I could clearly see that his smile had grown even wider.

"Don't worry, Cheryl," he said. "We'll all take initiative, like Morales."

"I'm glad to hear it." She nodded. Then, with her head held high, she walked triumphantly out of the booth.

Once Cheryl was out of sight, Ethan and Lea burst out laughing.

"Hey, Lea," Ethan said, pointing at me, "I want you to meet Joe Schmo."

"Hey, Joe," she said, her eyes practically tearing up with amusement, "how does it feel to be on Cheryl's shit list?"

I could already feel my face turning red as I put my phone back in my pocket. Cheryl's reprimand had embarrassed me, but I was more offended by her insinuation that I was somehow common. All of my life, I had been striving to be someone important. I wanted to prove that I was special, chosen, a cut above the rest, and there had always been a deeply rooted arrogance in that desire. I didn't just want to become a nun to help people; I wanted to become a saint so people would pray to me. I didn't just want to become an academic to foster education; I wanted to become a prized intellectual so people would revere me as a god. For years I had always been paralyzed by the fear that I would amount to nothing, and being called Joe Schmo was the deepest blow anyone could give me.

Ethan and Lea made more jokes through fits of laughter.

"Do you have any plans for tonight, Joe?"

"What kinds of games does Ms. Schmo like to play on her phone?"

Strangely, each new jibe softened the power of Cheryl's words. Whether they knew it or not, Ethan and Lea were reclaiming the insult for me. They were turning it into a badge instead of a slur, and I couldn't help myself from laughing along with them.

"Joe Schmo likes long walks on the beach."

"Joe Schmo likes margaritas at sunset."

Every iteration made me laugh a bit harder, and for the first time in more than a year, it felt like I truly belonged to this place. I wasn't anxious about my lack of prestige. I didn't feel stuck. I wasn't pining for something better.

All of the clichés I'd been told as a child came flooding back into view. *If you can dream it, you can do it! You're a unique flower with unlimited potential!* Perhaps that was so, but it wasn't the whole picture. Maybe, as a culture, we were all so enamored of our goddamned feelings of *specialness* that we were blinded to the toxic individualism that had engulfed our nation. We wanted to cling tightly to our ideologies with blinders over our eyes, remaining stubbornly enslaved to our self-righteousness, our self-importance, our individual pleasures, our individual stories, our individual beliefs, our individual pride. We preferred platforms where we didn't have to look too deeply at ourselves, where we didn't have to honor the complexity of people we didn't understand, where we didn't have to form communities with anyone who disagreed with us, where we could delete and ignore the realities that might contradict or complicate our own. Instead of community, we sought train wrecks, disasters, and scandals. We craved anything that piqued our adrenaline, because distraction was easier than dealing with the reality—and sometimes the messiness and mundanity—of who and what we are.

All of a sudden Ethan gasped and sat back in his chair. It seemed that he had been struck by a revelation.

"Oh my gosh," he said, "I'm gonna make a sticker for your hard hat that just says *J. Schmo*. You have to wear it everywhere."

I glanced down at the yellow hard hat, which was resting on the floor. Scuffs of dirt and oil had dulled its yellow sheen, and there were a few gouges on the top from the many times I had dropped it haphazardly onto the ground. The hard hat was no longer a shiny, pristine thing that looked unproved and untested, and the grit of the mill was so deeply embedded into the plastic that no amount of scrubbing would ever wash it clean. Never in my wildest dreams would I have envisioned myself in a hard hat, but maybe my wildest dreams had always focused too much on setting myself apart in a world that needed more connection.

"All right," I said, throwing my arms into the air with a smile, "you guys win. From now on, I'm a regular old Joe Schmo."

Tony and I didn't talk for months after the breakup. We went about our lives, healing the wounds we'd caused each other. I put the mementos of our relationship in boxes that held things from the past. The Christmas gifts he'd given me were slotted alongside old love letters from other boyfriends. Pictures and ticket stubs slid into a closet, out of sight. I was resigned to move on, and I figured Tony felt the same way. Then one night, while I was reading on the couch, he texted me out of the blue.

I know you probably don't want to talk to me, and I don't really expect you to respond. I just wanted to let you know that the Ohio Pinball Show is coming up. If you have any interest in going, it'd be great to see you there.

I read the message several times, trying to parse out his intentions, but I didn't answer right away. The next day, I consulted Lea and Ethan about the matter. They both cautioned me against reconnecting with an ex.

"You guys broke up for a reason," Lea said. She meant it as a warning, but to me it proved another point. Tony and I had been driven apart by a poorly managed mental illness, which was exacerbated by the mill's swing shifts. Now the bipolar disorder was being controlled with medications and the swing shifts were no longer an issue. My disease would never go away, but maybe it could be tamped down enough to give me and Tony another chance.

A few weeks later I went to the pinball convention with my stomach in knots. The balls inside a hundred different pinball machines smacked against bumpers, drained down gutters, and changed trajectory at the wallops of well-timed flippers. The machines dinged at various intervals and various pitches, sounding like a host of triangles being played by a group of unruly children, and the flashing lights of each playfield did little to brighten the dimly lit conference room where the machines had been organized into rows.

I scanned the room for an open machine, trying my best to avoid the popular games that were surrounded by long lines of pinball enthusiasts. The more people who were gathered around a machine, the more likely it would be that I would run into Tony. I had come to meet him, but now the thought of looking him in the eye for the first time produced a wave of anxiety. I made a beeline for *Black Hole*, which would hopefully give me a few minutes to catch my breath.

Every so often I looked up from the machine and searched for Tony, hoping I wouldn't find him. There was a part of me that wanted to sacrifice the twenty dollars I'd just paid to get into the conference and run for my car. Before Tony, I had always broken up with men before they could break up with me. I was always afraid that one of those men would get fed up with my bipolar symptoms and cut me loose, which would serve as proof that my disease made me undesirable. It seemed better to preempt the strike. It seemed better to avoid the proof.

With Tony, I had done something different. I had made an effort to overcome my usual urge to end things, partly because I knew that my worst impulses would always leave me lonely, and partly because I liked Tony more than all the others. He was nerdy, stable, and kind, and we were good complements to each other. We were yin and yang, salt and caramel, chicken and waffles, but when he broke up with me on that fateful winter night, I was smacked in the face with all of the proof I'd been avoiding for years. Our relationship didn't crumble because we were incompatible or unfaithful or dishonest. It fell apart because my disease turned me into someone that no one else wanted.

I played game after game of *Black Hole*, but I was too distracted to make much progress. As I pulled the plunger on yet another ball, I finally spotted Tony walking amid the crowd, wearing the blue *Star Trek* T-shirt that I'd gotten him for his birthday. His hair and beard were both longer than they were when we separated. Usually he kept his head neatly shorn and manicured, which fit well with his meticulous nature, but I always liked it when he let the clippers rest for a few weeks. I used to run my fingers through his hair, begging him to grow it longer. Now his usual buzz cut had sprouted into a thick brunette crown, and his equally lush beard formed a halo around his chin and cheeks.

I looked down at my flippers, hoping Tony hadn't seen me. A lump formed in my throat as *Black Hole* beeped and whined, but I knew there was only one cure for my dread. I had to muscle through it and confront Tony, so I drained my last ball and walked up to him.

"Hey," I said, but he didn't hear me over the constant dings and whistles.

He pulled the plunger on an antique machine, and a ball went flying into motion. I touched his elbow to get his attention.

"Hey, Tony," I said.

Tony glanced up from his machine, ignoring the ball that was still bouncing between the bumpers.

"Oh, hey," he said. "I wasn't sure if you were gonna make it."

He turned to give me a quick hug. Our bodies barely made contact, both of us rigid and unyielding, and I was relieved when we each took a step back. The awkwardness was almost too much to bear.

"Did you see that they have *The Hobbit* this year?" Tony asked, referring to a newer machine that was revered by pinball fanatics.

"No, I didn't see it yet," I told him.

"They have *The Wizard of Oz* again too," he said with the bright, expectant eyes of someone who hopes for too much. I knew him well enough to understand exactly what he was hoping for. We had played *The Wizard of Oz* before, back when we were still together, and I could sense that Tony was trying to re-create whatever we had felt during better times. He was like a child who believed that a simple pinball machine held enough magic to mend what had happened to us, which was a quality I found both endearing and naive.

We wandered over to *The Wizard of Oz* and played a few games together, taking turns on a pair of flippers that were shaped like ruby slippers. We went through the motions, sending flying monkeys into the air, conjuring the wizard in the throne room, seeking out the ever-elusive

Munchkin Multiball, but it wasn't the same as it had been when we were dating. Our smiles were stilted and insecure, and any closeness we'd once felt was burdened by a conversation that we desperately needed to have. The shining lights on the game couldn't change the fact that we had never really talked about what had happened on that winter night that led me to the shore of Lake Erie.

As always, Tony's scores far surpassed the measly numbers I was able to earn, and when a line of restless pinball fans formed behind us, we relinquished control of the machine and stepped outside into the rainy gray afternoon to get a break from the noise inside the convention.

We stood together beneath an overhang, lighting cigarettes and watching the water trickle from the gutters, and we exchanged the usual pleasantries invoked by strangers who once knew each other well. *What have you been up to? How's work? How are your parents?* Each answer was followed by an awkward silence until Tony exhaled a thin cloud of smoke and asked a far more pointed question.

"Have you been doing okay?" he said, and I could tell that he wasn't talking about general wellness. He wanted to know if my mind was still a mess.

"Actually," I said, staring out at a parking lot filled with wet cars, "I've been doing really well."

A strange thing happened after Tony had broken up with me. I got the proof that I had dreaded for so long, but I found that it didn't crush me completely. Instead it made me want to get well. For the first time in my life, I was being compliant with medication. I committed myself to seeing a psychiatrist on a consistent basis. I started exercising. I reconnected with friends, and I went to a practitioner of traditional Chinese medicine for acupuncture. The acupuncturist was short and soft-spoken, and she had one of the kindest smiles I'd ever seen. After one treatment, she put her hand on my stomach as I sat on a massage table.

"Your spirit is weak," she said with a thick accent that was difficult to understand, "but you are not alone. Saint Michael is there. You know Saint Michael?"

"Yes," I said, recalling the book of Revelation, which I had read so often as a child. In the stories, Michael the Archangel led God's armies against the forces of evil. He was known as the warrior saint, and Catholics often invoked him in times of spiritual struggle.

"Do you mind if I give you a book?" the acupuncturist asked.

I wasn't sure what she had in mind, but I was curious. "No, I don't mind."

Before I left the clinic, the woman handed me a tiny blue book that contained the New Testament of the Bible. It was the last thing I had expected from someone devoted to Eastern medicine. The woman had no idea that I had been raised Catholic or that I had once wanted to become a nun, and her gesture seemed too coincidental to ignore.

Later that night I opened the book at random, landing on a passage about the Miracle of the Swine. In the story, Christ approaches a demon-possessed man who lives in the tombs. The man is beyond hope. He cannot be controlled, and he spends his nights cutting himself with stones. The evil spirits inside the man beg Christ to show mercy. *Do not send us into the Abyss*, they say, so Christ casts the spirits into a herd of swine two thousand strong. Immediately this great throng of pigs runs into a nearby lake and drowns.

The story had always scared me as a child. I often imagined the possessed animals thrashing and gasping in the lake, their lifeless bodies floating on the surface of the water as flies and vultures gathered around. I used to wonder where all those evil spirits went once the pigs were dead. I figured that they flew through the air, looking for new victims to torment, but when I read the blue book the acupuncturist had given me, I also knew that the story offered a choice. You could focus on the drowned pigs, the dead bodies, the circling vultures. You could get caught up in the horror and spectacle of it all, or you could look to the man who had been afflicted. He had survived a great burden, which had crushed him for years, and now the evil had been vanquished, at least for the time being.

Outside the pinball convention, Tony and I finished our cigarettes in silence as the sound of thunder rumbled in the distance. I didn't tell him about the acupuncturist or the swine. It wasn't the place to talk about such things, so I left a short time later. When I got home, however, I couldn't help but feel that we had missed an opportunity for closure or reconciliation. There were too many things left unsaid, so I asked him to get a cup of coffee with me later in the week.

We met at a little café and sat down at a small table near the register, both of us daunted by the conversation that lay before us. Baristas bustled behind the counter, calling out orders, counting out loose change, filling white cups with steamy liquid.

"Why did you ask me to go to the pinball thing?" I said, trying to cut past the pleasantries.

Tony wrapped his hands around his coffee cup before answering. He hunched slightly in his chair, which wasn't normal for him. Usually he sat with relaxed shoulders and an open chest, and I could tell that his nerves were getting the best of him.

"Pinball used to be our thing," he told me. "When the convention rolled around, it made me think of you. I realized that I don't want to lose you forever."

"What does that mean, exactly?" I asked. I wasn't trying to be defensive, but my guard was up.

Tony shrugged and stared at me with pleading brown eyes.

"I want to be with you," he said. "I'm sorry I didn't realize it before."

My coffee was still piping hot, but I took a sip anyway. The liquid scalded my lips and tongue, but it allowed me to pause before responding. My stomach fluttered a little when Tony said that he wanted to be with me, but then a feeling of dread started to take over. Part of me kept thinking about Lea's advice. Exes always carried the same baggage with them, and getting back together usually ended poorly.

"Honestly, I'm afraid that we'll wind up in the same place," I said.

Tony looked down at his hands, which were still wrapped around his cup.

"I'm afraid of the same thing," he said, "but maybe we can both do things differently this time around."

I took a deep breath and picked at a hangnail that had formed on my thumb. "What do you mean by 'differently'?"

"I don't know," he said. "You seem to be doing really well right now.

You seem healthy. Maybe if you keep doing what you're doing—if you do whatever it takes to stay healthy—then things won't get as bad."

I bristled at the comment, even though I knew that Tony was right. I needed to keep myself healthy if I was going to have a meaningful relationship with anyone, but I resented the insinuation that everything was on my shoulders.

"I can do everything in my power to stay on the medicine and see a doctor," I said, sitting taller in my chair, "but there's always a chance that the symptoms will return. There's always a chance that the medicine will stop working, and I need to know that you'll stand by me if it does. You have to be willing to accept all of me, even my bipolar disorder, and I need you to be honest with me now. If you can't deal with the fact that I have a mental illness, that's fine. I get it. We'll go our separate ways, and I won't harbor any ill will about it. You have to do what's best for you."

Tony leaned forward and reached across the table, taking my hands in his.

"You're what's best for me," he said.

The skin on his palms felt rough and warm against my own, and I was struck by how natural it felt to touch him. Up until that point, we had been two strangers dancing awkwardly around each other's bodies, but this familiar bit of intimacy recalled all of the tenderness that had once been exchanged between us. I remembered the long walks by the lake at sunset, the nights on the couch watching *Star Trek*, the Saturday mornings spent with a lazy arm draped across my waist.

"I'm terrified that you'll abandon me if I get sick again," I whispered. "And I'm still angry that you abandoned me in the first place."

Tony and I stared at each other in silence, but there was nothing defensive or accusatory in our eyes. There was some sadness and a bit of regret, but the longer we sat with our hands entwined, the more we began to feel like two people who had never really left each other. The rest of the café moved in the background—a dozen conversations droned beneath the Muzak, a credit card machine buzzed between orders, and a few espresso machines hissed milk into a froth—but it felt like Tony and I were immune to the world around us. We were a bubble of stopped time. We were an island in the fog.

"I know you're angry," he told me. "You deserve to be angry, and I'm sorry. I panicked. It felt like we were drowning, and I thought a break might help us both."

"We were drowning," I said, "but I needed a life raft, not a hard shove off the boat. You can't do that to me again. I can do what I can to stay healthy, but this isn't going to be a one-way street. You can't just withdraw when I'm having trouble."

Tony paused for a moment, nodding slightly. As good as it felt to have his hands wrapped around my own, I still wasn't sure about getting back together. Maybe I was just craving what we could no longer have. Maybe I was lonelier than I thought.

"I know you might not believe me, but I won't make the same mistake twice," Tony told me, squeezing my hand. "I wasn't going to tell you this, but I've been going to church more over the past few months. One day I was sitting in Mass, and I got this feeling that we should be together. I don't know; I guess it was more than just a feeling. It was this little voice in the back of my head, but it felt like the voice came from somewhere else. Like, it just popped up out of nowhere and said that we were good for each other. It might have just been my imagination or something, but I like to think that the voice was right."

Like me, Tony was a Catholic who had fallen out of practice. Like me, he still felt the draw of the Church. My relationship to Catholicism had changed over the years, but I found that I could never abandon it completely. Even the bitterness I once felt toward the Church had faded with time, and I found myself called back to the ritual, the beauty. The same spirit I'd worshipped as a child was part of me, although I came to understand that we could take many paths to find it. Mine had brought me to the heart of the mill, and although the job broke me for a time, it taught me what it meant to take ownership of a life that I thought I couldn't control. The same problems that had been pushing me around for years—poverty, the rape, my disease—now felt manageable. I could move forward despite everything that had happened to me. I could repair what had been broken. I could rebuild the pieces that had been leveled by the tide, because faith didn't always live in a convent. Sometimes you could find it amid iron and steel, where you never thought to look.

I smiled at Tony as we sat inside the coffee shop, pondering the story he'd told me about the tiny voice in his head. The mill had made me stronger and more resilient, but I was still the gentle bright-eyed little girl who once followed the voice she'd heard in a church when she was nine years old.

"Okay," I said to Tony, just as the voice had once said to me.

I grasped his hands even tighter, but I didn't say goodbye.

"Let's start over." I nodded. "Let's try again."

As promised, everyone was slotted into different departments after the Temper Mill closed. Nelson, Morales, and Evelyn went to my old home in the Shipping Department. Ethan went to the Roll Shop, where he had worked before. Lea found a place in the Pickle Line, and Cheryl stayed on as a manager for the Re-Inspect Lines. As for me, I learned how to run a crane in the Hot Mill before transferring to #1 Steel Producing, which was the home of the orange flame. I worked directly beneath it, filling giant bins with dolomite, blendstone, and manganese. I suffered through the dust and the heat until I found my way into a forklift, which I had already learned to wield without fear.

Trump's tariffs went into effect a few months before the Temper Mill closed, but they weren't enough to save the two dozen jobs that were lost from Cleveland. In the end, the closure didn't have anything to do with Trump or Obama. The company wanted to streamline operations, partly because the equipment in the Cleveland Temper Mill was old and expensive to maintain, partly because demand for tempered steel had fallen, and partly because the company's Temper Mill in Indiana could easily process Cleveland's tonnage in addition to its normal workload. No matter how many tariffs you imposed, industry would always have a life of its own. It would expand and contract. Some parts would wither, other parts would grow, and older technologies would eventually give way to newer ones.

In the summer of 2018, when I was first learning to run the crane, I noticed that other tides seemed to be changing in the world outside the mill. Alexandria Ocasio-Cortez was elected to Congress, and I read news about her on my breaks, laughing at the protests she ignited.

"Ocasio-Cortez isn't qualified," people said. "She was a waitress before she got into politics! A waitress can't be a Congresswoman!"

I just shook my head. The Millennial Representative was the model of my generation. We were the products of an unexpected recession. The rug had been pulled out from under us on the eve of our long-awaited adulthoods, so we humbled ourselves, we carried on, we made do. We had to serve sandwiches before we could plate policies. We had to pour lattes before we could make an impact. We had to band coils before we could bind ourselves to the jobs that gave us meaning, but Ocasio-Cortez's election was an omen. It was the rainbow after the flood, a sign that the waters were receding, proof that something good could survive a stunning deluge. After years of minimum-wage jobs, underemployment, and a wealth of frustration, my generation was finally coming into its own.

Over the course of the next year, I would use my newly earned degree to apply for jobs as a professor. I didn't feel trapped or stifled by the mill anymore; I had simply grown into someone who was no longer afraid to reach for what she wanted. I went through rounds of rejection over the course of those twelve months. No one knew what to do with a steelworker who wanted tenure, and my paltry teaching experience did little to help my cause.

Then, when I was nearing my third anniversary as a steelworker, I got a job offer. It was only a part-time gig, but it would help me establish myself in the profession I had long envisioned for myself. It didn't matter that I would have to start at the bottom and work my way up, and it didn't matter that the new job would come with a huge pay cut. My life as a steelworker had given me enough confidence and financial security to take the risk, because the mill was more than just a job for me. It had become part of my identity. It was a second family, a second home, a second start. For everyone who worked within its borders, the mill put good food on the table. It put reliable cars in the garage. It provided money for retirement, and it paid for children's college tuition, giving the next generation a favorable start. At its core, the mill was always a stepping stone. It was the promise of something better.

Several months before the Temper Mill shuttered its doors, I was banding coils on the conveyor belt when a few mechanics went running past. I shrugged and kept banding.

Something must be on fire, I thought to myself, completely unfazed.

When I finished with the coil, I took off my gloves and set them on the steel table. As I did so, Ethan came running toward me. He leapt over the conveyor belt and ran behind a trio of tanks that sat near the exit end of the mill. Morales wasn't far behind him.

"Hey," I said to Morales, who slowed down for a split second. "What's going on?"

"There's a man down," he said, a little out of breath. Then, before I could ask him who it was, he started running again.

I looked on in confusion, unsure what to do, and Lea hurried out of the Conveyor Booth. I waved to get her attention.

"Who's hurt?" I asked.

"It's Frenchie," she told me.

We both rushed to the end of the Temper Mill and saw Frenchie lying on the ground below the same machines he had spent his life fixing.

"Do you know what happened?" I whispered to Lea.

"I think it was a heart attack."

The wrappings of Frenchie's uniform had been pushed aside to accommodate a defibrillator, and his bare chest surprised me for a moment. I had always seen him as the gruff, slightly angry man who made things work again, and yet his skin looked like a piece of oiled parchment. Blue veins ran along his sides, and a few wisps of hair sprung from an otherwise smooth chest.

Ethan kneeled beside him, along with a few mechanics who worked to revive him. They shocked him with the defibrillator and breathed into his parted lips, but Frenchie gave no signs of waking. I prayed as I stood there, hoping for a miracle that would rouse him. I said the same words I'd once learned as a child. The Our Fathers. The Hail Marys. The Glory Bes. As I did so, something prickled down my spine. It reminded me of the shiver that overtakes you when you hear something moving in the dark, but I wasn't afraid. Instead I imagined that every light in the place had dimmed in the way it does just before the power goes out, and I saw each person in the valley as a flicker in an otherwise dark mill. I could see down to the far end of the Finishing Department, across to the Hot Mill, and into the belly of the furnaces far beyond. We were these tiny sparks of consciousness burning fiercely amid the machines—each of us made of the same substance, each of us a pulse in the dark—and, taken together, we were the beating heart of this world.

Paramedics eventually came and took Frenchie away on a gurney, and everyone in the Temper Mill watched the lights flash on the ambulance as it drove away.

A few hours later Cheryl gathered the crew into the same conference room where we had learned that the Temper Mill was closing. The head manager of the Finishing Department stood beside her.

"I'm sorry to tell you all this," the manager said, "but Frenchie passed away this morning at the hospital."

The men who had tried to revive Frenchie took the news hard. Ethan put his head in his hands. One of the mechanics shook visibly, while another fought back tears. Everyone else in the room fell silent. We bowed our heads and looked at our laps. Some of us hunched our shoulders in disbelief. Others whispered prayers and intercessions. Still others recalled fond memories of the old days.

Inside that room, which was coated in layers of dirt, we conjured a deep reverence for one of our own. It didn't matter that Frenchie had been a company man. We didn't care that he was management through and through. The age-old divide between union and company wasn't important just then, and we mourned Frenchie's death deeply, not because we all knew him well, but because we were all steelworkers, Ohioans, Americans. We were a bunch of Joe Schmos who knew how to run a mill, and we all understood the value—and the risk—of donning a hard hat every day. In the end, the loss of Frenchie's life was the loss of a brother's life. There was no division so great that it could eclipse the unity that had been forged in the light of the mill's orange flame.

Even now I still remember what that flame looked like from the heart of the mill. Whenever I drove my buggy around the Finishing Department just before dusk, the flame shot into the pink sky like a second stretched sun. In the background, the Cleveland skyline slowly became a shadow of itself, while the men and women in yellow hard hats settled in for a long night beside the furnace. They tapped heats and gunned ladles and pulled dolomite from the bins, shaking their boots past buildings a century old, making tracks in the dust and graphite that had been there for years.

Every so often, the men and women stepped out into the dusk and looked up at the flame, which towered far above. Its color softened when you stood beneath it, as if proximity had tamed its orange rage, and you were left with a trail of gauze that lapped against the waning daylight, a testament to what we could create, what we could transform, what we could refine. When the pink of the sky finally faded and the edges of the skyline disappeared, the flame wagged its bright tongue at the darkness, burning away the memory of soot and grime and rust, lighting instead a vigil for the lives that were built and lost beneath it. If you looked at just the right angle, the sight of that flame could take your breath away. In its light, the mill seemed almost sacred.

ACKNOWLEDGMENTS

To my parents, Tom and Sandy, for your faith, strength, and encouragement over the years. Mom, for everything you've sacrificed for me. Dad, for everything you've inspired me to do. I couldn't have asked to be raised by better people. You both mean more than words to me.

To my sister, Laurel, for motivating me to be the best in everything. To Lance, her husband, for being the funny, loving, and stalwart spouse that my sister deserves. To their son, Collin, for your gentle spirit and meticulous nature, which remind me of the things I need to cultivate in myself. To their daughter, Abby, for your spunk and sensitivity, which reflect the best parts in both of us. You each remind me that innocence and beauty still exist in this world.

To Frank and Kathy, for being an amazing set of in-laws. Thank you for showing me compassion when I had to skip Sunday dinner to write.

To Tina, Kevin, Abby, Livi, and Finn, for being a wonderful adopted family. Tina, for your strength and competitive spirit. Kevin, for your easygoing humor. Finn, for your quirkiness. Abby, for your energy and charisma. Livi, for your quiet determination, which is so similar to my own.

To David Giffels, for believing in me when most others lost hope.

To my best friend, Jacqui, for commiserating with me in hard times and celebrating with me in good ones. For your willingness to seek out and appreciate good art. For the glasses of wine enjoyed in Cleveland

Heights. For the nights spent watching the Cleveland Orchestra at Blossom. Let's do that a million more times.

To my agent, Sarah Levitt, for helping me turn this book into a reality. It was your guidance that gave my fledgling idea substance, and I'm eternally grateful for all of the hours you spent guiding me forward. I couldn't have done any of it without your optimism, your support, and your advice.

To my editor, Bryn Clark, for your wisdom throughout the writing process, which allowed this book to evolve and grow. I am forever indebted to your candid feedback, which always made me excited to tackle the next few pages. I thank you for harnessing my impulses. And I'm especially grateful for your steady direction, which led me toward the revisions that helped to give this story shape.

To everyone at Flatiron Books who helped turn this book into a reality, especially Chris Smith, Claire McLaughlin, and Kaitlin Severini.

And to my husband, Tony, for being more than I imagined a husband could be. For the words of encouragement. For the moments of compassion and support. For the dinners I missed. For the walks I didn't take. I appreciate every sacrifice. I'm always humbled—and inspired—by your patience, your strength, and your character.

ABOUT THE AUTHOR

ELIESE COLETTE GOLDBACH was a steelworker at Arcelor-Mittal Cleveland. She received an M.F.A. in nonfiction from the Northeast Ohio Master of Fine Arts program. Her writing has appeared in *Ploughshares*, *Western Humanities Review*, *Alaska Quarterly Review*, *McSweeney's Internet Tendency*, and *The Best American Essays 2017*. She received the Ploughshares Emerging Writer's Award and a Walter Rumsey Marvin Grant from the Ohioana Library Association, which is given to a young Ohio writer of promise. She now works at John Carroll University and lives in Cleveland with her husband.